D1592138

the
PACKERS
EXPERIENCE

A YEAR-BY-YEAR CHRONICLE OF
THE GREEN BAY PACKERS

Lew Freedman

MVP
BOOKS

First published in 2013 by MVP Books, an imprint of MBI Publishing Company, 400 First Avenue North, Suite 400, Minneapolis, MN 55401 USA

© 2013 MVP Books

Photograph copyrights are as indicated with the individual images.

All rights reserved. With the exception of quoting brief passages for the purposes of review, no part of this publication may be reproduced without prior written permission from the Publisher.

The information in this book is true and complete to the best of our knowledge. All recommendations are made without any guarantee on the part of the author or Publisher, who also disclaims any liability incurred in connection with the use of this data or specific details.

We recognize, further, that some words, model names, and designations mentioned herein are the property of the trademark holder. We use them for identification purposes only. This is not an official publication. It has not been prepared, approved, or licensed by the Green Bay Packers or the National Football League.

MVP Books titles are also available at discounts in bulk quantity for industrial or sales-promotional use. For details write to Special Sales Manager at Quayside Publishing Group, 400 First Avenue North, Suite 400, Minneapolis, MN 55401 USA.

To find out more about our books, visit us online at www.mvpbooks.com.

Library of Congress Cataloging-in-Publication Data
Freedman, Lew.
 The Packers experience : a year-by-year chronicle of the Green Bay Packers / Lew Freedman.
    pages cm
 Includes index.
 ISBN 978-0-7603-4450-7 (hardcover)
 1. Green Bay Packers (Football team)--History. I. Title.
 GV956.G7F74 2013
 796.332'640977561--dc23
                                    2013013221

ISBN-13: 978-0-7603-4450-7

Printed in China

On the front cover: Forrest Gregg, 1960. *Photo by Robert Riger/Getty Images.*
On pages 2–3: Lambeau Field, January 15, 2012. P*hoto by Michael Heiman/Getty Images.*
On the facing page: © *Shutterstock*

Editor: Josh Leventhal
Design Manager: James Kegley
Layout: Laurie Young

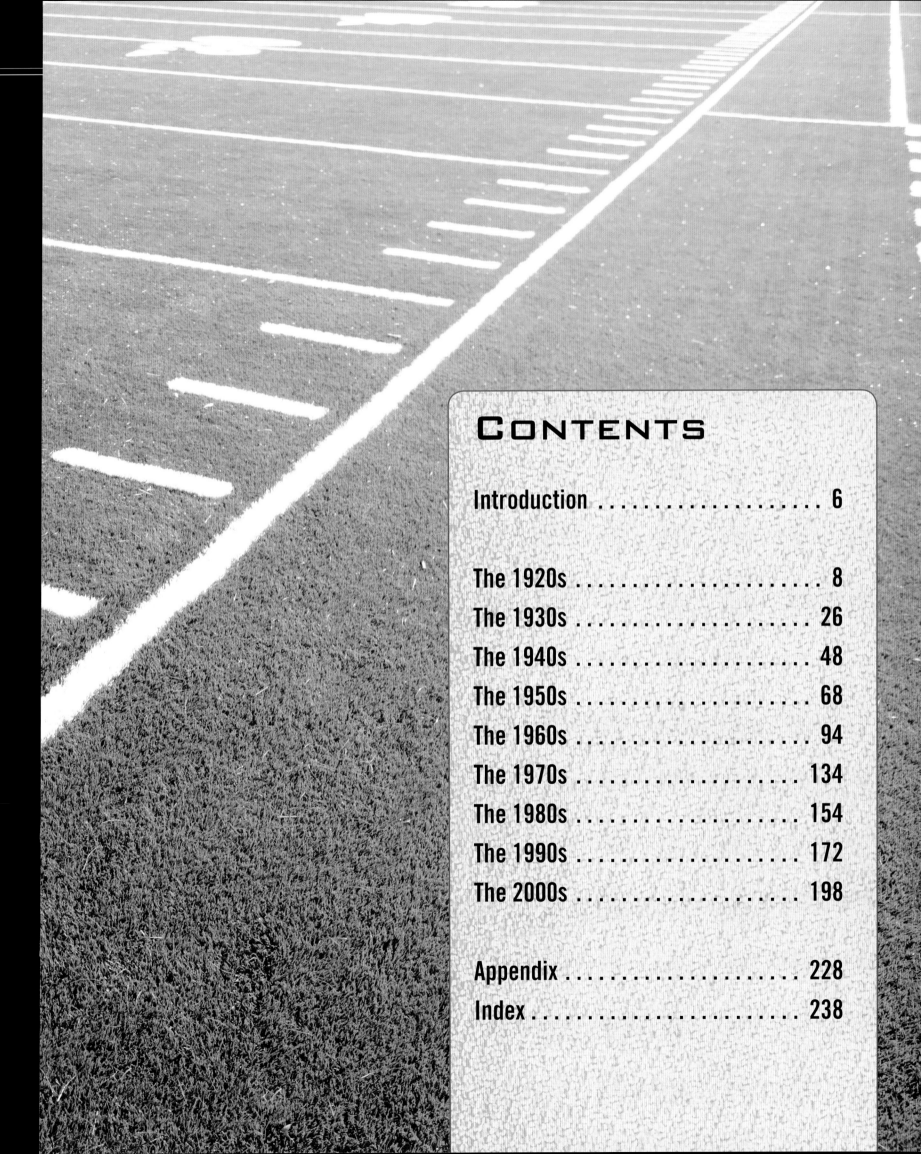

CONTENTS

GREEN BAY PACKERS: A TRADITION OF WINNING

F ew teams in sports represent a tradition of winning like the Green Bay Packers. With nine NFL titles in the pre–Super Bowl era to go along with four Super Bowl victories since 1966, Green Bay has rightly earned the nickname "Titletown." That legacy of success has been championed by an extensive list of Hall of Famers, All-Pros, Pro Bowlers, and hard-working if underappreciated players of all shapes and sizes who have worn the green and gold throughout the decades. The coaches who have roamed the sidelines include legendary names like Curly Lambeau and Vince Lombardi, while more recent sideline wizards Mike Holmgren and Mike McCarthy revived the winning ways for more recent generations of Packer backers.

Of course, not every Green Bay season has ended in celebration. In fact, the Packers and their fans have lived through some pretty grim times, when even a mere taste of the postseason was a pipe dream. But through it all, the Green Bay faithful have come out to Lambeau Field, and its predecessors old City Stadium and Milwaukee County Stadium, to cheer on their favorite team. The many-generations-long season-ticket waiting list, the ubiquitous cheesehead gear, and the legions of rabid face-painted, pom-pom waving everyday supporters are testament to the Packers tradition and the loyalty of their fans.

Wisconsinart/Dreamstime.com.

1959 Topps card. *MVP Books Collection*

THE GREEN BAY PACKERS

MVP Books Collection

Lambeau Field at night, 2004. *Wisconsinart/Dreamstime.com*

This year-by-year exploration of every Packers season reveals the highs and lows from more than nine decades of football in Green Bay. Beyond the wins and losses, each season has its unique storyline, its standout performances, its heartbreaking and uplifting moments, all providing a compelling saga of one team's rise and fall and rise again. Those stories, and the stories of the players and coaches who made it happen, are presented here to offer an in-depth and informative history of one of professional sports' most cherished and significant teams.

Aaron Rodgers in action, 2010 playoffs. *Scott Anderson/Dreamstime.com*

The Green Bay Packers, the oldest team in the National Football League, actually predate the founding of the NFL. They were founded due to the energy and efforts of Earl "Curly" Lambeau, the team's first coach, who also played quarterback.

With a 10–1 record, the Packers certainly were an artistic success for the Indian Packing Company, which fronted Lambeau the money to start the team—and which explains his choice of the nickname of Packers and his loyalty to the name. However, the sponsoring company began having financial difficulties and sold out to a different firm, the Acme Packing Company. The Packers played on against regional foes, but when Lambeau learned that a serious professional football league was being formed, he wanted in. Lambeau put down $50 in earnest money to bid for membership.

Green Bay agreed. The community wanted to be part of it. A representative of Acme Packing arrived at the league's organizational meeting in an automobile showroom in Canton, Ohio, to bid for a franchise. At the Canton gathering, the league that would become the National Football League was established, though it first used the name American Professional Football Association. The Green Bay Packers became a charter franchise.

Lambeau was the captain, coach, quarterback, and personnel director of the Packers, and he was dismayed when Acme folded. Lambeau, who was determined to stay in business, actually wished to discard the nickname "Packers" following

Pro football was still very much in its infancy in the 1920s, but the Packers were starting to see crowds turning out for games at home and away. *AP Photo/Pro Football Hall of Fame*

Program cover for Packers game against the Dayton Triangles on November 15, 1925.
MVP Books Collection

Illustration of Curly Lambeau in a Packers uniform from the early 1920s. *MVP Books Collection*

Acme's demise, but the local sportswriters kept referring to the team by that nickname in print, so it stuck.

The 1920s were a rocky period for the league. Teams came and went. Midsized cities took a beating. They could not sustain members in the new pro league. They didn't have the population base and they didn't draw enough fans. The Packers, though, were a beacon. Green Bay posted a winning record during every season of the 1920s. In 1929, the Packers had the best record in the league. While no playoff existed to determine a champion, the team with the finest mark was declared champ by acclamation. That season marks Green Bay's first title.

Underfunded, the Packers were cautious on money matters. For each home game, the team took out a rain insurance policy. This represented protection against an inch of precipitation or more, which might discourage fans from attending. Once, the team failed to collect on the policy because only 0.9 inches fell.

At first, the Packers were more successful on the field than at the box office. That changed when the team went public in 1923, offering 1,000 shares of stock to buyers at $5 apiece. Also, the team's bills were guaranteed by 100 local businessmen who put up $100 each to create their own sort of rainy day insurance.

When the new City Stadium opened in 1925, the Packers had a fine place to play and crowds began responding, coming out 6,000 strong. From there, both the stadium capacity and fan interest continued to grow.

Game-by-Game

9/14	W, 53–0, North End A.C.
9/21	W, 61–0, Marinette Northerners
9/28	W, 54–0, New London
10/5	W, 87–0, Sheboygan Company C
10/12	W, 76–6, Racine Iroquois
10/19	W, 33–0, at Ishpeming
10/26	W, 85–0, Oshkosh Professionals
11/2	W, 53–0, Milwaukee Maple Leaf A.C.
11/9	W, 46–0, Chicago Chilar A.C.
11/16	W, 17–0, at Stambaugh Miners
11/23	L, 0–6, at Beloit Fairies/ Professionals

Team Scoring

565 points scored

6 points allowed

PACKERS HEADLINE

Newly formed Packers football club destroys the competition in debut season.

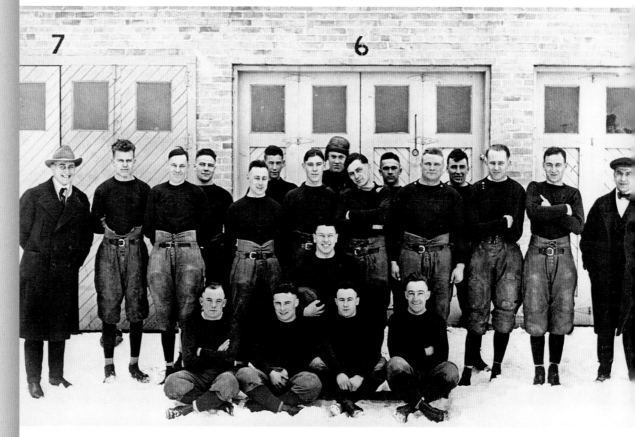

This motley crew represents the first organized Packers team. Known as the Acme Packers, the team was coached and quarterbacked by Curly Lambeau, seen here kneeling in the second row. *MVP Books Collection*

The Packers were organized and began play in 1919, when a native son named Earl "Curly" Lambeau gave up the idea of playing football for Knute Rockne at Notre Dame.

A lengthy illness caused Lambeau to return home from school, and instead of pursuing higher education when he recovered, Lambeau went to work for the Indian Packing Company. The young man was infatuated with football, and he persuaded his boss to sponsor a team to play other regional outfits. Lambeau did so after consulting with the sports editor of the local paper on whether or not the writer thought the idea might pan out.

After being funded for $500 worth of equipment and granted permission to practice in the company yard—a vacant lot—the football Packers did well representing the parent company. That year, with Lambeau as both player and coach, the Packers ran up a 10–1 record against such competition as the Sheboygan Company C. and the Milwaukee Maple Leaf A. C.

The schedule was dotted with teams that mean nothing to the modern football fan. Other competitors included the Marinette Northerners, Stambaugh Miners, and the Oshkosh Professionals.

Really, the Packers were a juggernaut, far too good for their opponents. They outscored their foes 565–6 until, in the last game of the season, they tripped over the Beloit Professionals, losing 6–0. By strict definition of the term, the Green Bay Packers were professionals because the players collected cash. When the season ended, profits were divided among the players. Each man was paid $16.75.

Another dominating season for the Packers includes eight shutout victories.

▶ 9–1–1 ◀

T he turn of the decade, into what became known as the Roaring '20s, got off with a roar for the Green Bay Packers. Once again under the tutelage of jack-of-all-trades Curly Lambeau, who coached and quarterbacked the team and picked the players, the season produced a 9–1–1 record.

The campaign began with a 3–3 tie against the Chicago Boosters, and once again Green Bay lost to Beloit. However, the Packers won the most important game on their schedule in a rout. Sometimes rivalries count double when teams savor victory, and the challenge put forth by the team situated in nearby De Pere was one of those contests for Green Bay.

There was a history between the two clubs. In 1919, in its eight games, De Pere won seven and had a scoreless tie with a total point differential in its favor of 261–6. De Pere challenged the mighty Packers to a game, but a flooded field compounded by a pure ice surface resulted in cancellation.

In October 1920, the teams met at Hagemeister Park in Green Bay to settle the issue. An estimated 3,500 fans turned out. On that day, the visitors learned rather bitterly that they were no match for the Pack. Green Bay crushed De Pere 62–0. That more than settled bragging rights for the duration.

The game remained close for a quarter, as Green Bay led just 7–0. But by halftime, the margin was 27–0. The difference grew to 41–0 after three periods, by which time De Pere was probably praying for rain and ice.

Game-by-Game

9/26	T, 3–3,	vs. Chicago Boosters
10/3	W, 56–0,	vs. KauKauna Legion
10/10	W, 3–0,	vs. Stambaugh Miners
10/17	W, 25–0,	vs. Marinette North End Badgers
10/24	W, 62–0, vs. De Pere Pros	
10/31	W, 7–0, vs. Beloit Fairies	
11/7	W, 9–0,	vs. Milwaukee All-Stars
11/14	L, 3–14, at Beloit Fairies	
11/21	W, 19–7,	vs. Menominee Professionals
11/25	W, 14–0,	vs. Stambaugh Miners
11/28	W, 26–0,	vs. Milwaukee Lapham A.C.

Team Scoring

227 points scored

24 points allowed

With Curly Lambeau again at the center of the team (seated, holding football), the Packers of 1920 took on pro, semi-pro, and traveling teams from throughout Wisconsin, Illinois, and Indiana, marching to 7 wins in 11 games. *MVP Books Collection*

Earl "Curly" Lambeau

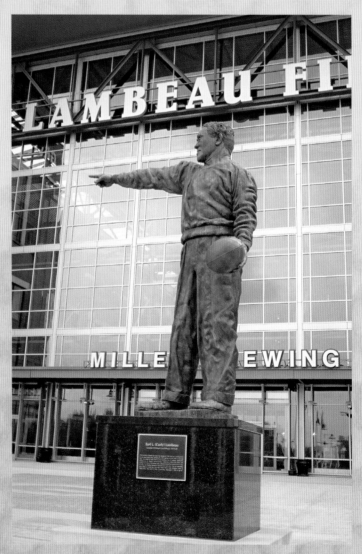

AP Photo

The man who now has the Packers' stadium named after him was the founder, coach, and star player for the team during an era that spread 31 years. Earl "Curly" Lambeau, given the nickname because of the twist of his hair, also worked to keep the team alive during the 1920s when it ran into financial crisis.

A passionate football fan, Lambeau became associated with the Packers even before there was a National Football League, and his acumen in acquiring top personnel and coaching championship teams helped keep the organization going strong in the depths of the Depression, when almost every other small-town team folded.

Lambeau was one of the first proponents of the forward pass as a big part of his offensive game plan, and he discovered what a weapon passing could be during a 1919 game. The opponent was Ishpeming, and the Packers suffered the loss of running backs due to injury. "So we just passed them silly and won 33–0," he said. "That was the day I realized how valuable the forward pass could be."

As the main thrower for the Packers during the 1920s before he retired from active duty, Lambeau once threw 45 times during a game and completed 37—the type of statistic more commonly associated with the 2000s.

Lambeau coached the Packers to NFL titles in 1929, 1930, and 1931. That was when championships were calculated by in-season records, not playoff success. It was the first time any team won three crowns in a row. Lambeau, who remained as coach through the 1949 season, won six titles in all for Green Bay. He then coached the Chicago Cardinals and the Washington Redskins.

Lambeau passed away from a heart attack in 1965 at the age of 67 and was voted into the Pro Football Hall of Fame in 1963, the first year of its existence.

"He was Mr. Green Bay," said Buckets Goldenberg, one of Lambeau's early stars. "If you won for him, and this is what he wanted most, you could ask for the world and the moon. If you lost, you stayed away from him."

During his NFL coaching career, Lambeau compiled a record of 231–133–23, a winning percentage of .627. Remembering back to the first season of the Packers' existence under the auspices of the Indian Packing Company, when the only money his fledgling pros were paid came from passing the hat to fans at games, he said, "We didn't do too good."

Regarded as an excellent judge of talent, Lambeau got great mileage out of signing players who were free agents, and then from plucking the right people in the draft once it started in the 1930s.

Running back Johnny "Blood" McNally was one of the most colorful and wild players Lambeau ever put up with, and while the two got along well for a while, they eventually had a falling out. Still, McNally admired how Lambeau took care of the Packers. "We traveled on the best trains," he said. "We stayed at the best hotels." Players made $75 to $100 a game, he said. "There weren't many guys our age earning that kind of money then."

Statue of Curly Lambeau outside the Packers' home stadium. *Shutterstock.com*

B y autumn of 1921, the new American Professional Football Association, under new commissioner Jim Thorpe, began play. The league had accepted 14 teams for its inaugural season, and the Green Bay Packers were one of them.

That initial season, teams played a short, irregular schedule. The Packers played four regional non-league teams—handling them easily by a combined 109–6 score—before beginning official APFA competition on October 23. The first league game brought to town the Minneapolis Marines, and the populace was excited enough to turn out 6,000 strong for a sellout.

Green Bay—in what history has marked as the team's first game in the NFL—prevailed 7–6 on its way to a 3–2–1 official season record. (They went 7–2–2 including non-league games.) The worst loss the Packers suffered was 20–0 to the Staleys, forerunners of the Chicago Bears. It was the first meeting between the clubs.

Winning the first game was special. Minneapolis scored first on a touchdown by halfback Ben Dvorak in the first quarter. The usually big-scoring Packers could muster little offense and went scoreless in the first, second, and third quarters. They even failed to cross the goal line in the third quarter after an interception provided a first down on the Minneapolis 20-yard line.

Green Bay got the break it needed with about five minutes left. Dvorak fumbled a punt, and the Packers started a series on the Marines' 35. A pass from Curly Lambeau to Buff Wagner put the ball on the 14. Soon, Art Schmael powered over from the 1-yard line to tie the game, and Lambeau drop-kicked the extra point for the win.

Game-by-Game

9/25	**W**, 13–6, vs. Chicago Boosters*
10/2	**W**, 49–0, vs. Rockford Olympics*
10/9	**W**, 40–0, vs. Chicago Cornell-Hamburgs*
10/16	**W**, 7–0, vs. Beloit Fairies*
10/23	**W**, 7–6, vs. Minneapolis Marines
10/30	**L**, 3–13, vs. Rock Island Independents
11/6	**W**, 43–6, vs. Evansville Crimson Giants
11/13	**W**, 14–7, vs. Hammond Pros
11/20	**T**, 3–3, at Chicago Cardinals
11/27	**L**, 0–20, at Chicago Staleys
12/4	**T**, 3–3, vs. Racine Legion*

* Non-league games

Team Scoring

182 points scored (6th)

64 points allowed (10th)

In 1921, the Packers first began play in an organized pro league, the American Professional Football Association, precursor to the National Football League. They won only three official league games that year. *MVP Books Collection*

PACKERS HEADLINE

Packers debut in APFA with mixed results, finishing 6th out of 21 teams in all. (Not all clubs played a full season.)

1922

Game-by-Game

10/1	**L**, 14–19, at Rock Island Independents
10/8	**L**, 6–10, vs. Racine Legion
10/15	**L**, 3–16, at Chicago Cardinals
10/22	**T**, 0–0, at Milwaukee Badgers
10/29	**T**, 0–0, vs. Rock Island Independents
11/5	**W**, 3–0, vs. Columbus Panhandles
11/12	**W**, 14–6, vs. Minneapolis Marines
11/19	**T**, 3–3, at Racine Legion
11/26	**W**, 13–0, vs. Milwaukee Badgers
12/3	**W**, 14–0, at Racine Legion

Team Scoring

70 points scored (11th)

54 points allowed (7th)

Defense produces five shutouts and allows a total of nine points in the final seven games of the season.

On June 24, 1922, the American Professional Football Association faded from the scene, officially giving way to the National Football League. The Packers were one of the league's 17 tenants. Not the best, not the worst, they finished eighth.

For the first several weeks of the season, the Packers could not get untracked. They opened the year with a loss to the Rock Island Independents, and in their first five encounters Green Bay lost three games and tied two. Although the offense never came around, the Packers won four of their last five, with one tie, to finish 4–3–3. They had an additional victory over the Duluth Kelleys, but the game was not an official contest.

Without a sturdy defense, the Packers would have been in serious trouble that season. After the shaky start, Green Bay recorded five shutouts. However, the Packers had no scoring punch all year, never once scoring more than two touchdowns in a game.

Something more notable than any single game during the year took place that fall. On September 13, 1922, the Green Bay Packers filed articles of incorporation.

Unfortunately, the Packers were flagged for using players competing under assumed names. Commissioner Joe Carr revoked the franchise in punishment. Curly Lambeau, the face of the franchise in all important football matters, pleaded for reinstatement of the team and was granted a reprieve. But by that season, the Packers were a failing financial entity.

Howard "Cub" Buck

If half of what the people in Wisconsin said about Howard "Cub" Buck's strength was true, he probably would have been better off with the circus as a strongman rather than playing tackle for the Green Bay Packers.

The legend surrounding Buck was that he once picked up two opposing players at the same time by their belts. During an era in which players were more likely to weigh 185 pounds than 285, Buck was one of the few around who tipped the scales at the higher weight.

An All-American at the University of Wisconsin, Buck was lured to the Packers by coach Curly Lambeau's sizzling offer of $75 per game in 1921. Buck, who already had spent a season with the Canton Bulldogs, played for the Packers until 1925 before leaving to start the University of Miami football program as coach. Besides tackle, Buck also punted and did the placekicking for the Packers.

Buck wore tailor-made clothes because of his size, never swore, and said he had only one fight in his life and that he nearly killed the other guy. At Miami, where he learned he didn't like coaching, Buck felt that his players weren't tough enough. When he got down in his three-point stance to show them how it was done, he broke his star player's leg and lost him for the season.

The paramount order of business for 1923 was ensuring financial solvency. Curly Lambeau had no money to invest in the Packers, but a friend of his sold his roadster for $1,500 and donated the money on the condition that Coach Lambeau put him into a game. The deal was consummated, and Lambeau's friend played a few minutes.

While the Packers were on their way to a best-ever 7–2–1 record, Lambeau still had to worry about the big picture. A group of businessmen who became known as the "Hungry Five" backed him with their bankrolls and ensured that the Packers would endure. The behind-the-scenes ownership group included Andrew Turnbull, general manager of the *Green Bay Press-Gazette*; Jerry Clifford, an attorney; Lee Joannes, owner of a grocery-store chain; a doctor named W. Webber Kelly, who acted as team physician; and Lambeau himself. Stock was also sold in the team, creating broad-based local ownership.

Once again in 1923, the Packers' success was measured by how well the defense played. The most number of points Green Bay put on the board in a game was the 19 it totaled in a shutout of the Hammond Pros in the final game of the season. The Packers recorded seven shutouts in 10 games and remarkably allowed just 34 total points. Even more amazing, 24 of those points were scored in a single game, a loss to the Racine Legion.

The Packers, who made their debut at Bellevue Park for home games, finished third in the league standings. In Week 3, Green Bay lost 3–0 to the Chicago Bears, the first time the longstanding rivals played each other under the names they both still use.

The community-owned team announced that profits from the Green Bay Football Corporation would be awarded to the Sullivan Post of the American Legion.

▶ 7–2–1   3rd place ◀

Game-by-Game

9/30	W, 12–0, vs. Minneapolis Marines
10/7	T, 0–0, vs. St. Louis All-Stars
10/14	L, 0–3, vs. Chicago Bears
10/21	W, 12–0, vs. Milwaukee Badgers
10/28	L, 3–24, vs. Racine Legion
11/4	W, 3–0, at St. Louis All-Stars
11/11	W, 16–0, at Racine Legion
11/18	W, 10–7, at Milwaukee Badgers
11/25	W, 10–0, vs. Duluth Kelleys
11/29	W, 19–0, vs. Hammond Pros

Team Scoring

85 points scored (7th)

34 points allowed (3rd)

Packers and Bears players take a breather during their meeting at Bellevue Park in Green Bay on October 14. Chicago eked out a 3–0 victory in the game—the only three points the Packers allowed in the first four games of the season. *AP Photo/Pro Football Hall of Fame*

PACKERS HEADLINE

The "Hungry Five" group of local businessmen ensure the survival of the club, which enjoys its best NFL finish to date.

1924

Game-by-Game

9/28	**L**, 3–6, at Duluth Kelleys	
10/5	**L**, 0–3, at Chicago Cardinals	
10/12	**W**, 16–0, vs. Kansas City Blues	
10/19	**W**, 17–0, vs. Milwaukee Badgers	
10/26	**W**, 19–0, vs. Minneapolis Marines	
11/2	**W**, 6–3, vs. Racine Legion	
11/9	**W**, 13–0, vs. Duluth Kelleys	
11/16	**W**, 17–10, at Milwaukee Badgers	
11/23	**L**, 0–3, at Chicago Bears	
11/27	**W**, 17–6, at Kansas City Blues	
11/30	**L**, 0–7, at Racine Legion	

Team Scoring

108 points scored (7th)

38 points allowed (2nd)

PACKERS HEADLINE

Player-coach-owner Curly Lambeau propels a high-scoring offense to complement the typically stingy Packers defense.

One thing Curly Lambeau could do was produce winners. Every year under his supervision, the Packers won more than they lost. They had another solid season in 1924, going 7–4 despite the rough scheduling of having their last four games on the road.

By modern standards, the Packers defense continued to be phenomenally stingy, surrendering just 38 points in 11 contests. Green Bay posted four shutouts, and it gave up double-figure points in a game just once all year.

The Packers finished sixth in the league standings. Numerous teams in the league were soon doomed to fail, including the 1924 champion Cleveland Bulldogs. The Packers seemed to have adjusted well to Bellevue Park. Green Bay won all five of its home games.

As an illustration of how the game was different, Lambeau's completion percentage at quarterback was just 41.9. The forward pass was rarely used by many teams, but Lambeau threw 179 times. He gained 1,094 yards through the air and also ran for 457 yards, but he threw only eight touchdown passes compared to a whopping 29 interceptions.

Lambeau really was a do-everything player. He intercepted five passes playing in the defensive backfield, was the leading punt returner with a 10.6 average, was the backup punter, and caught seven passes. He even kicked a field goal. Moreover, Lambeau was still coaching the team, selecting the players, and doing everything short of sweeping the stadium.

The Milwaukee Badgers lasted only five seasons in the NFL (1922–1926), and Green Bay never lost a game to its intrastate rival (9–0–1). The Packers shut out the Badgers in eight of their ten meetings, including this 17–0 win on October 19, 1924. *MVP Books Collection*

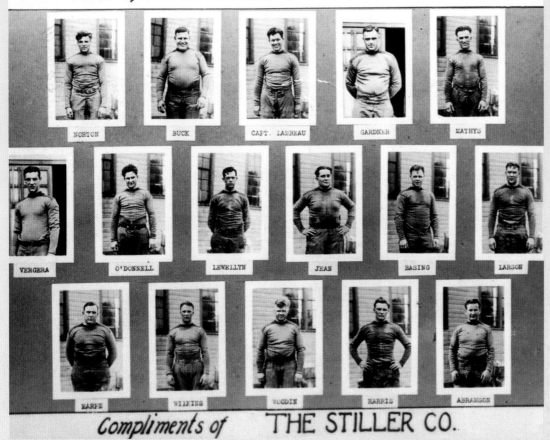

THE 1925 PACKER FOOTBALL TEAM.

NORTON — BUCK — CAPT. LAMBEAU — GARDNER — MATHYS

VERGERA — O'DONNELL — LEWELLYN — JEAN — BASING — LARSON

EARPE — WILKINS — WOODIN — HARRIS — ABRAMSON

Compliments of THE STILLER CO.

In 1925, the Packers were still a few years away from championship contention, and only one member of the 1925 squad was still in uniform in 1929: Verne Lewellen (middle row, third from left). Curly Lambeau (top, middle) remained as coach and owner. *MVP Books Collection*

Game-by-Game

9/20	W, 14–0,	vs. Hammond Pros
9/27	W, 14–10,	vs. Chicago Bears
10/4	L, 0–3,	at Rock Island Independents
10/11	W, 31–0,	vs. Milwaukee Badgers
10/18	W, 20–0,	vs. Rock Island Independents
10/25	W, 33–13,	vs. Rochester Jeffersons
11/1	W, 6–0,	at Milwaukee Badgers
11/8	L, 6–9,	at Chicago Cardinals
11/15	W, 7–0, vs.	Dayton Triangles
11/22	L, 0–21, at Chicago Bears	
11/26	L, 0–31,	at Pottsville Maroons
11/28	L, 7–13,	at Frankford Yellow Jackets
12/6	W, 13–10,	at Providence Steam Roller

Team Scoring

151 points scored (3rd)

110 points allowed (11th)

The big news in 1925, a year in which the Packers finished 8–5, was the completion of construction of a new stadium. Hagemeister Park had been the team's first home, and a new high school was built on the site. Bellevue Park was a baseball stadium.

When City Stadium opened on September 20, 1925, the Packers had a home of their own—and one that was plush for the times. They were lucky the building was ready for habitation when the Hammond Pros came to town. The Packers won that game 14–0.

A week later, on September 27, the Packers recorded a milestone victory, defeating the Chicago Bears 14–10. It was the first triumph for the Packers in that historic rivalry, although the Bears beat them 21–0 in Chicago later that season.

Though the Packers finished ninth in the league standings that year, they were on sounder financial footing, not only because of the local backers but because attendance for home games was excellent.

While the Packers defense was still king, the offense did more damage during the 1925 season. The club creamed the Milwaukee Badgers 31–0 and the Rochester Jeffersons 33–13. During that era, scoring was more difficult because the ball was rounder, less aerodynamic, and thus much more difficult to throw.

Lambeau, however, was more of a risk-taker than most quarterbacks. At a time when teams averaged only six passes per contest, he threw 17 times a game.

PACKERS HEADLINE

First victory over the Chicago Bears and six wins in first seven games ends with ninth-place finish.

1926

Game-by-Game

9/19	W, 21–0,	vs. Detroit Panthers
9/26	T, 6–6,	vs. Chicago Bears
10/3	T, 0–0,	vs. Duluth Eskimos
10/10	L, 7–13,	vs. Chicago Cardinals
10/17	W, 7–0,	vs. Milwaukee Badgers
10/24	W, 35–0,	vs. Racine Tornadoes
10/31	W, 3–0,	at Chicago Cardinals
11/7	W, 21–0,	at Milwaukee Badgers
11/14	W, 14–0,	vs. Louisville Colonels
11/21	L, 13–19,	at Chicago Bears
11/25	L, 14–20,	at Frankford Yellow Jackets
11/28	W, 7–0, at Detroit Panthers	
12/19	T, 3–3, at Chicago Bears	

Team Scoring

151 points scored (3rd)

61 points allowed (5th)

In a year when the Packers finished 7–3–3 for fifth overall in the National Football League standings, Green Bay was visited by an interesting and competitive Duluth Eskimos opponent.

The headline on the *Green Bay Press-Gazette* story of the October game summarized the City Stadium matchup this way: "Eskimos Put Up Good Fight Against Boys; Nevers Tears Off Feature Run Of Game."

It rained throughout the game, holding down attendance to about 2,500 fans, and the muddy field likely contributed to the inability of the teams to score. Duluth's star player, Ernie Nevers, was an attraction. An iron-man player, Nevers was still a few years away from scoring a record six touchdowns in a game.

In what became a 0–0 result, Lambeau's passing was inhibited and the slop was difficult to maintain footing in, to the extent that most players took pratfalls into the muck at various times during the game. Nevers negotiated a 75-yard run that brought him close to the Packers end zone, but he was hauled down by defender Moose Gardner and the Eskimos failed to score.

Players from both teams had their uniforms so covered in mud that the newspaper's game report remarked that the cleaning bill would be outrageously high.

That season, the Packers played the Bears three times, twice in Chicago. All games were tough battles. Two tie games—6–6 and 3–3—bookended a 19–13 victory by the Bears.

Halfback Verne Lewellen is an All-Pro after scoring seven touchdowns for the third-ranked Packers offense.

Official Program

Published By The
Green Bay Football Corporation

National League

Green Bay
Packers.

vs.

Milwaukee

SUN., SEPT. 11, 1927

2:00 P. M.

JIMMY CROWLEY
making a gain against
Leland Stanford U

Price 10c

The Packers were scheduled to play the Milwaukee Badgers for the season opener on September 11, but the Badgers folded before the start of the season. They were one of several teams to fold in the late 1920s, while the team from Green Bay continues on decade after decade. *AP Photo/NFL Photos*

Curly Lambeau and George Halas, owner and coach of the Chicago Bears, didn't like one another, but the bigger deal was that the Bears became an irritant to the Packers on the field. During the 1927 season, the Packers went 7–2–1—and both losses were to Chicago, 7–6 and 14–6.

However, the Packers had the pleasure of humbling a notable player with Chicago connections. Red Grange, the brilliant halfback, had been an All-American at the University of Illinois, and after completing college play he immediately joined the Bears for an exhibition tour in 1925.

In 1927, though, Grange was committed to his own team, the football New York Yankees, and they came to town in October. The largest crowd to date to watch a football game in Green Bay turned out 11,000 strong to see the heralded Grange. Better for them, they witnessed their Packers whip New York 13–0.

The problem for the fans and the Yankees was that Grange could only watch from the bench because of a leg injury he had suffered in a previous game. With Grange walking with a cane instead of carrying the football, New York displayed little offense. Grange wasn't even supposed to travel. Doctors had ordered him to remain in the hospital, but he made the journey to Wisconsin.

Green Bay scored a touchdown and extra point in the first quarter and added another touchdown in the second period. The 13–0 halftime lead held up.

The Packers defeated the Dayton Triangles by a 6–0 score on November 13, 1927. The Triangles never scored a point in five meetings against Green Bay before the team folded in 1929. Dayton was one of five teams the Packers played against in 1927 that were gone from the league within five years. *MVP Books Collection*

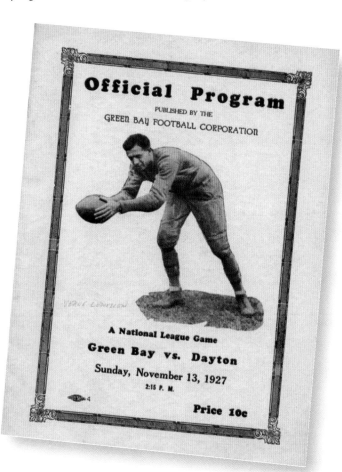

Official Program

PUBLISHED BY THE
GREEN BAY FOOTBALL CORPORATION

VERNE LEWELLEN

A National League Game

Green Bay vs. Dayton

Sunday, November 13, 1927

2:15 P. M.

Price 10c

▶ 7–2–1   2nd place ◀

Game-by-Game

9/18	W, 14–0, vs. Dayton Triangles
9/25	W, 12–7, vs. Cleveland Bulldogs
10/2	L, 6–7, vs. Chicago Bears
10/9	W, 20–0, vs. Duluth Eskimos
10/16	W, 13–0, vs. Chicago Cardinals
10/23	W, 13–0, vs. New York Yankees
11/6	T, 6–6, at Chicago Cardinals
11/13	W, 6–0, vs. Dayton Triangles
11/20	L, 6–14, at Chicago Bears
11/24	W, 17–9, at Frankford Yellow Jackets

Team Scoring

113 points scored (3rd)

43 points allowed (2nd)

PACKERS HEADLINE

A pair of losses to the rival Chicago Bears thwart an otherwise stellar season for Green Bay.

Verne Lewellen

One of the Packers' earliest stars, Verne Lewellen was on the roster from 1924 to 1932 (other than a three-game stint with the New York football Yankees in 1927), long enough to help shepherd Green Bay from a good team to great, from runner-up to champion. He was a First-Team All-Pro in 1926, 1928, and 1929. Then in the 1950s, Lewellen became the Packers' general manager.

Lewellen had already earned a law degree at the University of Nebraska by the time he became a pro football player. While competing for the Packers, he was elected district attorney of Brown County, where Green Bay is located.

An outstanding punter whose official records were lost to time, Lewellen scored 50 touchdowns from his halfback spot for the Packers. Some suggested that Lewellen averaged 50 yards per punt in the 1920s, and there are anecdotes about his brilliant placement ability.

"He was way ahead of his time in ability," said teammate Charlie Mathys. "From 60 yards, if he aimed, he put it out of bounds on the 5-yard line. He had almost dead accuracy."

Lewellen was not a latecomer to punting, either. He trained his whole life, from childhood, for the role. "I remember as a kid my coach used to have me punt 40 or 50 times a day," Lewellen said. "Not any old way, but to different men scattered at different fielding positions. He always emphasized absolute control of the ball."

Lewellen's coach, Curly Lambeau, and Chicago Bears coach George Halas were always at odds, but they could agree on one thing: how good Lewellen was as a punter. "Who was ever better?" Halas said.

Lavvie Dilweg

Prior to Don Hutson, the first offensive end to make an impact for the Packers was Lavvie Dilweg. Dilweg was an All-American at Marquette, played one year for the Milwaukee Badgers, and then joined Green Bay in 1927, where he proceeded to have five straight All-Pro seasons. He was the featured pass catcher on the championship teams of 1929, 1930, and 1931 before retiring in 1934.

Like teammate Verne Lewellen, Dilweg had already obtained a law degree before breaking into pro football, and he practiced law in Green Bay while playing for the Packers. Dilweg practiced with the Packers in morning sessions and then went to his law office in the afternoon.

"Everybody was very understanding," Dilweg said. "If I needed a continuance because of road trips, I'd generally get it."

Later, Dilweg served one term in Congress representing the area, and he also became a Big Ten official.

Dilweg retired the year before Hutson arrived to play end. They may have made for intriguing teammates. "I had a couple of more years left, I think," Dilweg said, "but I could see myself slowing down."

This Packers game from the late 1920s illustrates how far professional football has come since its first decade. Although helmets were the norm by this time, the stadiums in which the teams played were rudimentary, to say the least. *AP Photo/Pro Football Hall of Fame*

1928

▸ 6–4–3   4th place ◂

Game-by-Game

9/23	**L, 9–19,** vs. Frankford Yellow Jackets
9/30	**T, 12–12,** vs. Chicago Bears
10/7	**L, 0–6,** vs. New York Giants
10/14	**W, 20–0,** vs. Chicago Cardinals
10/21	**W, 16–6,** at Chicago Bears
10/28	**W, 17–0,** vs. Dayton Triangles
11/4	**W, 26–14,** at Pottsville Maroons
11/11	**T, 0–0,** vs. New York Yankees
11/18	**W, 7–0,** at New York Giants
11/25	**L, 0–26,** at Pottsville Maroons
11/29	**L, 0–2,** at Frankford Yellow Jackets
12/2	**T, 7–7,** at Providence Steam Roller
12/9	**W, 6–0,** at Chicago Bears

Team Scoring

120 points scored (5th)

92 points allowed (4th)

Relations between the Packers and Bears, or probably more precisely between Curly Lambeau and George Halas, grew tenser in 1928 as Green Bay finished 6–4–3. These two rivals faced each other three times.

The trio of games began in Green Bay in late September, and the squads tied 12–12. Three weeks later, the Packers traveled to Chicago, where they won 16–6 at Wrigley Field. Some 15,000 fans turned out, making it the largest crowd to ever watch Green Bay play football to that date. The teams met a third time in the last game of the season in Chicago, and in front of 14,000 fans the Packers won again, 6–0.

It was standard sportsmanship for the head coaches to shake hands after the final whistle. Lambeau and Halas, hard-driving men, did not shake hands with one another.

"Shake hands?" Lambeau said. "That would have been a lie. If I lost, I wanted to punch Halas in the nose. If he lost, Halas wanted to punch me."

The frosty relationship between the coaches permeated the attitude between the teams as well.

One major difference for the Packers on the field in 1928 was that Lambeau began seriously limiting his role as a player. He threw just one touchdown pass that year and only one the next as he eased himself into street clothes permanently. Lambeau suited up for 11 seasons, counting pre-NFL days, but after that he only wore suits without numbers.

PACKERS HEADLINE

Curly Lambeau recedes into the background as a player while All-Pro Verne Lewellen continues to shine.

Cal Hubbard

Whether playing offensive or defensive tackle, Cal Hubbard was so tough that he made opponents wish they had run the other way or blocked some other guy. At 6-foot-4 and 250 pounds, the muscular Hubbard was not only big for the era, he was quick, and that made him extra deadly to deal with for Packers foes.

Hubbard, who started his pro career in 1927 with the New York Giants, joined the Packers for the longest stretch of his playing days in 1929. He was one of coach Curly Lambeau's important hires that year, and he was a cornerstone of the Green Bay championship teams of 1929, 1930, and 1931.

A three-time All-Pro, Hubbard was inducted into the Pro Football Hall of Fame and the Baseball Hall of Fame after a second career as a prominent umpire.

When Hubbard said you were out on the gridiron, you were out there, too, not just on the diamond, and it was probably because Hubbard made the tackle. "There never was a better lineman," said Chicago Bears coach George Halas.

Hubbard intimidated others with hard-nosed play and speed. Steve Owen, later the New York Giants coach, once said of Hubbard, "A giant of a man who could outrun any back in the league for 30 yards."

Going both ways felt just right to Hubbard. "I can't imagine playing less than half a game," he said. "We had to be in shape, and we were—or we'd have been killed."

MVP Books Collection

Cal Hubbard at his induction into the Pro Football Hall of Fame, September 1963. *AP Photo*

Johnny "Blood" McNally

Johnny McNally, the whippet halfback who took his nom du football from a movie marquee to become Johnny Blood, was a free spirit on the field and especially off of it. He was a dangerously quick and slick runner who could elude tacklers, catch balls, and outrun defenders to the end zone.

He was so good that he was selected for the Pro Football Hall of Fame's charter class in 1963, but he could be such a fun-loving guy that he moved from team to team because he wore out his welcome. Packers coach Curly Lambeau discovered he could not even pay Blood not to drink.

When Blood first came to the Packers in 1929, Lambeau offered him $110 per game if he did not drink from Wednesday until after the weekend game. Blood made a counter offer. "Make it $100 a game and let me drink on Wednesday," he said. Lambeau said Blood was so up-front about his drinking that he would give him the $110 anyway and "still let you drink on Wednesday." The late-night habits and moving from team to team led to the player acquiring the nickname "Vagabond Halfback."

Another time Lambeau pitched Blood in a different manner. He told him he had to promise not to drink during the season. Lambeau gave Blood only $25 a week and held the rest of his pay in escrow. Each day after practice, Blood picked up a couple quarts of milk and adjourned to the home of the *Green Bay Press-Gazette* editor to read because he knew he had a first-rate library. If Blood drank that season, Lambeau never knew it.

Later in life, Blood was asked what games he would never forget. "Our first championship in 1929 was a big thrill for all of us," Blood said. "Eleven men played 60 minutes."

He expressed a particular fondness for the 1936 championship triumph over the Detroit Lions as well. "They were ahead in the last five minutes," Blood said. "I made a great catch for a touchdown, and we beat them 20–18."

During that same game, Blood was benched for a time by Lambeau because he had called a pass play in the huddle that Lambeau had banned. The throw was intercepted. The fans were believers, though, and they chanted "We want Blood!" so loudly that Lambeau thought they might draw blood from his eardrums. He put Blood back in the game, and Johnny won it for him.

Blood played for the Packers from 1929 through 1933 and again in 1935 and 1936. When he joined Pittsburgh as player-coach in 1937, he scored on a 92-yard kickoff return on his first play, and as he passed owner Art Rooney on the sideline, he said, "Nice coaching, huh?"

MVP Books Collection

Stories like that followed Blood from Green Bay to Pittsburgh and beyond, but later in life he questioned their authenticity. "They're mostly legend," he said, "interesting but inaccurate."

1929

Game-by-Game

9/22	W, 9–0, vs. Dayton Triangles
9/29	W, 23–0, vs. Chicago Bears
10/6	W, 9–2, vs. Chicago Cardinals
10/13	W, 14–2, vs. Frankford Yellow Jackets
10/20	W, 24–0, vs. Minneapolis Red Jackets
10/27	W, 7–6, at Chicago Cardinals
11/3	W, 16–6, at Minneapolis Red Jackets
11/10	W, 14–0, at Chicago Bears
11/17	W, 12–0, at Chicago Cardinals
11/24	W, 20–6, at New York Giants
11/28	T, 0–0, at Frankford Yellow Jackets
12/1	W, 25–0, at Providence Steam Roller
12/8	W, 25–0, at Chicago Bear

Team Scoring

198 points scored (2nd)

22 points allowed (1st)

Titletown Is Born.
The Packers put together an undefeated season.

As the first decade of the existence of the Green Bay Packers came to an end, Curly Lambeau and his team gave the small community in northern Wisconsin its biggest reason to cheer yet. The Packers finished the NFL regular season with a 12–0–1 record and secured the franchise's first championship.

The championship was won simply by piling up the best record. There were no playoffs in those days of the NFL, no head-to-head championship games, only a total mark compiled over the course of a season that ran from September to December.

Green Bay had a hard-fought 0–0 contest with the Frankford Yellowjackets late in the year, but they won all other league games. It was an astonishingly dominating defensive performance for the Packers. They posted eight shutouts, did not allow more than six points in any game, and allowed just 22 total points all year. Green Bay had a potent offense as well, ranking second in the league in points scored.

The Bears appeared on the schedule three times in 1929, much to Lambeau's delight, as it turned out. Chicago did not score a point on Lambeau's defense in the three games. Three shutouts in one season of the hated Bears! How grand life was for coach Lambeau. The scores were 23–0, 14–0, and 25–0.

Attendance was growing around the league, too, and each of the first two games against the Bears attracted 13,000 fans. More impressively, a November game against the New York Giants in New York drew 25,000 fans to the Polo Grounds—a new record for any Packers game anywhere.

As well as the Packers played, besting the Giants 20–6 represented the crux of the season. New York finished 13–1–1, but the Packers won the league title because of the head-to-head win and a better winning percentage—1.000.

The Packer defense struggles to tackle New York tailback Benny Friedman on this play at the Polo Grounds on November 24, but Green Bay still secured a 10th consecutive victory with this 20–6 win. *AP Photo*

GREEN BAY PACKERS 1929 © STILLER'S 1929
WORLD CHAMPIONS

Team photo of the first World Champion squad in franchise history. *MVP Books Collection*

One reason the Packers were so exceptional in 1929 was the acumen displayed by Lambeau in adding new faces to the roster. He signed three players who made their debut for that team and eventually became members of the Pro Football Hall of Fame: Johnny "Blood" McNally, Cal Hubbard, and Mike Michalske.

Michalske had played on the New York Yankees team that was formed by promoter C. C. Pyle to capitalize on Red Grange's name, but which went belly-up. That left Michalske, a two-way guard, looking for work, and Lambeau found him.

"Charlie Pyle owed me $400 when the Yankees disbanded," Michalske said, "so I became a free agent. I figure I still have the $400 coming. I also figure I'm not going to collect it."

After the Packers won their first championship, the town threw a celebratory banquet. By then, the team also had a fight song for spectators to chant at home games titled "The Locomotive." Lyrics included, "U! Rah! Rah! Packers." The two-way banter between a lead cheerleader and the crowd went this way: "What's the matter with the Packers?" "They're all right." "Who's all right?" "The Packers." "Who says so?" "We all say so." "Who are we?" "The Bay! The Bay!"

While the Packers were at the pinnacle of the sport, the stock market crash that led to the Great Depression occurred during the middle of the season. When the schedules were completed, teams representing several of the smaller teams in the league folded. Out went the Pottsville Maroons, Detroit Wolverines, and Duluth Eskimos.

The Packers were the anomaly—the little engine that could.

OFFICIAL PROGRAM
Sunday, October 20, 1929

Final
Game
Of
The
Season
At
Home

10¢

KICK-OFF
2 P. M.

Coach Curley Lambeau

Minneapolis vs. Green Bay

Published by
Green Bay Football Corporation

Green Bay defeated the Minneapolis Red Jackets, 24–0, at home on October 20, 1929. Four days later, the stock market crash on "Black Thursday" set the country spiraling into the Great Depression. *MVP Books Collection*

The decade that began with the Great Depression and ended with the United States on the verge of war was the greatest of decades for Curly Lambeau in leading the Green Bay Packers.

Riding the high of the first championship in franchise history in 1929, the Packers carried their success into the new decade with a repeat championship in 1930 and a three-peat in 1931. Then, as had been since the National Football League was founded, the title winner was determined by the best record compiled over the course of the season.

The rules changed in 1932, when the Bears ended the Packers' run. The Bears won the first crown decided by a face-to-face championship game by beating the Portsmouth Spartans. The game was arranged because the teams finished with identical records. However, in 1933 the league split in half, with teams placed in Eastern and Western conferences and the winners meeting for a championship game. The Packers, who were placed in the Western Conference, were joined there by the Chicago Bears.

The Packers swiftly bounced back, winning the 1936 title, reaching the championship game in 1938, and winning the crown once more in 1939.

Green Bay had been blessed with a strong core of players, several new to the 1929 squad, and they helped carry the club through the beginning of the next decade. But Lambeau demonstrated his acumen as a talent judge. After that little lull in the early 1930s, he acquired new greats who brought the Packers back to the top.

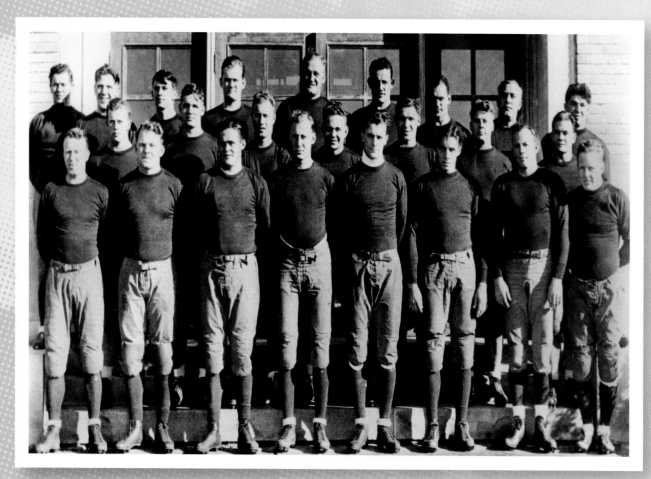

The 1931 Packers represented three-time repeat NFL champions. Green Bay would accumulate four league titles in the decade under coach Curly Lambeau. *AP Photo/Pro Football Hall of Fame*

"OLD CITY STADIUM"
GREEN BAY - 1938

Aerial view of Green Bay's City Stadium in 1938.
MVP Books Collection

As a proponent of the passing game, Lambeau searched for the right players to fit his system. Obtaining a top quarterback was imperative, but it was just as important to find someone who could catch the ball and make big plays. Lambeau targeted Alabama end Don Hutson, an acclaimed All-American, as his game-changer. Only a few other NFL teams recognized Hutson's value.

Hutson came out of school in 1935, and the NFL draft did not start until the next year, so teams could bid for rookies. Hutson signed with Green Bay and Brooklyn. Commissioner Joe Carr awarded Hutson's rights to the Packers because he had signed that contract earlier. The decision changed history. Brooklyn went out of business and Green Bay thrived.

Hutson became a pioneer receiver, demonstrating skills and savvy well ahead of his time and inventing pass routes that are still used. Almost 70 years after his retirement, Hutson is still considered one of the best football players in history. His acquisition for the Packers was huge.

In between capturing four championships in the '30s, Green Bay did have its first losing record ever under Lambeau in 1933. But it was a blip on the screen, and whatever rebuilding Lambeau felt was needed was accomplished on the fly without a prolonged slump. The key new faces from 1929—Johnny "Blood" McNally, Cal Hubbard, and Mike Michalske—were still around in the 1930s, but they were supplemented by quarterback Arnie Herber, Hutson, Clarke Hinkle, Joe Laws, and Milt Gantenbein.

Leather helmets had become commonplace by the 1920s, and in 1938 the first hard-shell helmet was manufactured. The very last players in the league who failed to wear protective headgear were gone by 1940.

Most importantly for Lambeau and the Packers, passing rules were liberalized and the ball was streamlined. No team was better equipped than Green Bay to take advantage of the changes. Already having Herber on the roster made it easier for Lambeau to recruit Hutson.

"I remember Curly Lambeau telling me over the telephone that Green Bay had the best long passer in pro football," Hutson said.

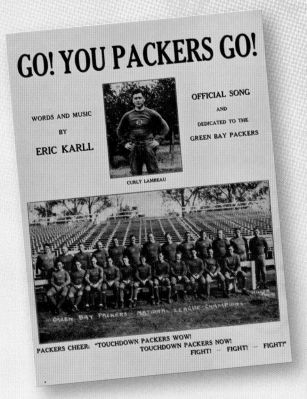

Sheet-music cover for "Go! You Packers Go!" fight song.
MVP Books Collection

1930

▶ 10–3–1   1st place ◀

Game-by-Game

9/21	W, 14–0, vs. Chicago Cardinals
9/28	W, 7–0, vs. Chicago Bears
10/5	W, 14–7, vs. New York Giants
10/12	W, 27–12, vs. Frankford Yellow Jackets
10/19	W, 13–0, at Minneapolis Red Jackets
10/26	W, 19–0, vs. Minneapolis Red Jackets
11/2	W, 47–13, vs. Portsmouth Spartans
11/9	W, 13–12, at Chicago Bears
11/16	L, 6–13, at Chicago Cardinals
11/23	L, 6–13, at New York Giants
11/27	W, 25–7, at Frankford Yellow Jackets
11/30	W, 37–7, at Staten Island Stapletons
12/7	L, 0–21, at Chicago Bears
12/14	T, 6–6, at Portsmouth Spartans

Team Scoring

234 points scored (2nd)

111 points allowed (4th)

PACKERS HEADLINE

Packers' 8–0 start extends unbeaten streak to 23 games, dating back to November 1928.

Since the Packers ended their 1929 season with an extracurricular game against Memphis, which they lost, they had no carryover winning streak. But they had not lost an NFL game since the third-to-last game of the 1928 season.

When Green Bay spurted to an 8–0 start in 1930, it lifted the team's unbeaten streak to 23 games. It was an impressive run, and particularly satisfying in 1930 when two games against the Chicago Bears went into the win column, 7–0 and 13–12.

The Packers were not as dominating, but with a 10–3–1 record, they were good enough to claim a second championship in a row. The Giants, with whom Green Bay split their two meetings, placed second at 13–4. The November game in New York was witnessed by 37,000 fans. The Bears won a third game versus the Pack, 21–0.

Especially early on, Green Bay's key offensive player was Verne Lewellen. In the opening rout of Oshkosh, Lewellen scored a touchdown. In the second game against the Chicago Cardinals, he scored on a 10-yard run. In the third game against the Bears, he scored on a 1-yard run. In the first Giants game, Lewellen threw a touchdown pass. He was always around the ball, and those offensive snaps didn't include his long-distance punting.

"I scored a lot of touchdowns on pass receiving," Lewellen said. "I had Michalske and Hubbard on that side of the line, and they did a pretty good job of clearing the way."

The Packers took on the Portsmouth Spartans for the first time on November 2, 1930, and defeated them handily, 47–13, in Green Bay's highest scoring output of the season. It was the beginning of a long rivalry between the two clubs, as the Spartans would go on to become the Detroit Lions, beginning in 1934. *AP Photo/NFL Photos*

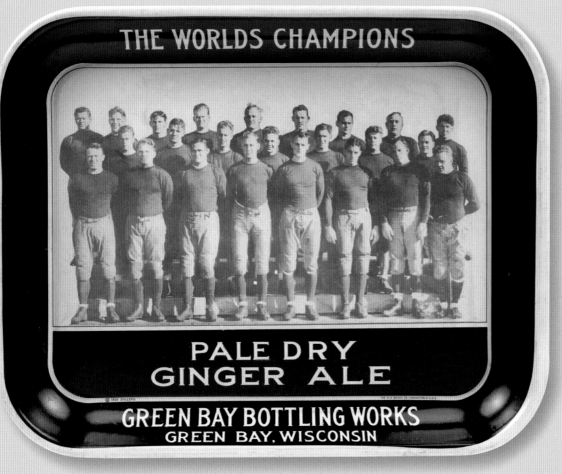

THE WORLDS CHAMPIONS

PALE DRY
GINGER ALE

GREEN BAY BOTTLING WORKS
GREEN BAY, WISCONSIN

A third straight world championship made the Packers the toast of the town, and of all the NFL, in 1931.
MVP Books Collection

Game-by-Game

9/13	**W**, 26–0,	vs. Cleveland Indians
9/20	**W**, 32–6,	vs. Brooklyn Dodgers
9/27	**W**, 7–0, vs. Chicago Bears	
10/4	**W**, 27–7,	vs. New York Giants
10/11	**W**, 26–7,	vs. Chicago Cardinals
10/18	**W**, 15–0,	vs. Frankford Yellow Jackets
10/25	**W**, 48–20,	vs. Providence Steam Roller
11/1	**W**, 6–2, at Chicago Bears	
11/8	**W**, 26–0,	vs. Staten Island Stapletons
11/15	**L**, 13–21,	at Chicago Cardinals
11/22	**W**, 14–10,	at New York Giants
11/26	**W**, 38–7,	at Providence Steam Roller
11/29	**W**, 7–0,	at Brooklyn Dodgers
12/6	**L**, 6–7, at Chicago Bears	

Team Scoring

291 points scored (1st)

87 points allowed (2nd)

The way the Packers dominated most of the season, it was surprising they even lost a game. Green Bay finished 12–2 and won a third straight championship. In 11 of 14 games, the defense allowed zero or one touchdowns and posted four shutouts.

Probably the single biggest out-of-character game of the season was a 48–20 victory over the Providence Steam Roller. That was Green Bay's highest point total of the year, but it was almost its highest number of points allowed. In a 26–7 win over the Cardinals, Johnny Blood scored three times on pass plays. Mildly irritating was an end-of-season loss to the good old Chicago Bears, 7–6.

The final scores of the other two games of the season against the Bears—both triumphs—sounded more like pitching matchups than football results. Green Bay won 7–0 and 6–2.

Winning three straight titles made Curly Lambeau a household name, not only in his home area but throughout Wisconsin. And with pro football gaining in status around the country, he was becoming known elsewhere as well.

Having Arnie Herber gave the Packers an advantage over most teams, because his ability to throw was far advanced over most of the other quarterbacks in the league. Herber, who joined the Packers from the New York Giants in 1930, was one of those players who disdained using a helmet until the NFL mandated it.

"I didn't wear headgear because it was too heavy," Herber said, "and I felt it slowed me down."

PACKERS HEADLINE

Top-ranked offense and second-ranked defense lead Packers to 12–2 record and third straight championship.

Football's First Three-Peat Champions

Recording the team's first NFL championship in 1929, the Green Bay Packers stayed on a roll into the new decade and became the first team to capture three straight titles by adding the 1930 and 1931 crowns.

Defense paved the way for the Pack in 1929, when the squad allowed just 22 points all season. The defense was still strong in 1930 and 1931, but the two sides of the ball were better balanced. Green Bay could score, too.

There was a fair amount of turnover on the roster for 1929 and 1930, but not among key players. One of those changes was Curly Lambeau quitting as a player-coach and just sticking around as coach. Verne Lewellen, Cal Hubbard, Lavvie Dilweg, Mike Michalske, and Johnny "Blood" McNally still represented the core of the lineup. In 1931, end Milt Gantenbein joined the crew.

Lewellen was in the midst of leading the Packers in touchdown scoring for five straight years. His skein began in 1927 and ended in 1931.

During that three-year championship stretch, the Packers won 12 games, 10 games, and 12 games. They owned the NFL. Several big-city franchises found this difficult to believe, and concurrent with their snobby outlook there was disparagement of Green Bay as a hole-in-the-wall town.

After a few years of continued success, though, the Packers gained serious respect around the league, and some of the big-city writers began to look at Green Bay as a charming entrant in the NFL.

During one of the post-championship celebrations on the train ride back to Green Bay, the always-mischievous Blood got to teasing Dilweg by throwing wet napkins at him. Despite Dilweg's growing anger, the sophomoric Blood refused to stop. Dilweg came after him, and Blood ran through train cars with Dilweg pursing. As Blood ran out of room, Dilweg believed he had him cornered.

However, Blood went out the back door, climbed the railing, and hauled his body onto the roof of the train car. Then as the train kept rolling, Blood ran over the car tops and climbed back down into the train. "When we stopped in Green Bay, I got out, ran up to the locomotive, climbed next to the engineer, and let everybody think I'd made the whole trip on top of the train," Blood said.

During the Packers' 1929–31 victory stretch, there were no culminating championship games. The team's regular-season record provided the title, but celebrations were still in order. When the Packers began the 1930 season with a home game against the Chicago Cardinals, provisions were made for a pre-game ceremony a half hour before kickoff.

The activities were announced in the *Green Bay Press-Gazette*. An article read, "Pepped up all over again over the championship won last year, the first in Green Bay's history, the football corporation has made plans for an appropriate celebration." Those plans included a parade on the field, the playing of "On Wisconsin," and then the raising of a pennant with the words "National Champions, 1929."

Three-peat champs pose before the 1932 season.

Verne Lewellen sets franchise record
with his 301st point scored,
while the defense holds opponents to seven scoreless games.

G reen Bay's championship winning streak came to an end during the 1932 season, even though the Pack finished 10–3–1.

That was the year in which Verne Lewellen established a Packers scoring record and completed the year with his fiftieth touchdown in a Green Bay uniform. Lewellen had begun collecting his touchdowns starting in 1924, and this was his ninth campaign. Lewellen set the team record of 301 points, ranking far ahead of Johnny Blood and Curly Lambeau.

Some of the wackiest scores in the long rivalry with the Bears were recorded that season. The first contest was a 0–0 tie. The second game was 2–0 Packers, and the third game was 9–0 Bears. Green Bay did not score a touchdown against the Chicago defense that season. The Bears also compiled the peculiar record of 7–1–6, which was good enough to win the title.

Ordinarily, Portsmouth was not as fierce a rival as the Bears, but the 1932 game became a grudge match. The Spartans and their fans issued several insults to the Packers before the October 9 game. The anger dated back to the 1931 season.

The Spartans refused to play in Green Bay, and they felt they secured a commitment from Lambeau to play in Portsmouth. When Lambeau indicated he had signed no contract and wouldn't bring the Packers to town, there was outrage. The team was called "The Green Bay Pikers" and "Cheese Champions." But the Packers won the October 1932 game, 15–10.

1932

▶ 10–3–1   2nd place ◀

Game-by-Game

9/18	W, 15–7, vs. Chicago Cardinals
9/25	T, 0–0, vs. Chicago Bears
10/2	W, 13–0, vs. New York Giants
10/9	W, 15–10, vs. Portsmouth Spartans
10/16	W, 2–0, at Chicago Bears
10/23	W, 13–0, vs. Brooklyn Dodgers
10/30	W, 26–0, vs. Staten Island Stapletons
11/6	W, 19–9, at Chicago Cardinals
11/13	W, 21–0, vs. Boston Braves
11/20	L, 0–6, at New York Giants
11/24	W, 7–0, at Brooklyn Dodgers
11/27	W, 21–3, at Staten Island Stapletons
12/4	L, 0–19, at Portsmouth Spartans
12/11	L, 0–9, at Chicago Bears

Team Scoring

152 points scored (2nd)

63 points allowed (2nd)

1933

Game-by-Game

9/17	T, 7–7, vs. Boston Redskins
9/24	L, 7–14, vs. Chicago Bears
10/1	L, 7–10, vs. New York Giants
10/8	W, 17–0, vs. Portsmouth Spartans
10/15	W, 47–0, vs. Pittsburgh Pirates
10/22	L, 7–10, at Chicago Bears
10/29	W, 35–9, vs. Philadelphia Eagles
11/5	W, 14–6, at Chicago Cardinals
11/12	L, 0–7, at Portsmouth Spartans
11/19	L, 7–20, at Boston Redskins
11/26	L, 6–17, at New York Giants
12/3	W, 10–0, at Philadelphia Eagles
12/10	L, 6–7, at Chicago Bears

Team Scoring

170 points scored (2nd)

107 points allowed (6th)

PACKERS HEADLINE

Franchise suffers first losing season, but ushers in new era of home games at Milwaukee.

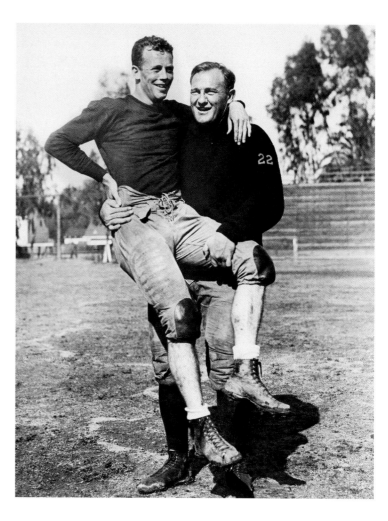

The 250-pound tackle Cal Hubbard gives a lift to 180-pound halfback Roger Grove in early 1933. Hubbard was an All-Pro selection that season, while Grove led the Packers with 17 pass receptions. Grove spent five seasons with Green Bay (1931–1935) before leaving pro football. *AP Photo*

All of a sudden in 1933, the Green Bay Packers were no longer championship material, and for the first time since the founding of the franchise in 1919, they were not a winning team. The club suffered through its first losing campaign, 5–7–1, and the highlights were much harder to come by.

The timing could have been better, but this was the first season in which the Packers played some home games in Milwaukee instead of hosting all of them at City Stadium. Borchert Field was the home away from home. The first time Green Bay played in the facility, on October 1, 1933, the Packers faced the New York Giants.

The reason for the part-time switch was to play in a bigger stadium and hopefully attract bigger crowds than were turning out in Green Bay, so as to produce a windfall. Attendance was just 12,467 for the 10–7 loss to New York, which was probably only slightly larger than it likely would have been in Green Bay. The Pack fell behind early, trailing 10–0 at the half, and could not come back. The only Packers touchdown was scored by Buckets Goldenberg on a three-yard run.

Most of the season, the Packers had difficulty scoring, but they did have two explosive games. In mid-October, they smashed the Pittsburgh Pirates (who would soon be renamed the Steelers) 47–0, and two weeks later they crushed the Philadelphia Eagles 35–9.

Goldenberg and Bob Monnett, both rookies, each scored two touchdowns in the Pittsburgh win.

Clarke Hinkle

Although Clarke Hinkle played college football at little Bucknell University in rural Pennsylvania, Green Bay Packers coach Curly Lambeau found him anyway.

Hinkle was one of the most versatile players of his time. He was a bruising fullback on offense and a bruising tackler on defense, and he played both ways for the Packers. Running the ball, kicking it, or bringing down men who tried to carry it past him, Clarke was a superb player during his tenure with the Packers (1932–1941).

"Clarke Hinkle was the greatest all-around fullback ever to play in the National Football League," Lambeau said. "Hinkle rams the middle, runs wide, blocks and tackles viciously, punts and placekicks with the best, can do a good job as a pass receiver, and on defense against the aerial attack, he has no superior in professional football."

Hinkle rushed for 3,860 yards, caught 48 passes, and was chosen All-Pro four times as a fullback.

He could also tackle. Bronko Nagurski, the battering-ram running back for the Chicago Bears, said Hinkle was the "toughest man I ever played against, and we collided in at least 25 games."

Hinkle never said tackling Nagurski was easy. Sometimes he brought the king-sized runner down, but sometimes he had to stay down himself after contact. "One time I hit him and wound up with seven stitches to patch up a cut on my chin," Hinkle said.

When balloting took place in 1994 for an all-time NFL team of the old, 60-minute, two-way performers, Hinkle was selected.

AP Photo

MVP Books Collection

1934

Game-by-Game

9/16   **W**, 19–6,
vs. Philadelphia Eagles

9/23   **L**, 10–24,
vs. Chicago Bears

9/30   **W**, 20–6,
vs. New York Giants

10/7   **L**, 0–3, vs. Detroit Lions

10/14   **W**, 41–0,
vs. Cincinnati Reds

10/21   **W**, 15–0,
vs. Chicago Cardinals

10/28   **L**, 14–27,
at Chicago Bears

11/4   **W**, 10–0,
at Boston Redskins

11/11   **L**, 3–17, at New York Giants

11/18   **L**, 0–9,
vs. Chicago Cardinals

11/25   **W**, 3–0,
at Detroit Lions

11/29   **L**, 0–6,
at Chicago Cardinals

12/2   **W**, 21–14,
at St. Louis Gunners

Team Scoring

156 points scored (3rd)

112 points allowed (7th)

PACKERS HEADLINE

Financial struggles compound on-field losses, but local businessmen raise funds to keep team solvent.

Arnie Herber, Clarke Hinkle, Hank Bruder, and Joe Laws practice their kicking in preparation for the upcoming game against the Giants in New York, November 8, 1934. The Packers lost to the Giants to fall to 5–4 with four games to play. *Corbis/Bettman*

This was hardly the best season in Packers history. On the field, the team finished 7–6, a winning record and thus an improvement over 1933. However, Green Bay was a distant third in the Western Division standings behind the Chicago Bears and the Detroit Lions, who were the transplanted Portsmouth Spartans.

The Depression gripped the country, and money was tight. When a fan took a fall out of the stands at City Stadium and won a $5,000 judgment, the team felt it was covered by its insurance policy. However, the insurance company went out of business.

As a result, the Packers went into receivership. Rallying behind the hometown Packers once again, a team of local businessmen spearheaded by the "Hungry Five," raised $15,000 to keep the gates open.

The Packers had played their first "home" game in Milwaukee in 1933, but this season they formalized the arrangement and committed to two home games in the beer city at State Fair Park for the next three years. The idea was to potentially raise more revenue in a stadium that held 32,000 fans rather than City Stadium's 22,000. The Packers definitely needed the money.

Green Bay displayed little offensive punch during the season. The Packers had the gifted-throwing Arnie Herber, but they lacked receivers. Herber completed just 42 passes all season, and his leading receiver was Clarke Hinkle with 11 catches. Hinkle, who was at the beginning of a Hall of Fame career, was also the leading running back with 359 yards.

▶ 8–4   2nd place ◀

Don Hutson was the story of the 1935 season. The arrival of the Alabama All-American transformed the Packers into a more dangerous offensive team. Quarterback Arnie Herber had someone to throw to who could ruin defenses. The Packers finished 8–4, second in the standings. Coach Curly Lambeau was piecing together a strong team that included some holdovers, but it was built around the 6-foot-1, 185-pound Hutson. Hutson was faster and trickier and had better hands than any receiver seen in the game before.

On the first play of his professional career against the Chicago Bears on September 22, Hutson collaborated with Herber on an eye-opening play. After the hike, Herber faked a pass to Johnny Blood McNally and then looked downfield, where Hutson was running away from coverage. He hauled in the long pass and scored on an 83-yard play.

It was a spectacular moment that not only sent a message that Hutson was a new and exciting weapon, but that the Packers were on their way back to the top. That touchdown was the only score in a 7–0 victory over the Bears. Later in the season, Green Bay edged Chicago 17–14 after a dramatic finish.

That win was tremendously satisfying. The Bears appeared to have the game locked up in the fourth quarter, and many of the 30,000 fans at Wrigley Field were departing. However, the Packers rallied with two touchdowns in the last three and a half minutes. Both of them came on tosses from Herber to Hutson, covering 69 and four yards.

Don Hutson's arrival in Green Bay in 1935 ushered in a new era for the Packers and for pro football. He revolutionized the position of wide receiver and helped lead the Packers to 11 straight winning seasons. *AP Photo/Robert Walsh*

Game-by-Game

9/15	L, 6–7, vs. Chicago Cardinals
9/22	W, 7–0, vs. Chicago Bears
9/29	W, 16–7, vs. New York Giants
10/6	W, 27–0, vs. Pittsburgh Pirates
10/13	L, 0–3, vs. Chicago Cardinals
10/20	W, 13–9, vs. Detroit Lions
10/27	W, 17–14, at Chicago Bears
11/10	W, 31–7, vs. Detroit Lions
11/17	L, 10–20, at Detroit Lions
11/24	W, 34–14, at Pittsburgh Pirates
11/28	L, 7–9, at Chicago Cardinals
12/8	W, 13–6, at Philadelphia Eagles

Team Scoring

181 points scored (3rd)

96 points allowed (1st)

PACKERS HEADLINE

Newcomer Don Hutson sparks offense while defense holds opponents to league-low 96 points.

Don Hutson

Don Hutson was special from the moment he put on a Green Bay Packers uniform. Still regarded as one of the greatest players in football history, Hutson turned pro in 1935 after an All-American career at Alabama.

Other teams did not think Hutson would be a valuable pro because of his slight build. However, Green Bay's Curly Lambeau, who had already cast his lot with the forward pass, recognized how important the young player could be.

Hutson revolutionized the game. He invented the modern position of receiver, invented pass routes, and scored 105 touchdowns (99 through the air) for Green Bay in an 11-season career spanning 1935 to 1945.

Hutson scored a touchdown on his first play from scrimmage, an 83-yard pass play, and at times it seemed as if he could score at will. During his rookie year, Hutson made one of his grander statements against the Chicago Bears. Green Bay bested the Bears 7–0 early in the season, and then in a late-October rematch Chicago seemed poised to gain a split. With the Bears leading 14–3 in the fourth quarter, fans began leaving Chicago's Wrigley Field.

"I got hit sometime in the game," Hutson recalled. "I was dizzy and I was out of the game for a while. Then Curly put me back in with two and a half minutes left. Herber threw a little flat pass to me, and I went the rest of the way for a touchdown." The Packers got the ball back quickly, and Hutson scored on another touchdown pass.

Hutson stood 6-foot-1 and weighed around 180 pounds. Until they went up against him, defensive backs couldn't figure out just how he got free so easily.

"I remember the first time I played against him," said Dwight Sloan, who faced Hutson from 1938 to 1940. "He came out for a pass and I had no trouble keeping up with him. 'This isn't too hard,' I thought to myself. And then I couldn't find him. Suddenly, I looked behind me and he was far up the field taking in the pass. He had shifted into high gear and left me standing there."

While it was undeniable that Hutson was speedy and talented and could make catches other ends could only dream of, he said he worked very hard at his craft.

MVP Books Collection

"For every pass I caught in a game," Hutson said, "I caught a thousand in practice."

Hutson worked closely with Arnie Herber as quarterback first, and then Cecil Isbell. Herber ended up in the Hall of Fame. Isbell played only five seasons but had the stronger arm. Isbell was amazed with what he had to work with when looking downfield for Hutson.

"Hutson is the only man I ever saw who can feint in three different directions at the same time."

—Hall of Fame coach Greasy Neale

"He had triple speed," Isbell said. "The man could do the most amazing things. He had finesse. He could freeze a defensive back better than anybody I've seen."

Although it seemed as if he was still at the top of his game, Hutson retired after the 1945 season to become a Packers assistant coach.

Hutson set 22 league records, some for receiving and some broader in scope. Many of his records lasted for decades. Among those achievements were leading the NFL in scoring five times and five times in a row; most times leading the league in touchdowns scored, eight; and most times leading the league in passes caught, eight.

He held the record for most passes caught in a game (14), most receptions in a season (74), and most passes caught in a career (488). Hutson also had his name next to the record for most receiving yards in a game (209), a season (1,211), and a career (7,991). Hutson held the records for most touchdowns in a game (four), most TDs in a season (17), and most receiving touchdowns in a career (99). Hutson, who also kicked at times, scored a record-setting 823 points in his career.

Don Hutson Jockey Underwear ad, mid-1940s. *MVP Books Collection*

Don Hutson Wheaties ad, mid-1940s. *MVP Books Collection*

1936

Game-by-Game

9/13	W, 10–7,	vs. Chicago Cardinals
9/20	L, 3–30,	vs. Chicago Bears
10/4	W, 24–0,	vs. Chicago Cardinals
10/11	W, 31–2,	vs. Boston Redskins
10/18	W, 20–18, vs. Detroit Lions	
10/25	W, 42–10,	vs. Pittsburgh Pirates
11/1	W, 21–10,	at Chicago Bears
11/8	W, 7–3, at Boston Redskins	
11/15	W, 38–7,	at Brooklyn Dodgers
11/22	W, 26–14,	at New York Giants
11/29	W, 26–17, at Detroit Lions	
12/6	T, 0–0,	at Chicago Cardinals

Playoffs

12/13	W, 21–6,	vs. Boston Redskins

Team Scoring

248 points scored (1st)

118 points allowed (4th)

PACKERS HEADLINE

Packers win fourth title in franchise history and win in their first postseason appearance.

After a few years of famine, the Packers were rejuvenated. In 1936, Green Bay won its fourth championship with a 10–1–1 record—and first title under the procedures that included a postseason playoff.

The Packers averaged 20 points per game during the regular season, and the only defeat was an aberration—a 30–3 loss to the Chicago Bears. After that loss, the team knocked off nine consecutive wins, four at home and five on the road. They played to a scoreless tie in the season finale against the Chicago Cardinals, but Green Bay had already locked up the Western Division crown and the best record in the league.

No longer a rookie and adapting well to the pros, Hutson brought out the best in quarterback Arnie Herber. He caught 34 passes for eight touchdowns and averaged 15.8 yards per catch. Clarke Hinkle led the ground attack with 476 yards and five touchdowns on 100 carries.

During the regular season, the Packers outgained opponents by 600 yards and outscored them by 130 points.

Coach Curly Lambeau, who had become enamored with Hollywood, took the team on a postseason tour of the western United States, with stops for exhibition games in Denver and San Francisco and for three more in Los Angeles. It was all about making money for the Packers coffers. They even played the Bears twice in L.A.

The Packers' 21–6 victory over the Boston Redskins secured the franchise's third NFL title after a five-year hiatus. Here the Redskins attempt, and miss, the extra point following their lone touchdown of the contest. *MVP Books Collection*

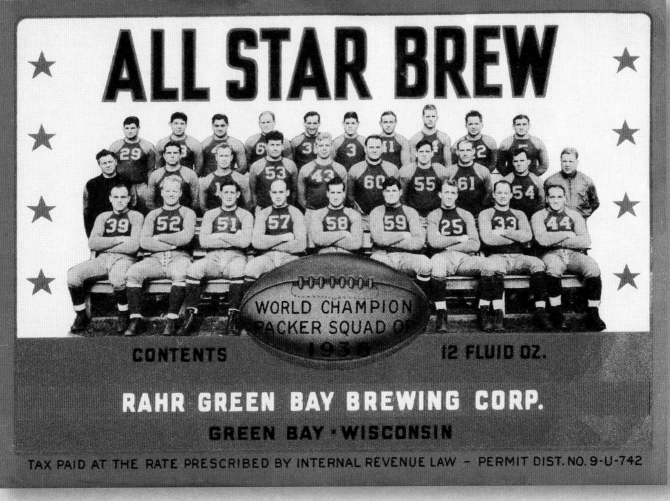

MVP Books Collection

1936 Championship Game

Once Curly Lambeau and the Packers discovered the taste of celebratory champagne in 1929, they decided they liked having banquets and parades at the end of the season. After the run of three straight NFL crowns in 1929, 1930, and 1931, the Packers went through a little lull, but they came back in the middle of the decade with fresh troops.

The league divided into two conferences after the 1932 season, and in 1936, the Packers won the Western Division for the first time since the change. They finished with a league-best record of 10–1–1, but instead of being anointed champs based on regular-season record, the Packers now had to face the Eastern Division victors for the title.

On December 13, 1936, Green Bay faced the Boston Redskins in New York. The Redskins had been founded in 1932 by owner George Preston Marshall and played home games in Boston's Fenway Park. However, even as the team rallied to capture the NFL's Eastern Division with a 7–5 record, attendance at the Redskins' last home game was under 5,000. Marshall was so unhappy that he didn't care about a home-field advantage, and that's why the game was moved to

New York. After the season, the team became the Washington Redskins.

The Packers, meanwhile, were pretty much unveiling their new weapon, receiver Don Hutson, on the national stage. Hutson had been a rookie in 1935, but the Packers had placed second in their division that year, so he was still largely unknown to the football-watching public.

Although the Polo Grounds was a neutral site, the 1936 Championship Game attracted nearly 30,000 fans.

Green Bay won its fourth title, 21–6, in a game that was close until the fourth quarter. The Packers led 7–0 after the first quarter, 7–6 at the half, and 14–6 after three quarters. Green Bay got touchdowns from Hutson, Milt Gantenbein, and Bob Monnett. Most of the key plays revolved around passes from quarterback Arnie Herber. The Packers got a break after a fumble was picked up by Boston and returned 90 yards for a score. It was called back on a penalty. The Packers also blocked two punts.

The win secured the franchise's fourth league title. And more were still to come.

August "Mike" Michalske

Playing eight seasons for the Packers, starting in 1929 with the first championship squad, Mike Michalske was an undersized lineman of 210 pounds. What he lacked in size he made up for in fire. Such competitiveness helped him become the first guard elected to the Pro Football Hall of Fame.

In older age, Michalske reflected on how much had changed in pro football and how much bigger the linemen were. "They're bigger than they were then," Michalske said, "and I guess they're faster. But I don't know whether their hearts are growing any bigger—that's pretty important in this game."

Michalske played his college ball at Penn State, and many years later he coached Iowa State. In Green Bay, he was a six-time All-Pro guard. Curiously, he wore nine different uniform numbers with the team.

For the Packers, Michalske played both ways, usually all 60 minutes a game. He picked up the nickname "Iron Mike" after playing two seasons with the old New York Yankees. "Forty years ago, they played because they liked it," said Michalske.

The aggressive lineman was a regular on Green Bay's first three championship teams, 1929 to 1931. One of Michalaske's favorite memories was picking up a fumble and running 70 yards with it to score a touchdown against the Chicago Bears.

"Mike was not only a smart player," said fellow guard Buckets Goldenberg, "but he had a fine mind for football and a great interest in the game from all standpoints. He sold Lambeau on quite a few of his ideas."

MVP Books Collection

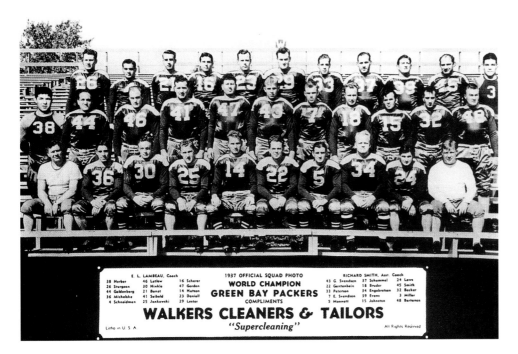

Green Bay dropped back to second place in 1937, but this roster still produced the highest-scoring offense in the league. All but one of the Packers' seven wins were by double digits. *MVP Books Collection*

The Packers' 1937 season was afflicted with a certain amount of schizophrenia. Green Bay lost to both Chicago teams, the Bears and the Cardinals, to start the season, and to the New York Giants and renamed Washington Redskins to end the season. Yet in between, the Packers won seven games in a row.

One satisfying win was a 34–13 thumping of the Cardinals in a return bout in Milwaukee. Ed Jankowski, the team's No. 1 draft pick out of Wisconsin, had one of his best days, scoring on a 46-yard run. During the season, his first of five with the team, Jankowski rushed for 324 yards on 61 attempts for a 5.3 yards-per-carry average.

Another had-to-have-it win after the slow start came in Detroit against the Lions. The Packers won 14–13 on Ernie Smith's extra point in the closing minutes. Detroit led 13–0, but Jankowski dashed for a 36-yard touchdown run, and Clarke Hinkle's two-yard TD run set up Smith's game-winning boot.

Following the 0–2 start, the Packers were making a move to crawl into contention for the divisional crown, but they missed out with the season-ending two straight losses. End of miracle comeback.

Lambeau really did do just about every Green Bay job, and that included playing general manager. "Contract negotiations with Curly were like a three-act play," said Buckets Goldenberg. "You started out full of hope. Then Curly started to talk down your demands. At the end, you felt like a bad guy trying to rob the Packers."

Goldenberg's loyalty to the Packers lasted 13 years. Born in Odessa, Russia, in 1911, Goldenberg and his family fled as refugees to the United States, where he became a star football player, first for the University of Wisconsin and then the Packers, for whom he remained a fixture on the line from 1933 to 1945.

"I loved to block," Goldenberg said. "I loved to knock down those fellows on the other side to give our ballcarriers running room. And on defense, I liked to clobber somebody, anybody, just as long as he wore a different jersey."

▶ **7–4   2nd place** ◀

Game-by-Game

9/12	L, 7–14,	vs. Chicago Cardinals
9/19	L, 2–14, vs. Chicago Bears	
10/3	W, 26–6, vs. Detroit Lions	
10/10	W, 34–13,	vs. Chicago Cardinals
10/17	W, 35–10,	at Cleveland Rams
10/24	W, 35–7,	vs. Cleveland Rams
10/31	W, 14–13, at Detroit Lions	
11/7	W, 24–14,	at Chicago Bears
11/14	W, 37–7,	vs. Philadelphia Eagles
11/21	L, 0–10,	at New York Giants
11/28	L, 6–14,	at Washington Redskins

Team Scoring

220 points scored (1st)

122 points allowed (5th)

PACKERS HEADLINE

Packers again dominate on offense, but two two-game losing streaks to start and finish the season doom championship hopes.

41

1938

Game-by-Game

9/11	W, 26–17, vs. Cleveland Rams
9/18	L, 0–2, vs. Chicago Bears
9/25	W, 28–7, vs. Chicago Cardinals
9/28	W, 24–22, at Chicago Cardinals
10/9	L, 7–17, vs. Detroit Lions
10/16	W, 35–7, vs. Brooklyn Dodgers
10/23	W, 20–0, vs. Pittsburgh Pirates
10/30	W, 28–7, at Cleveland Rams
11/6	W, 24–17, at Chicago Bears
11/13	W, 28–7, at Detroit Lions
11/20	L, 3–15, at New York Giants

Playoffs

12/11	L, 17–23, at New York Giants

Team Scoring

223 points scored (1st)

118 points allowed (3rd)

PACKERS HEADLINE

Championship game loss to Giants brings disappointing end to promising season.

For the first time, the Packers reached the NFL Championship Game but didn't win it. They fell to the New York Giants 23–17 at the Polo Grounds before the biggest championship-game crowd to date of 48,120.

The Giants scored first and held the lead right through a scoreless fourth period. Although Arnie Herber threw a touchdown pass of 40 yards to Carl Mulleneaux, Don Hutson was nowhere to be found on the score sheet. Even Tiny Engebretsen kicked a field goal for Green Bay.

One thing that made the 1938 season unique was air travel. This was coach Curly Lambeau's idea, and several players were edgy about it. "I know we did fly to California," said guard Mike Michalske. "It was quite a change for everybody, including me. On my first trip to Green Bay, I came by bus." Some connected with the team believed that no one besides Lambeau favored flying.

New York beat the Packers 15–3 during the regular season, too, so no one disputed who was the best team. In another odd score, Green Bay lost to the Chicago Bears 2–0.

It also became apparent that Arnie Herber was near the end of his tenure behind center. Cecil Isbell, five years younger, and faster, threw more passes than Herber and also ran for 445 yards. He represented the future. Green Bay saw 13 players catch passes that season, including Isbell when Herber was throwing and Herber when Isbell was throwing.

Fullback Clark Hinkle gets some blocking as he heads up field against the Giants during a losing effort in the NFL Championship Game at New York's Polo Grounds on December 11, 1938. *NY Daily News Archive via Getty Images*

Arnie Herber

Arnie Herber was born in Green Bay nine years before the Packers were founded, and the team was ready for him when he took over as quarterback in 1930. Herber remained with the Pack through 1940 and was an early inductee to the Pro Football Hall of Fame in Canton, Ohio.

Known for his ability to throw the long-range pass, Herber paired perfectly and explosively with Don Hutson once he arrived in 1935. Three times Herber led the NFL in passing, and he won the first official passing title in 1932.

"A lot of guys today can throw the ball as far or maybe farther," coach Curly Lambeau said of Herber in the 1960s, "but none as well for distance. The guy was phenomenal."

It was an achievement for Herber to make the team at age 19 in 1930. Green Bay was the defending league champion, and there were only 18 men on the roster. It was not an easy way to get rich, either; Herber was paid $75 a game.

"In my first two years with the Packers, I played without a headgear," Herber said. "It was pretty rough."

Compared to the wide-open passing style of the modern game, the rules inhibiting forward passing were difficult to cope with during Herber's first seasons. "You had to be at least five yards behind the line of scrimmage to pass, and if you threw a pass over the goal line you lost the ball," he said.

Ad featuring Arnie Herber for the "Big Ten Football Game," late 1930s.

AP Photo/Pro Football Hall of Fame

MVP Books Collection

1939

Game-by-Game

9/17	**W**, 14–10,	vs. Chicago Cardinals
9/24	**W**, 21–16,	vs. Chicago Bears
10/1	**L**, 24–27,	vs. Cleveland Rams
10/8	**W**, 27–20,	vs. Chicago Cardinals
10/22	**W**, 26–7, vs. Detroit Lions	
10/29	**W**, 24–14,	vs. Washington Redskins
11/5	**L**, 27–30, at Chicago Bears	
11/12	**W**, 23–16,	at Philadelphia Eagles
11/19	**W**, 28–0,	at Brooklyn Dodgers
11/26	**W**, 7–6, at Cleveland Rams	
12/3	**W**, 12–7, at Detroit Lions	

Playoffs

12/10	**W**, 27–0,	vs. New York Giants

Team Scoring

233 points scored (3rd)

153 points allowed (4th)

PACKERS HEADLINE

Packers get revenge on Giants in Championship Game to claim franchise's fifth NFL crown.

Cecil Isbell, Green Bay's top rusher in 1939, eludes a Giants defender during the NFL Championship Game played at the State Fair Grounds on December 10. The Packers won, 27–0, before crowd of more than 32,000 for the NFL title. *AP Photo*

Capping the decade, the Packers won the title again. They qualified by going 9–2, then beat the New York Giants 27–0 in the NFL Championship Game in Milwaukee.

This was the Packers' fourth NFL title in the 1930s and their fifth appearance in the championship game. Plus, all of those achievements followed a 1929 season that produced still another title. Coach Curly Lambeau had five league crowns on his résumé.

It was Green Bay weather for the championship contest, even though the game was held in Milwaukee. The temperature was 28 degrees, and while it was sunny, 35-miles-per-hour winds ripped through the stadium. Most satisfying, despite the brisk day, was that the game brought out 32,279 fans.

"They were really one of the great ballclubs," said running back Clarke Hinkle. "Our '39 bunch was very versatile. While there were 33 players on the roster, we relied on 16 men who played a lot of the 60 minutes each game. Those fellows stayed healthy through a tough, 11-game schedule."

Against the Giants, the Packers took a 7–0 lead in the first period on a touchdown pass from Arnie Herber to end Milt Gantenbein. The defense did the rest, bottling up New York the rest of the day. The Giants accumulated 154 total yards. Green Bay added 10 points in each of the second-half quarters to pull away.

Cecil Isbell, who was the team's top rusher during the regular season, threw a touchdown pass to Joe Laws, Ed Jankowski ran for a TD, and the Packers also got field goals from two different players.

1939 Championship Game

After securing the 1936 NFL title, the Packers missed the postseason in 1937 by finishing in second place and then reached the title game after winning the West Division in 1938. However, the Packers lost to the New York Giants in that year's championship game, marking the first time that Green Bay was in position to win a crown and did not come through.

In 1939, the Packers got a second chance against the same foe, and this time they overwhelmed New York, winning 27–0.

"They really were one of the great ballclubs," said fullback Clarke Hinkle of that championship team. Saying that team could do it all, Hinkle singled out the end opposite Hutson for his contributions. "Milt Gantenbein was the best blocking end who ever lived."

The Packers crushed New York in front of 32,379 fans at the Dairy Bowl in West Allis, Wisconsin, on December 10. They took the lead early and never permitted the Giants to penetrate the end zone.

Gantenbein scored the go-ahead touchdown on a seven-yard throw from Herber, and Paul "Tiny" Engebretsen kicked the extra point. He also had a 29-yard field goal in the third quarter. It was interesting that the Packers, regarded as a pass-happy team, attempted only 10 in the contest while the Giants, forced to come from behind, threw 26 times.

One of the Packers' additions in 1939 was the hard-hitting Larry Craig, who stepped in at defensive end and moved Hutson to defensive back. Some say that the move prolonged Hutson's career. Hutson was appreciative and said, "Craig is my defense and Isbell is my offense."

SOUVENIR
Official Program
GREEN BAY PACKERS
vs.
NEW YORK GIANTS
STATE FAIR PARK MILWAUKEE
SUNDAY DEC. 10 1939
PRICE 25ᶜ
KICKOFF 1:30 P. M.

MVP Books Collection

THE 1930s RECORD BOOK

Team Leaders

(**Boldface** indicates league leader)

Scoring Leaders (Points)
1930: Verne Lewellen, 54
1931: Johnny "Blood" McNally, 78
1932: Johnny "Blood" McNally
& Hank Bruder, 24
1933: Buckets Goldenberg, 42
1934: Bob Monnett, 30
1935: Don Hutson, 43
1936: Don Hutson, 54
1937: Clarke Hinkle, 56
1938: Clarke Hinkle, **58**
1939: Don Hutson, 38

Rushing Leaders (Carries / Yards / TDs)
1930: NA
1931: NA
1932: Clarke Hinkle, 95 / 331 / 3
1933: Clarke Hinkle, 139 / 413 / 3
1934: Clarke Hinkle, 144 / 359 / 1
1935: Bob Monnett, 68 / 336 / 1
1936: Clarke Hinkle, 100 / 476 / 5
1937: Clarke Hinkle, 129 / 552 / **5**
1938: Cecil Isbell, 85 / 445 / 2
1939: Cecil Isbell, 132 / 407 / 2

Passing Leaders (Completions / Attempts / Yards)
1930: NA
1931: NA
1932: Arnie Herber, **37** / **101** / **639**
1933: Arnie Herber, 50 / 124 / 656
1934: Arnie Herber, **42** / **115** / **799**
1935: Arnie Herber, 40 / 106 / 729
1936: Arnie Herber, **77** / **173** / **1,239**
1937: Arnie Herber, 47 / 104 / 684
1938: Cecil Isbell, 37 / 91 / 659
1939: Arnie Herber, 57 / 139 / 1,107

Receiving Leaders (Receptions / Yards / TDs)
1930: NA
1931: NA
1932: Johnny "Blood" McNally, 14 / 168 / 3
1933: Roger Grove, 18 / 215 / 0
1934: Clarke Hinkle, 12 / 113 / 1
1935: Johnny "Blood" McNally, 25 / 404 / 3
1936: Don Hutson, **34** / **536** / 8
1937: Don Hutson, **41** / 552 / 7
1938: Don Hutson, 32 / **548** / 9
1939: Don Hutson, 34 / 846 / 6

MVP Books Collection

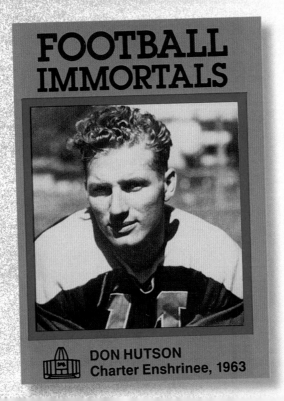

FOOTBALL IMMORTALS

DON HUTSON
Charter Enshrinee, 1963

MVP Books Collection

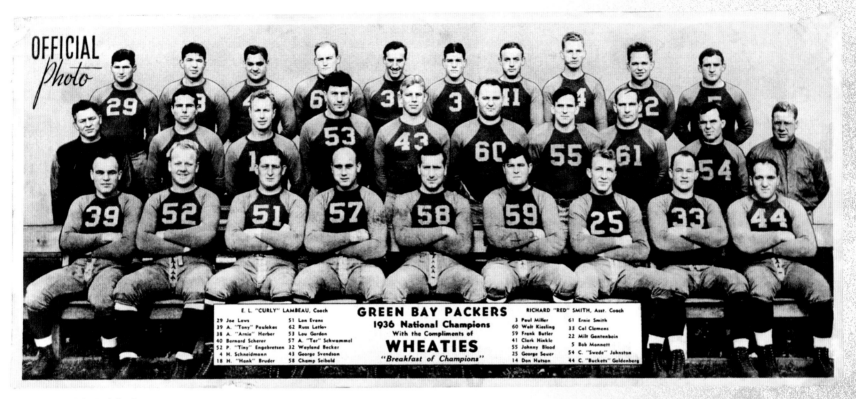

E. L. "CURLY" LAMBEAU, Coach

GREEN BAY PACKERS
1936 National Champions
With the Compliments of
WHEATIES
"Breakfast of Champions"

RICHARD "RED" SMITH, Asst. Coach

29 Joe Laws	51 Lon Evans
39 A. "Tony" Paulekas	62 Russ Letlow
38 A. "Arnie" Herber	53 Lou Gordon
40 Bernard Scherer	57 A. "Tar" Schwammel
52 P. "Tiny" Engebretsen	32 Wayland Becker
4 H. Schneidmann	43 George Svendson
18 H. "Hank" Bruder	58 Champ Seibold

3 Paul Miller	61 Ernie Smith
60 Walt Kiesling	33 Cal Clemens
59 Frank Butler	22 Milt Gantenbein
41 Clark Hinkle	5 Bob Monnett
55 Johnny Blood	54 C. "Swede" Johnston
25 George Sauer	14 Don Hutson
	44 C. "Buckets" Goldenberg

MVP Books Collection

First-Team All-Pros

1930: Lavvie Dilweg, End
1930: Mike Michalske, G
1931: Lavvie Dilweg, End
1931: Cal Hubbard, T
1931: Mike Michalske, G
1932: Arnie Herber, Back
1932: Cal Hubbard, T
1932: Tom Nash, End
1933: Cal Hubbard, T
1935: Clarke Hinkle, Back
1935: Ade Schwammel, T
1936: Lon Evans, G
1936: Milt Gantenbein, E
1936: Clarke Hinkle, FB
1936: Ernie Smith, T
1937: Clarke Hinkle, FB
1938: Clarke Hinkle, FB
1938: Don Hutson, End
1939: Don Hutson, End

Pro Bowl Selections

1938: Clarke Hinkle, FB
1938: Cecil Isbell, TB
1938: Russ Letlow, G

1st-Round Draft Picks

1936: Russ Letlow (7), G, San Francisco
1937: Eddie Jankowski (9),
    Back, Wisconsin
1938: Cecil Isbell (7), Back, Purdue
1939: Larry Buhler (9), Back, Minnesota

RED TOP CABS
CLEAN - SAFE - EFFICIENT
PHONE HOWARD 50

Beaumont
Coffee
Shop

Before
the Game

—

FOOTBALL
LUNCHEON

—

Quick Service

—

YOUR SELECTION OF
EXCELLENT FOOD

E. L. LAMBEAU
Coach

Coach Curly Lambeau, who got his grid-iron start at East high school, Green Bay, and later played under Rockne at Notre Dame, has been associated with the Pack-ers ever since the team's organization. He has started his 18th consecutive sea-son with the Green Bay Club, and has seen its growth from a small packing company squad to a football machine of international reputation. Lambeau took an active part in the team's play for a number of years, but for the past several seasons has directed the squad from the bench.

Beaumont
Hotel

After
the Game

—

DINNER
DE LUXE

THE MOST UP TO DATE
TAVERN IN THE STATE
OF WISCONSIN

5:30 to 8 P.M.

—

SEVENTY-FIVE
CENTS THE PLATE

1

MVP Books Collection

In his final decade with the team, Coach Curly Lambeau—seen here on the sideline during a game against the Chicago Cardinals in October 1947—led the Packers to eight winning seasons and one more NFL championship. *AP Photo*

The Packers of the 1940s—until the last two years of the decade—continued to be one of the most prominent teams in the National Football League. In 1944, they won another world championship.

Despite the interruption of World War II, Green Bay continued with a run of success that dated back to 1929. The war was paramount to the country, and team personnel was drastically affected for all the clubs in the league. Many teams lost all their stars. They replaced them with over-aged players coming out of retirement, players with physical defects who were rejected by the armed forces, and young players before they went off to war.

Although the war did not affect his status, the early departure of star quarterback Cecil Isbell for the coaching life was the first major surprise of the decade for Packers fans. Isbell had thrown for a remarkable (for the times) 24 touchdowns during the 1942 season, but he then abruptly retired. By the end of the decade, he had moved from a college coach to a pro coach with the Baltimore Colts of the upstart All-America Football Conference.

The Packers were fortunate to hold onto the great Don Hutson throughout the war. By the beginning of the decade, he was a genuine superstar and the cornerstone of the offense. However, he remained active only through the 1945 season. After 11 seasons, he retired at the relatively youthful age of 32.

Before he completed his playing days, Hutson became an assistant coach for Lambeau in 1944, and he stayed on as an assistant through the 1948 season. The retirement of Hutson as an active player stunned Green Bay fans.

Even more surprising in this series of unconnected events was the unraveling of the Packers near the end of the 1940s. From the 1934 season through the 1947

WISCONSIN DAIRY PRODUCTS BUILD CHAMPIONS

Star player Don Hutson and Coach Curly Lambeau on a program for an exhibition game in 1946. *MVP Books Collection*

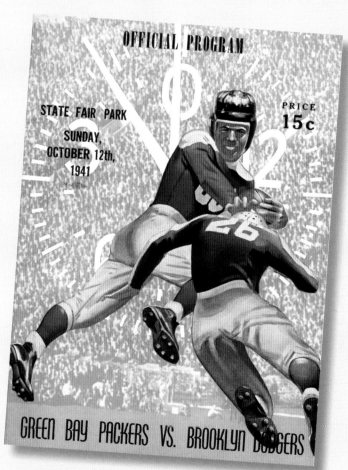

Program cover for Packers game against the Brooklyn Dodgers on October 12, 1941. *MVP Books Collection*

campaign, Green Bay under coach Curly Lambeau recorded a winning record every year. However, in 1948 the Packers finished 3–9, and in 1949 they were even worse at 2–10. One reason for this dip in the win column was the Packers' inability to find new players who matched the high standards of predecessors. Lambeau lost draft choices to the All-America Football Conference.

In the front office, a chasm grew between Lambeau and his team of financial backers. He stopped listening to them, and he angered them by replacing longtime Packers benefactors and supporters.

Compounding this misery on the field was the feeling that Lambeau, who was Mr. Packer since the founding of the team in 1919, was no longer committing his full efforts to the job and that he was being distracted by other interests off the field. Lambeau led the Packers to six championships and was one of the most revered figures in Green Bay—until he lost his public.

Under pressure because of his seemingly indifferent attitude and the slump of the team, Lambeau left Green Bay and accepted a job as coach of the Chicago Cardinals beginning with the 1950 season. The long and glorious run of Earl Lambeau in the little northern Wisconsin town was over.

1940

Game-by-Game

9/15	**W**, 27–20,	vs. Philadelphia Eagles
9/22	**L**, 10–41,	vs. Chicago Bears
9/29	**W**, 31–6,	vs. Chicago Cardinals
10/13	**W**, 31–14,	vs. Cleveland Rams
10/20	**L**, 14–23, vs. Detroit Lions	
10/27	**W**, 24–3,	vs. Pittsburgh Steelers
11/3	**L**, 7–14, at Chicago Bears	
11/10	**W**, 28–7,	at Chicago Cardinals
11/17	**L**, 3–7, at New York Giants	
11/24	**W**, 50–7, at Detroit Lions	
12/1	**T**, 13–13,	at Cleveland Rams

Team Scoring

238 points scored (2nd)

155 points allowed (6th)

PACKERS HEADLINE

End Don Hutson leads offense with 45 receptions and 7 touchdowns, leads defense with 6 interceptions.

Green Bay was the defending NFL champion in 1940, but although the Packers finished second in the Western Division to the Bears, they didn't play nearly as well. Finishing 6–4–1 didn't cut it, and losing twice to Chicago was the difference. The Bears had the upper hand, winning 41–10 and 14–7.

Some all-time team greats, from end Don Hutson to quarterback Cecil Isbell, were still with the Packers, and with others supporting them the team was sound. Joe Laws excelled as a punt returner and was a solid blocker. Second-year man Charlie Brock gave Green Bay brilliant play at center, regularly good enough to make second-team all-league. As a linebacker, Brock had a nose for the ball.

Against the Chicago Cardinals, who Green Bay swept, Brock returned an interception for a touchdown. "It was the first time I stole a ball and scored a touchdown," Brock said. "I ran about 35 yards. We had to win to stay in contention."

Ed Jankowski was a solid football player who proved his ability many times, but he was stuck at second string at fullback behind Clarke Hinkle. Still, coach Curly Lambeau recognized that Jankowski could be a very useful player.

"I knew what I was up against," Jankowski said. "The Packers had Hinkle, and there was only one Hinkle. But Curly Lambeau gave me a break, used me a lot when Hinkle was tired or hurt, and I did get in a lot of plays."

Running back Andy Uram—seen here looking for yardage against the New York Giants on November 17, 1940—had a career-high 71 carries in 1940. Drafted in 1938, he stayed with the Packers through 1943. *AP Photo*

Packers finish regular-season in a first-place tie with the Bears but lose in one-game playoff for trip to NFL title game.

Game-by-Game

9/14	W, 23–0, vs. Detroit Lions
9/21	W, 24–7, vs. Cleveland Rams
9/28	L, 17–25, vs. Chicago Bears
10/5	W, 14–13, vs. Chicago Cardinals
10/12	W, 30–7, vs. Brooklyn Dodgers
10/19	W, 17–14, at Cleveland Rams
10/26	W, 24–7, at Detroit Lions
11/2	W, 16–14, at Chicago Bears
11/16	W, 17–9, vs. Chicago Cardinals
11/23	W, 54–7, at Pittsburgh Steelers
11/30	W, 22–17, at Washington Redskins

Playoffs

12/14	L, 14–33, at Chicago Bears

Team Scoring

258 points scored (2nd)

120 points allowed (2nd)

Quarterback Cecil Isbell is hit by a Bears defender just after he unleashed a throw during the Western Division playoff at Wrigley Field on December 14, 1941. In the first-ever postseason meeting between the two rivals, Chicago pulled off a 33–14 victory. *AP Photo/Press-Gazette*

Before the 1941 season began, the NFL, under new commissioner Elmer Layden—one of the famed "Four Horsemen" of Notre Dame—implemented some new rules. For the first time, the league provided for a playoff in case two teams tied for first in either division. And sure enough, it happened immediately.

The Packers swept to a 10–1 record, dominating everyone except the familiar Chicago Bears, who posted the same record. Naturally enough, the teams split two games, with Chicago winning 25–17 and the Packers winning 14–7.

The teams met for a third time in a playoff. Before a crowd of 43,425 fans at Wrigley Field, the Bears trounced the Packers 33–14. That ended Green Bay's season and sent the Bears into the title game.

The regular season ended in late November for the Packers, a week before the Japanese bombed Pearl Harbor on December 7. The playoff against the Bears took place on December 14, and the championship game was set for December 21 in Chicago between the Bears and Giants. The Bears won the title with barely more than 13,000 fans in attendance, as the stunned nation mobilized for war.

In what seemed to be a peculiar move to Packers fans, Lambeau cut former star quarterback Arnie Herber, placing more weight on Cecil Isbell. Lambeau got limited help from his top picks in the college draft. However, with their sixth-round pick the Packers came up with a bargain. Running back Tony Canadeo would play 11 years and become a Hall of Famer.

Cecil Isbell

A star at Purdue, Cecil Isbell became one of the Packers' first top draft choices after the National Football League introduced a player draft in 1936. Isbell was Green Bay's No. 1 pick in 1938.

One of four college-football-playing brothers from Houston, Isbell shared the quarterback spot with Arnie Herber and then became the field leader throwing to Don Hutson.

Isbell spent only five years with the Packers before retiring at 27 to coach. The 1942 season, his last one, saw Isbell throw for 24 touchdowns and pass for more than 2,000 yards. Isbell knew that he benefited from playing with the swift and agile Hutson. "If I ever got the ball close to him, he never missed the catch," Isbell said, "whether it was high or low."

Isbell had a big fan of his own in coach Curly Lambeau, who called him the best quarterback of the era, ranking him higher than Sammy Baugh and Sid Luckman.

"Isbell was the best," Lambeau said, "with Luckman of the Bears a close second and Sammy Baugh of the Redskins a long third. Luckman wasn't as versatile, and Baugh couldn't compare on the long ones."

One Isbell mark was throwing a touchdown pass in 23 straight games. He could have extended that record, but the chance to coach his alma mater in West Lafayette, Indiana, lured him off the field.

"We felt we could move with the pass anywhere on the field, and we could," Isbell said of his Green Bay days.

AP Photo

The only two Green Bay losses in 1942 were to the Chicago Bears, and once again the rivals from Illinois kept the Packers out of the playoffs. The Packers tied one game against the New York Giants, but otherwise they won their eight remaining regular-season games.

It was the same old story, with Curly Lambeau's Packers and George Halas' Bears fighting it out—only this time there was a twist. Halas, an ensign in the Navy during World War I, joined up again with the rank of lieutenant commander. He left the Bears for 20 months during World War II.

Quarterback Cecil Isbell led the NFL with 2,021 yards passing, but the Packers fell just short of the playoffs. Don Hutson set league records for most catches in a single season (74), most yards gained (1,211), and most touchdowns (17) through the air. It was by far the best season ever recorded by a receiver to that point in NFL history.

One Packers player missing from the lineup after spending two years as a guard with the team was Smiley John Johnson. Johnson joined the Marines after Pearl Harbor was bombed, and he was killed before the end of the war. He was the only Green Bay Packers player ever killed in combat while serving his country.

The season opened on August 29 in Brooklyn against the Dodgers, and attendance was sparse with just under 10,000 paid admissions. The crowd included 1,209 servicemen.

The league-leading passing of Cecil Isbell (left) and the record-breaking catching of Don Hutson (right) helped propel the 1942 Packers to 10 wins and 300 points scored during the season. Unfortunately, two losses to the Bears kept them out of postseason play. *AP Photo*

Game-by-Game

9/27	L, 28–44, vs. Chicago Bears
10/4	W, 17–13, at Chicago Cardinals
10/11	W, 38–7, vs. Detroit Lions
10/18	W, 45–28, vs. Cleveland Rams
10/25	W, 28–7, at Detroit Lions
11/1	W, 55–24, vs. Chicago Cardinals
11/8	W, 30–12, at Cleveland Rams
11/15	L, 7–38, at Chicago Bears
11/22	T, 21–21, at New York Giants
11/29	W, 7–0, at Philadelphia Eagles
12/6	W, 24–21, vs. Pittsburgh Steelers

Team Scoring

300 points scored (2nd)

215 points allowed (8th)

PACKERS HEADLINE

Don Hutson sets league marks for most receptions (74), most yards gained (1,211), and most touchdown catches (17).

1943

Game-by-Game

9/26	T, 21–21,	vs. Chicago Bears
10/3	W, 28–7,	at Chicago Cardinals
10/10	W, 35–14,	vs. Detroit Lions
10/17	L, 7–33,	vs. Washington Redskins
10/24	W, 27–6,	at Detroit Lions
10/31	W, 35–21,	at New York Giants
11/7	L, 7–21,	at Chicago Bears
11/14	W, 35–14,	vs. Chicago Cardinals
11/21	W, 31–7,	at Brooklyn Dodgers
12/5	W, 38–28,	at Steagles

Team Scoring

264 points scored (2nd)

172 points allowed (4th)

PACKERS HEADLINE

World War II depletes Green Bay's roster, but the fans continue to come out to see the Packers play.

Coach Curly Lambeau confers with Tony Canadeo (3), Irv Comp (51), and Don Huston (14) at practice during the 1943 season. Canadeo and Comp accounted for the bulk of the Packers' passing that season, while Hutson pulled in a league-best 47 receptions and 11 touchdown catches. *Bettmann/Corbis*

Departure of players throughout the league and other effects of World War II on the national mood, economy, and day-to-day living were felt by the NFL and the Packers, much as they were in the rest of the country.

Before the season, coach Curly Lambeau predicted that his team would be okay with 13 returning players out of the 25 on the roster. Most of the other dozen from 1942 had joined the military.

"We'll have one of the hardest-running, heaviest, and best defensive teams we've had around here in years," Lambeau said, while admitting the Packers would miss retired Cecil Isbell.

Green Bay put together another strong season, going 7–2–1, but as usual the Chicago Bears were the main nemesis, accounting for one loss and one tie on the overall record. That left the Packers in second place in the Western Division.

Somewhat surprisingly, given the much more important aspects of the war, the number of people that watched the Packers play during the 1943 season was the greatest by far—278,905. There were crowds of more than 40,000 for games in Detroit, New York, and Chicago.

One illustration of the changes in the 1940s was Green Bay's opponent in the last game of the season. By a score of 38–28, Green Bay defeated the Steagles. The Steagles represented a temporary merger of the Pittsburgh Steelers and the Philadelphia Eagles because of the player shortage and financial ills suffered by those franchises due to the war.

Tony Canadeo

An all-around back known as the "Gray Ghost," stemming from his football days at Gonzaga when his hair was already turning gray, Tony Canadeo was the Packers' back of the decade in the 1940s.

A Chicago native, Canadeo trekked to Washington to play college football because some of his friends were doing so, and he had no better opportunities. It was not until he showed his talents during his freshman year that he was given a scholarship.

Canadeo broke in with Green Bay in 1941 and played through 1944, before missing a year to military service during World War II. He returned to his old spot in the lineup after the war and held it from 1946 to 1952. Chosen for the NFL's team of the 1940s, Canadeo rushed for a total of 4,171 yards, logged a 4.1-yards-per-carry average, and scored 31 touchdowns in his career.

One of Canadeo's greatest accomplishments was rushing for 1,052 yards during the 1949 season—making him only the third player ever to rush for more than 1,000 yards in a season. He was named as a first-team All-Pro in 1943, when he completed 56 passes as quarterback while leading the team with 489 yards rushing.

When Canadeo wasn't taking handoffs and running from scrimmage, he threw some passes (including 16 TD heaves), returned kickoffs and punts, and was the team's punter. He also played defense and intercepted nine passes in his career.

After he quit playing, Canadeo remained with the team as a radio broadcaster. His No. 3 jersey was retired by the organization in 1952, the second player so honored.

Canadeo, who was not known for his speed, said instinct was more important. "You don't have to be so fast to catch passes," he said. "You just got to wait and go at the right time."

Canadeo was also known for his toughness with Green Bay. "I missed a couple of games my rookie year because of a broken hand," he said. "But after that, I never missed any playing time because of injuries. I had a few injuries in the preseason games. Once the league started, I was ready for every play."

With World War II raging, Canadeo did not make it through the entire 1944 season before the Army called. He played in just four games while on furlough, and though he was a member of the title team that season, he was not present and accounted for when the game was played. By then, he was serving in England.

Canadeo did not retire in 1952 because of injury or the feeling he was incapable of going on longer with his football career. "It was more that I felt I had played long enough and it was time to settle down," he said.

Canadeo settled down right in Green Bay. Not only did he continue his association with the Packers through broadcasting, but he did so as a member of the club's board of directors.

In 1974, Canadeo was chosen for enshrinement in the Pro Football Hall of Fame.

AP Photo

Ted Fritsch

A member of the Green Bay Packers Hall of Fame, Ted Fritsch was a star running back for the team from 1942 to 1950 and was a member of the 1944 championship team. His son Ted Fritsch Jr., who was born in Green Bay, played in the NFL, too, with the Atlanta Falcons and Washington Redskins.

One of the keys to Fritsch's successful career with the Packers stemmed from misfortune earlier in life. He had a punctured eardrum, so he was classified 4-F by the draft board during World War II. He might never have played for the Packers if Clarke Hinkle, Ed Jankowski, and George Paskvan hadn't all left because of military service.

During his Green Bay career, Fritsch rushed for 2,200 yards and scored 32 touchdowns. He led the NFL in touchdowns in 1946 with nine.

An excellent all-around athlete, Fritsch played minor-league baseball as well as professional basketball with the Oshkosh All-Stars, a forerunner to teams in the NBA.

Fritsch said it was easy to pick out his biggest thrill with the Packers. "Winning the world championship against the Giants," he said. "The fact I scored both touchdowns."

Fritsch never pressured Ted Jr. to follow in his footsteps, but his son always had enthusiasm for the game.

"It was really a household item in our family," Fritsch said of football. "He never really fought it or complained. Practice was always a drag. Games were always too short."

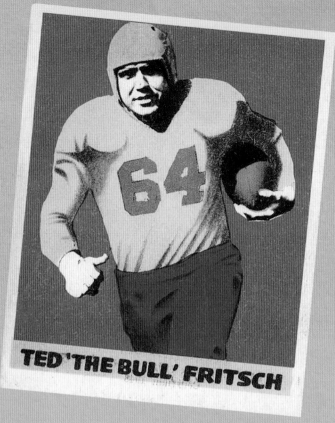

TED 'THE BULL' FRITSCH

MVP Books Collection

Another championship. After a five-year gap between titles, the Packers added a sixth crown to coach Curly Lambeau's résumé. It was to be the last championship won under Lambeau's tutelage, although no one knew it at the time.

Green Bay finished 8–2, and two victories came over another mixed version of a squad formed by tough times during World War II. The Steagles were no more, but this season the Pittsburgh Steelers partnered with the Chicago Cardinals. In one of the worst-sounding names of all time, that club was called Card-Pitt, short for Cardinals and Pittsburgh.

The Packers lost to the New York Giants 24–0 in New York in a game played before a huge crowd of 56,481. But after capturing the Western Division, the Packers had to face the Giants again. Seeking warm weather for training, Lambeau decided to hold a mini-camp in Charlottesville, Virginia. The combination of food rationing and train rescheduling due to the war caused a late arrival in Virginia.

Lambeau called for two-a-day practices and studied game film as if he were watching a favorite movie repeatedly. "I saw the motion pictures so often that I could coach the Giants myself," Lambeau said.

The knowledge he gathered apparently paid off. In one of the more memorable games in Packers history, Green Bay upset New York 14–7 at the Polo Grounds, a month after the humiliating shutout. Interestingly, 10,000 fewer fans turned out for the title game than at the first game in New York.

▸ 8–2   1st place ◂

Game-by-Game

9/17	W, 14–7, vs. Brooklyn Tigers
9/24	W, 42–28, vs. Chicago Bears
10/1	W, 27–6, vs. Detroit Lions
10/8	W, 34–7, vs. Card-Pitt
10/22	W, 30–21, vs. Cleveland Rams
10/29	W, 14–0, at Detroit Lions
11/5	L, 0–21, at Chicago Bears
11/12	W, 42–7, at Cleveland Rams
11/19	L, 0–24, at New York Giants
11/26	W, 35–20, at Card-Pitt

Playoffs

12/17	W, 14–7, at New York Giants

Team Scoring

238 points scored (3rd)

141 points allowed (3rd)

PACKERS HEADLINE

Six-game winning streak to start the season catapults Packers to another league championship.

Curly Lambeau with fullback Ted Fritsch after the Packers' 14–7 victory over the New York Giants in the 1944 NFL title game.
AP Photo

Sixth time's a charm. The Green Bay Packers celebrate in the locker room following the 14–7 win over the New York Giants for the 1944 NFL Championship. Getting a boost from the players are game hero Ted Fritsch (64) and coach Curly Lambeau. *AP Photo*

1944 Championship Game

The Packers adapted to defeat well. A month after being thoroughly trounced in a 24–0 loss to the New York Giants during the 1944 regular season, Green Bay topped New York 14–7 for the NFL championship.

Coach Curly Lambeau, now a six-time champ after 26 years of coaching in the league, gained credit for the way he helped his players learn from the loss and execute a better game plan. After a scoreless first period, Green Bay scored twice in the second quarter on touchdowns by Ted Fritsch. Each was followed by a Don Hutson extra point.

Although Hutson played the whole game, he was mostly used on offense as a decoy. The Giants, who had several players injured, focused on shutting down Hutson. But instead of targeting him frequently, the Packers limited their air attack and sent Fritsch on misdirection plays.

New York finally scored in the late stages of the game on a run by Ward Cuff. That was more than offset by the Packers offense and a defense that pinned the Giants in their own territory regularly. Packers defensive back Joe Laws intercepted three passes and rushed for 74 yards. He said

Green Bay's play repertoire was fundamental, but open to suggestions, too. "I only used two plays for myself that day," Laws said.

Laws, who called the plays, said Lambeau told him to avoid stodgy football. "You have permission to call anything you want, Joe," Lambeau said. "We're going to do things a little unorthodox."

"Which we did," Laws added. "We elected to kick off instead of receive, which we normally did when we won the toss."

Green Bay let the Giants spend their best defensive player, linebacker Mel Hein, covering Hutson. But when the Packers running game was juiced up and playing untouchable football, the Wisconsin reps didn't mind at all. The Packers stuck with the working plan rather than forcing the ball to Hutson.

This all worked out marvelously for Fritsch, the fullback. Hein dropped back into pass coverage instead of rushing, so Fritsch had no one to block. "As a result, the whole sideline was open for me all afternoon," Fritsch said later. Fritsch scored his first touchdown on a two-yard burst up the middle. He scored his second touchdown on a 10-yard pass from Irv Comp. "There was nobody within 15 yards of me when he finally did throw it to me," Fritsch said.

Fritsch did get tackled in the game occasionally, and he recalled being hit hard by New York's 6-foot-6, 250-pound Al Blozis. They talked on the ground, where Big Al told Fritsch he couldn't get past him twice.

The championship game was played on December 17. Blozis, known as the "Jersey City Giant," had already been accepted into the Army. He was shipped to France, where he died on January 21, 1945. "The tragedy of it was that I don't think he ever got to see his championship game check," Fritsch said.

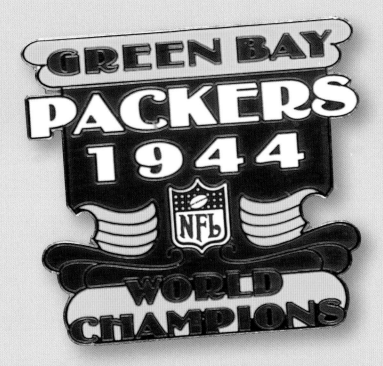

MVP Books Collection

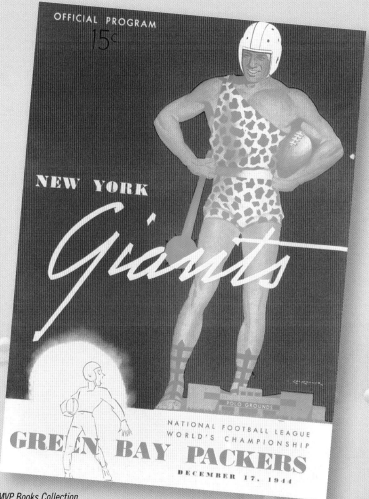

MVP Books Collection

▶ 6–4   3rd place ◀

Game-by-Game

9/30	W, 31–21,	vs. Chicago Bears
10/7	W, 57–21, vs. Detroit Lions	
10/14	L, 14–27,	vs. Cleveland Rams
10/21	W, 38–14, vs. Boston Yanks	
10/28	W, 33–14,	vs. Chicago Cardinals
11/4	L, 24–28, at Chicago Bears	
11/11	L, 7–20, at Cleveland Rams	
11/18	W, 28–0, at Boston Yanks	
11/25	W, 23–14,	at New York Giants
12/2	L, 3–14, at Detroit Lions	

Team Scoring

258 points scored (2nd)

173 points allowed (4th)

In his farewell season, future Hall of Famer Don Hutson leads the league in receptions (47) for the fifth year in a row and is named First-Team All-Pro for the eighth straight year.

After the Packers won the 1944 NFL championship, "The Alabama Antelope," Don Hutson, announced in the locker room that he was going to retire. He changed his mind and played the 1945 season, but after the 6–4 campaign ended, he really did quit as an active player. So did Joe Laws after that season.

Green Bay's schedule was a little bit peculiar in that the team played its first five games at home and its last five games on the road. The Packers were 4–1 at home and 2–3 away. For the second time in three years, more people than ever before watched the Packers play football. Season attendance was recorded at 291,947, and for the first time almost every single game topped 20,000 fans. The October 28 game in Green Bay versus the Chicago Cardinals attracted 19,221.

One sturdy Packer who competed for Green Bay only during the war years was Joel Mason, who was on the active list from 1941 to 1945. After watching departed quarterback Cecil Isbell and Hutson work together, he felt that the Packers deserved credit for modernizing the sport. "I believe that Green Bay, with its famed passing attack, was responsible for opening up the game," he said.

Another prominent Packer, Carl Mulleneaux, rejoined the team in 1945 after excelling before World War II. Mulleneaux played for Green Bay from 1938 to 1941 and then again in 1945 and 1946. Hutson provided personal pass-catching lessons to Mulleneaux, and Mulleneaux scored Green Bay's first touchdown in the 1938 title game.

Coach Lambeau and his staff prepare for the 1945 season at training camp in August. With Lambeau are (left to right) Walt Kiesling, Lambeau, assistant coach and player Don Hutson, and Eddie Kotal, scout and assistant. A disappointing 6–4 record left the team far short of a repeat title. *AP Photo*

The Packers took on the Chicago Cardinals at Comiskey Park on November 10 and came away with a 19–7 victory, but it wasn't enough to catapult the team to the postseason as a 2–2 finish left them with a 6–5 season record. *Bettmann/Corbis*

Game-by-Game

9/29	L, 7–30, vs. Chicago Bears	
10/6	L, 17–21, vs. Los Angeles Rams	
10/13	W, 19–7, at Philadelphia Eagles	
10/20	W, 17–7, vs. Pittsburgh Steelers	
10/27	W, 10–7, vs. Detroit Lions	
11/3	L, 7–10, at Chicago Bears	
11/10	W, 19–7, at Chicago Cardinals	
11/17	W, 9–0, at Detroit Lions	
11/24	L, 6–24, vs. Chicago Cardinals	
12/1	W, 20–7, at Washington Redskins	
12/8	L, 17–38, at Los Angeles Rams	

Team Scoring

148 points scored (8th)

158 points allowed (2nd)

PACKERS HEADLINE

Team stumbles to 6–5 record as the Packers are outscored by their opposition over the course of the season for the first time in franchise history.

For the first time in many years, the 1946 Green Bay Packers looked shaky. While they achieved a winning record, they were barely over .500 at 6–5. Although the Packers had been around since 1919, the 1946 season marked 25 years in the NFL, and a silver anniversary was celebrated.

Two losses to the Chicago Bears were detrimental, but with Don Hutson retired and Arnie Herber and Cecil Isbell—the star quarterbacks of the previous decade and a half—gone, the Packers needed offensive punch. Green Bay scored 148 points during the season, a stunning 110 fewer than the preceding year—despite an additional game.

The defense was a little stingier, permitting only 158 points compared to 178 in 1945. However, this was the first time in team history that the offense did not score more points than the defense allowed.

Quarterback Irv Crump did not have anyone of Hutson's caliber to throw to, and the Packers ratcheted back on the passing game. They became a double-barreled ground team with Ted Fritsch (444 yards, nine touchdowns) and Tony Canadeo (476 yards) sharing the load in the backfield.

When the Bears clobbered the Packers 30–7 in late September, Green Bay did not complete a pass until the fourth quarter—telling evidence of how things had changed.

After losing their first two league games, plus an exhibition, the Packers captured their first victory of the year, 19–17, over the Philadelphia Eagles in mid-October. Fritsch scored all three touchdowns.

1947

Game-by-Game

9/28	**W**, 29–20, vs. Chicago Bears
10/5	**W**, 17–14, vs. Los Angeles Rams
10/12	**L**, 10–14, vs. Chicago Cardinals
10/19	**W**, 27–10, vs. Washington Redskins
10/26	**W**, 34–17, vs. Detroit Lions
11/2	**L**, 17–18, vs. Pittsburgh Steelers
11/9	**L**, 17–20, at Chicago Bears
11/16	**L**, 20–21, at Chicago Cardinals
11/23	**T**, 24–24, at New York Giants
11/30	**W**, 30–10, at Los Angeles Rams
12/7	**W**, 35–14, at Detroit Lions
12/14	**L**, 14–28, at Philadelphia Eagles

Team Scoring

274 points scored (5th)

210 points allowed (1st)

PACKERS HEADLINE

High-scoring season on both sides of the ball leads to third straight playoff absence for Green Bay.

n the big picture, the 1947 season wasn't much different, or much better, for the Packers than 1946. Green Bay finished 6–5–1, and missed the playoffs for the third straight season, as scoring went up around the league.

Coach Curly Lambeau got some higher production out of his offense, and the team's 274 points scored were its most since 1942. And although the 210 points that the defense allowed were also the most since 1942, they still ranked first in the league with fewest points allowed. The defense failed to post a shutout, and every single opponent reached double figures—but even the champion Cardinals allowed 21 more points during the year.

Strategically, Lambeau did return to his roots. He found a new quarterback with a good arm, and the player known as "Indian" Jack Jacobs did a solid job. Of Creek Indian heritage, Jacobs was a second-round pick out of Oklahoma and went on to play six years in the NFL and five more in the Canadian Football League with the Winnipeg Blue Bombers.

In 1947, Jacobs completed 108 passes for 1,615 yards and 16 touchdowns for Green Bay. Nolan Luhn caught 42 passes, and Clyde Goodnight hauled in 38. Jacobs would actually gain much greater fame in Canada. After spending three seasons with Green Bay, he became, with Winnipeg, the first pro to throw for more than 3,000 yards in a season.

With the Pack in 1947, Jacobs led the NFL in punting.

Tony Canadeo eludes a Chicago defender during Green Bay's 29–20 loss to the Bears on September 28 at City Stadium. Canadeo's 464 yards rushing on the year ranked third-best in the league. *Vernon Biever/Getty Images*

1948

With no Pro Bowlers on the roster and a seven-game losing streak to close the season, Green Bay begins a decade-long skid without a winning season.

▶ 3–9   4th place ◀

The 1948 season was the most stunning year in Packers history to date because it was so bad. At that time it was the worst since the club was founded in 1919, and the results represented an abrupt fall.

Although the preceding two years had not been up to the usual Green Bay standard, they were both winning seasons. In 1948, however, everything fell apart. The Packers lost their last seven games and finished 3–9.

Even worse, the Packers were dominated on the scoreboard. Overall, Green Bay was outscored by an embarrassing 290–154 margin. The Packers lost games by such scores as 45–7 to the Chicago Bears, 38–7 to the Pittsburgh Steelers, 49–3 to the New York Giants, and 42–7 to the Chicago Cardinals.

The 1948 draft brought in no new stars and only a small number of players who made the roster and stuck for a few years. This was the height of competition between the National Football League and the All-America Football Conference, so the talent pool was being depleted and the Packers did not get their share of new guys.

Although Jack Jacobs was still at quarterback, he gained only half as many yards (848) through the air as in 1947 and threw 21 interceptions. The number of catches by key receivers was down across the board. Tony Canadeo was the offensive star with 589 rushing yards and 4.8 yards per carry.

Game-by-Game

9/17	W, 31–0, at Boston Yanks
9/26	L, 7–45, vs. Chicago Bears
10/3	W, 33–21, vs. Detroit Lions
10/10	L, 7–17, vs. Chicago Cardinals
10/17	W, 16–0, vs. Los Angeles Rams
10/24	L, 7–23, vs. Washington Redskins
10/31	L, 20–24, at Detroit Lions
11/7	L, 7–38, at Pittsburgh Steelers
11/14	L, 6–7, at Chicago Bears
11/21	L, 3–49, vs. New York Giants
11/28	L, 10–24, at Los Angeles Rams
12/5	L, 7–42, at Chicago Cardinals

Team Scoring

154 points scored (10th)

290 points allowed (7th)

1949

Game-by-Game

9/25	**L**, 0–17, vs. Chicago Bears
10/2	**L**, 7–48, vs. Los Angeles Rams
10/7	**W**, 19–0, at New York Bulldogs
10/16	**L**, 14–39, vs. Chicago Cardinals
10/23	**L**, 7–35, at Los Angeles Rams
10/30	**W**, 16–14, vs. Detroit Lions
11/6	**L**, 3–24, at Chicago Bears
11/13	**L**, 10–30, vs. New York Giants
11/20	**L**, 7–30, vs. Pittsburgh Steelers
11/27	**L**, 21–41, at Chicago Cardinals
12/4	**L**, 0–30, at Washington Redskins
12/11	**L**, 7–21, at Detroit Lions

Team Scoring

114 points scored (10th)

329 points allowed (8th)

PACKERS HEADLINE

Curly Lambeau ends his 31-year run as head coach of the Packers with a last-place finish.

As an example of the Packers' bad luck in 1949, after Cardinals end Mal Kutner bobbled this pass from quarterback Jim Hardy in the end zone, he grabbed it to secure one of Chicago's four first-quarter touchdowns on November 27. The Packers lost 41–21, one of eight losses they suffered by 20 points or more. *AP Photo/Charles Knoblock*

The 1948 season seemed like the nadir of the Green Bay franchise, but in 1949 fans discovered things could get worse. The record got even lousier at 2–10, and the Packers were outscored by a greater overall margin, 329–114. The defense completely crumbled.

Green Bay took major beatings almost every week, defeating only the New York Bulldogs, 19–0, and the Detroit Lions, 16–14.

The organization was about to undergo major changes. After 31 seasons with founder Curly Lambeau as coach and the key figure in all Packers decisions, he had lost the faith of the community. People believed he was too distracted by outside interests, including spending considerable time in Hollywood. They felt he had lost his touch in recruiting new players, and that his social life was too controversial.

At the same time, the Packers franchise was basically broke. An assessment of the books with two games remaining in the season showed that the team was going to lose $90,000. The crisis threatened the continued existence of the franchise. Green Bay was by far the smallest city in the league, and the big-city owners had long held a grudge against Green Bay as a potential drag on league finances. They now lobbied for the NFL to replace the city in the 10-team lineup.

Lambeau took a voluntary cut in pay, helped with a massive fund-raising project that included an exhibition game and an appeal for money to Green Bay businesses, and brought back old-time stars for appearances. Then he left for the Chicago Cardinals.

Saving the Team

Late in the 1949 season, front-office personnel reviewed the books and discovered that the Packers were on a super-speed path to bankruptcy. With just two weeks remaining in a disastrous 2–10 season, things were worse behind the scenes. The team was going to finish the year $90,000 in debt.

Plans were hurriedly formulated to raise money, and on a cold and snowy Thanksgiving Day, the Packers played an exhibition game between the Blues and Golds, the team's split groups. They played in front of 18,000 hardy, devoted Green Bay spectators, who paid for the experience knowing that the money was being used to save their beloved team from extinction.

Former Packers stars turned out at snowbound City Stadium to help the cause. Don Hutson, Arnie Herber, Jug Earp, Verne Lewellen, Lavvie Dilweg, Johnny Blood, Joe Laws, and Charlie Brock joined coach Curly Lambeau (helmet included, harkening back to his playing days) in a photo. They all mingled some with the fans, too. On a day that could have been ruined by the icy field and a heavy snowfall, they withstood the elements to provide warm memories and badly needed cash. At halftime, this group put on a show for the fans.

"It was a really cold day," said end Nolan Luhn. "There was snow and ice on the field. They took a grader and cleaned it off."

The players and team officials were amazed by the size of the turnout, which was a testimony to the fans' passion for the team after they had realized that the club needed their help. People did not throw up their hands and say there was nothing they could do. They reached into their pocketbook to help out.

Because of the nature of Mother Nature, combined with the fact that it was an exhibition game, running back Tony Canadeo said it was almost like touch football. Nobody crashed to the ground hard. "We faked the hell out of that game," he said. Everyone was extremely careful to avoid injury.

Other entertainment that day included the Packers' "Lumberjack Band," and one of the musical numbers was "In the Good Old Summertime."

The existence of the financial crisis was a secret from most everyone in the community until the public appeals began. One leading businessman, who was among the first approached for help, was Jerry Atkinson, the overseer of Prange's Department Store. It was his idea to hold the exhibition game, and he brought the plan to Lambeau.

Atkinson was most surprised by the need for it at all. He was among the majority who thought the Packers were doing just fine at the box office and in the team coffers.

"I was dumbfounded," Atkinson said of his first reaction.

The combination of fund-raising efforts produced $50,000, and that was enough to carry the Packers into the next year without repercussions from an anxious NFL.

Old-timers' game at City Stadium, 1949. *MVP Books Collection*

THE 1940s RECORD BOOK

Team Leaders

(**Boldface** indicates league leader)

Scoring Leaders (Points)
1940: Don Hutson, **57**
1941: Don Hutson, **95**
1942: Don Hutson, **138**
1943: Don Hutson, **117**
1944: Don Hutson, **85**
1945: Don Hutson, 97
1946: Ted Fritsch, **100**
1947: Ted Fritsch, 56
1948: Ted Fritsch, 29
1949: Ted Fritsch, 32

Rushing Leaders (Carries / Yards / TDs)
1940: Clarke Hinkle, 109 / 383 / 2
1941: Clarke Hinkle, **129** / 393 / 5
1942: Ted Fritsch, 74 / 323 / 0
1943: Tony Canadeo, 94 / 489 / 3
1944: Ted Fritsch, 94 / 322 / 4
1945: Ted Fritsch, 88 / 282 / 7
1946: Tony Canadeo, 122 / 476 / 0
1947: Tony Canadeo, 103 / 464 / 2
1948: Tony Canadeo, 123 / 589 / 4
1949: Tony Canadeo, 208 / 1,052 / 4

Passing Leaders (Completions / Attempts / Yards)
1940: Cecil Isbell, 68 / 150 / 1,037
1941: Cecil Isbell, **117** / 206 / **1,479**
1942: Cecil Isbell, **146** / 268 / **2,021**
1943: Tony Canadeo, 56 / 129 / 875
1944: Irv Comp, 80 / **177** / **1,159**
1945: Irv Comp, 44 / 106 / 865
1946: Irv Comp, 27 / 94 / 333
1947: Jack Jacobs, 108 / 242 / 1,615
1948: Jack Jacobs, 82 / 184 / 848
1949: Jug Girard, 62 / 175 / 881

Receiving Leaders (Receptions / Yards / TDs)
1940: Don Hutson, 45 / 664 / 7
1941: Don Hutson, 58 / **738** / 10
1942: Don Hutson, **74** / **1,211** / 17
1943: Don Hutson, 47 / **776** / 11
1944: Don Hutson, 58 / **866** / 9
1945: Don Hutson, 47 / 834 / 9
1946: Clyde Goodnight, 16 / 308 / 1
1947: Nolan Luhn, 42 / 696 / 7
1948: Clyde Goodnight, 28 / 448 / 3
1949: Ted Cook, 25 / 442 / 1

Interceptions (Number / Yards / TDs)
1940: Don Hutson, 6 / 24 / 0
1941: Hal Van Every, 3 / 104 / 1
1942: Don Hutson, 7 / 71 / 0
1943: Irv Comp, 10 / 149 / 1
1944: Ted Fritsch, 6 / 115 / 1;
　　　　Irv Comp, 6 / 54 / 0
1945: Charley Brock, 4 / 122 / 2;
　　　　Don Hutson, 4 / 15 / 0
1946: Herman Rohrig, 5 / 134 / 0
1947: Bob Forte, 8 / 140 / 1
1948: Ted Cook, 6 / 81 / 0
1949: Ted Cook, 5 / 52 / 0

THE PACKER PICTORIAL REVIEW

TED FRITSCH GAINS 11 YARDS VS. BEARS
SEPT. 28, 1947

PRICE 25¢

CHICAGO CARDINALS EDITION
CITY STADIUM
SUNDAY OCTOBER 12, 1947

MVP Books Collection

the Record Book

First-Team All-Pros

1940: Don Hutson, End
1941: Clarke Hinkle, FB
1941: Don Hutson, End
1942: Don Hutson, End
1943: Tony Canadeo, Back
1943: Don Hutson, End
1944: Don Hutson, End
1945: Charley Brock, C
1945: Don Hutson, End
1946: Ted Fritsch, FB

Pro Bowl Selections

1940: Charley Brock, C
1940: Clarke Hinkle, FB
1940: Don Hutson, End
1940: Carl Mulleneaux, End
1941: Larry Craig, Back
1941: Don Hutson, End
1941: Cecil Isbell, TB
1942: Charley Brock, C
1942: Larry Craig, Back
1942: Don Hutson, End
1942: Cecil Isbell, TB

1st-Round Draft Picks

1940: Hal Van Every (9), Back, Minnesota
1941: George Paskvan (7), Back, Wisconsin
1942: Urban Odson (9), OT, Minnesota
1943: Dick Wildung (8), OT, Minnesota
1944: Merv Pregulman (7), G, Michigan
1945: Walt Schlinkman (11), Back, Texas Tech
1946: Johnny Strzykalski (6), Back, Marquette
1947: Ernie Case (6), Back, UCLA
1948: Earl "Jug" Girard (7), Back, Wisconsin
1949: Stan Heath (5), Back, Nevada-Reno

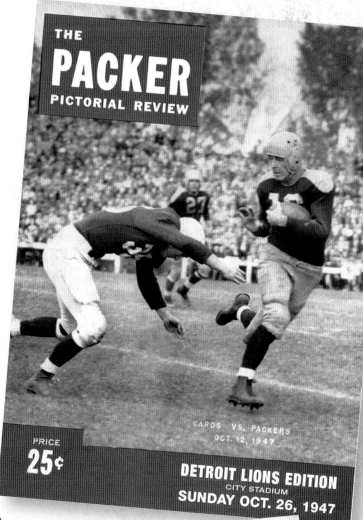

MVP Books Collection

MVP Books Collection

THE 1950s

The decade of the 1950s was the most schizophrenic in the history of the Green Bay Packers. It was both the worst of times and the best of times—in that order—and the upbeat ending of the decade could not have been foreseen.

Green Bay completed the 1949 season on shaky footing. The team parted ways with founder Curly Lambeau, the only coach the club had ever known, and was in financial peril.

Financial rescue came about in an odd manner. Lambeau had steered the purchase of a remote training facility called the Rockwell Lodge, about 15 miles from Green Bay. On January 25, 1950, the building caught fire. The structure was decimated, a total loss, and the Packers collected $75,000 in insurance money, which was badly needed for operations.

With Lambeau gone to the Chicago Cardinals, the Packers needed a new coach. Between Lambeau's coaching acumen, his personnel know-how, and his flamboyance, he was not easy to replace. And just how difficult that was became clear once a new man was on the job.

Gene Ronzani became the second head coach in Green Bay history for the 1950 season, and he was the boss through most of the 1953 season before departing with two games left. It was not as if Ronzani inherited a cupboard full of talent from Lambeau, either. The Packers were dismal during Lambeau's last two seasons, and during Ronzani's first two years they were no better, going a combined 6–18. There were signs of improvement the third year when the Pack climbed back to 6–6, but when the 1953 season represented regression, he was ousted.

Ronzani's most memorable, longest-lasting contribution was to change the color of the Packers' game uniforms, swapping green for blue while keeping the gold, thus instituting the iconic Packers look associated with the team.

The Packers were hardly living the high life during the 1950s, with the only winning campaign coming in the decade's final season. Here Green Bay is in the process of losing to the 49ers at home in October 1957. *Vernon Biever/Getty Images*

GREEN BAY PACKERS

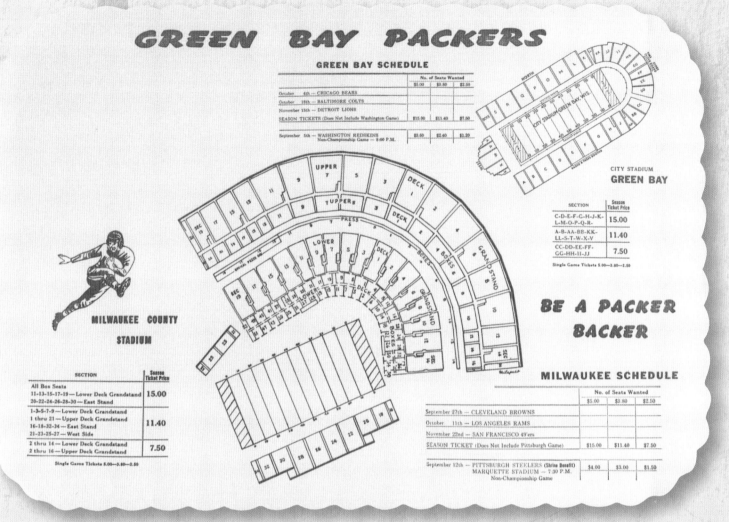

Packers home schedule for the 1953 season. *MVP Books Collection*

Of all things, at the tail end of the '53 campaign when Ronzani left, Packers management made Hugh Devore and Ray McLean co-head coaches for the final two games. With the goal of starting fresh in 1954, Lisle Blackbourn became the next head coach.

The Blackbourn years showed little improvement. In the four seasons he was in command from 1954 through 1957, the best Packers year was 6–6. The other three featured losing records.

McLean, whose nickname was "Scooter," returned as the head man for the 1958 season, but his single-season tenure was the worst of all and the worst in the history of the team. That year, the Packers finished 1–10–1 and McLean was fired. Packers fans had suffered through a decade of on-field misery and off-field uncertainty. The last championship had come in 1944. Fans and management were desperate for a turnaround.

The hiring of the next coach was pivotal. It just would not do to remain the worst team in the league. Green Bay was already the smallest city in the NFL, and for self-preservation the team's image needed revamping. The man tapped to be the next leader was Vince Lombardi.

While Lombardi became one of the greatest coaches of all time in any sport, his credentials did not guarantee such results. He had no ties to the Packers or Wisconsin. He was a notable offensive assistant with the New York Giants, and before that he had been an assistant coach at Fordham, his alma mater, and the U.S. Military Academy. He came well recommended, but there was nothing on his résumé suggesting that Lombardi was a miracle worker.

Only he was. In 1959, Lombardi's first season in Green Bay, the team went 7–5. It was just the beginning.

Program cover for Packers game against the Detroit Lions on October 5, 1958. *MVP Books Collection*

▶ **3–9**   **5th place** ◀

Game-by-Game

9/17   **L, 7–45, vs. Detroit Lions**

9/24   **W, 35–21,**
         vs. Washington Redskins

10/1   **W, 31–21,**
         vs. Chicago Bears

10/8   **L, 31–44,**
         vs. New York Yanks

10/15   **L, 14–28, at Chicago Bears**

10/19   **L, 17–35,**
         at New York Yanks

11/5   **L, 21–41,**
         at Baltimore Colts

11/12   **L, 14–45,**
         vs. Los Angeles Rams

11/19   **L, 21–24, at Detroit Lions**

11/26   **W, 25–21,**
         vs. San Francisco 49ers

12/3   **L, 14–51,**
         at Los Angeles Rams

12/10   **L, 14–30,**
         at San Francisco 49ers

Team Scoring

244 points scored (8th)

406 points allowed (12th)

PACKERS HEADLINE

New head coach brings same subpar results, as Gene Ronzani takes over on the sidelines.

Hall of Fame running back Tony Canadeo carried the ball a team-high 93 times in 1950, but he tallied only 247 yards, for an average of 2.7 yards per carry. Here Canadeo (3) runs upfield against the 49ers at snowy City Stadium on November 26, 1950. *Vernon Biever/Getty Images*

Being hired as the head coach of the Green Bay Packers, a job that hadn't been vacant in 31 years, probably seemed like a dream opportunity for Gene Ronzani. He had played his college ball at Marquette, had played for the Chicago Bears, and was working as an assistant coach in Chicago. George Halas wasn't going anywhere anytime soon, since he was the owner as well as coach of the Bears.

Ronzani was a creative coach who tinkered with formations. He wanted to make a splash, so he changed uniform jerseys from blue to green. And he signed the first African American player for the Packers, Robert Mann out of Michigan. Not surprisingly given the times, Ronzani was criticized for that.

He was loaded with good ideas, but Ronzani couldn't win, and a coach who can't win is not going to last. In his 1950 debut season, Ronzani's Packers finished 3–9. They showed well at first, starting 2–1 and beating the Bears 31–21, but then six straight losses followed, including the rematch with Chicago.

Green Bay's biggest problem was defense. While the offense averaged 20 points a game, the defense allowed a whopping 406 points, or 33.8 points per game.

Breaking in as a rookie at quarterback was Tobin Rote. Rote was 22, and the season earlier he had led Rice to a 10–1 record. Rote would have a long and successful career with several teams and make a couple of Pro Bowl appearances, but in 1950 he was too inexperienced.

Bob Mann

Although very talented, Bob Mann was a controversial hire when he joined the Packers in 1950 as the first African American player in team history. Mann had already broken that barrier with the Detroit Lions, but a salary dispute sent him to the New York Yanks. Then he was cut, and there were suggestions that he was being kept out of the league.

Mann played football first at predominantly black Hampton Institute, but he transferred to the University of Michigan because he thought of becoming a doctor after football.

Mann was a free agent when Packers coach Gene Ronzani signed him. For the Lions in 1949, Mann caught 66 passes for 1,014 yards. In 1951 for Green Bay, he hauled in 56 passes for 696 yards and eight touchdowns.

Traveling with the Packers was often a trial for Mann. Sometimes he faced discrimination at hotels or from taxi drivers. One of Mann's best friends on the team was a 250-pound lineman named Dick Afflis, who stood up for him in such discouraging circumstances. Afflis later became much more famous as the pro wrestler Dick the Bruiser.

Mann played for the Packers into 1955, but when he injured a knee in an exhibition game and was cut, he sued the team for $25,000. That's how Mann's pro football career ended. He later went on to a successful career in Michigan as an attorney, and years later he was inducted into the Green Bay Packers Hall of Fame.

Vernon Biever/Getty Images

Tobin Rote

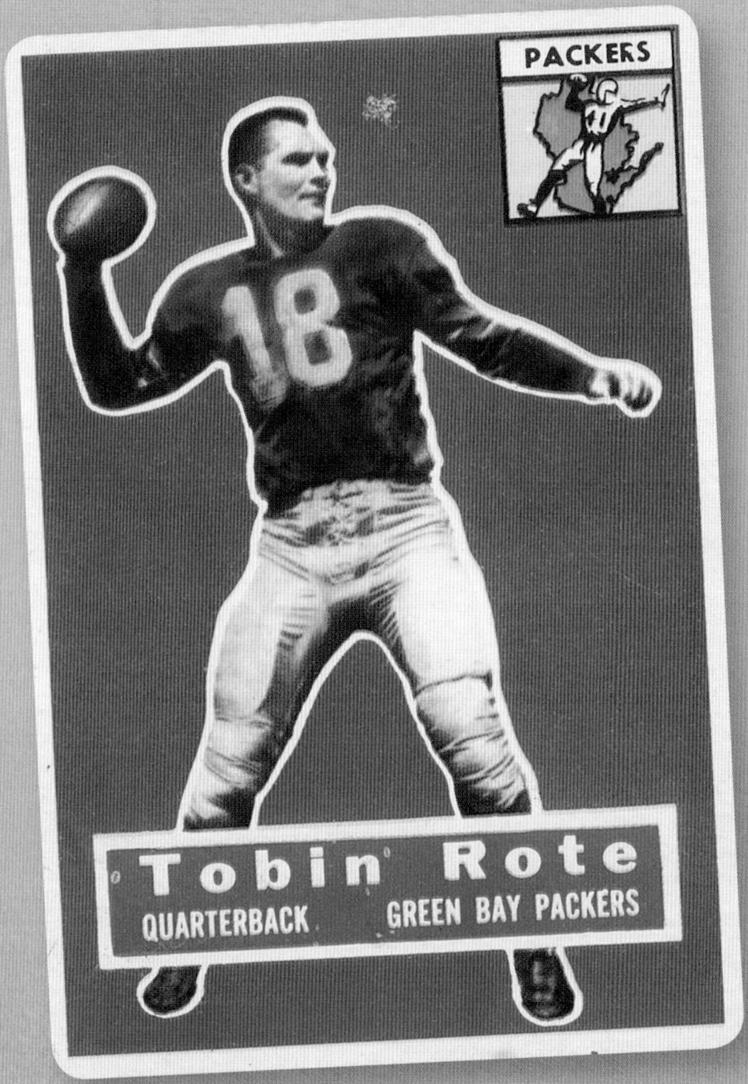

The 1950s NFL was a league for drop-back quarterbacks, not a scrambler's paradise. But Tobin Rote could both throw and run, and he enjoyed gaining yards on his own during the years he started for the Packers before continuing a long and varied career elsewhere.

Rote broke in with the Packers in 1950 and remained with the club through 1956. It was not the best time to be the signal-caller in Green Bay. Rote's performance was a bright spot through the losing seasons. His best Green Bay year was his last one, when he led the league in passes completed, passes attempted, yards gained through the air, and touchdown passes.

From Green Bay, Rote went to the Detroit Lions, the Toronto Argonauts of the Canadian Football League, and the San Diego Chargers in the early days of the American Football League. He finished up with the Denver Broncos in 1966.

Although Rote and Cleveland Browns coach Paul Brown proved to be ahead of their time, Brown described Rote's combination of talents as representing "the new type of T-formation quarterback—a fellow who threatens you with the run as well as the pass."

The 6-foot-3, 210-pound Rote won an NFL title with the Lions, copped an AFL title with the Chargers, was a two-time NFL All-Pro, and was the Associated Press 1963 Most Valuable Player of the AFL. Not including his time in Canada, Rote threw 148 touchdown passes and gained 18,850 yards through the air.

PACKERS

Tobin Rote
QUARTERBACK   GREEN BAY PACKERS

MVP Books Collection

Gene Ronzani's first year was a tough one. He was following on the heels of other bad years during the waning days of the Curly Lambeau administration, so it was important to show improvement in 1951. But if there was improvement that season, it was subtle, because the team went an identical 3–9.

After losing the season opener to the Chicago Bears, the Packers won two in a row. They lost another game and won another to move to 3–2, but they then lost their last seven games in a row. Wins were recorded over the Pittsburgh Steelers, Philadelphia Eagles, and New York Yanks.

Scoring was up a bit, but the holes in the defense shrunk only slightly, with the Packers still surrendering 375 points. The least number of points any opponent scored against Green Bay was 24.

With a year of experience, quarterback Tobin Rote showed great growth and was the key figure on offense. In the 11 games Rote played, he threw for 1,540 yards and 15 touchdowns and rushed for 523 yards and three more scores.

Tackle Dick Wildung, a No. 1 draft pick out of the University of Minnesota in 1942, who survived the lean years with the franchise, was chosen for the Pro Bowl. So, too, was halfback Billy Grimes, who did a little of everything. Grimes, the "Commanche Kid" out of Oklahoma State, rushed for 123 yards, caught 15 passes, and did much of the punt and kick returning.

Fullback/kicker Fred Cone (66) boots the winning field goal with 11 seconds left to cap the Packers' 23-point final period and defeat the New York Yanks, 29–27, at Yankee Stadium on October 28. It was Green Bay's third and final win of the season. The Yanks would win only one game in 1951, the final season in the franchise's brief history. AP Photo/Harry Harris

1951

▶ 3–9   5th place ◀

Game-by-Game

9/30	**L**, 20–31, vs. Chicago Bears
10/7	**W**, 35–33, vs. Pittsburgh Steelers
10/14	**W**, 37–24, vs. Philadelphia Eagles
10/21	**L**, 0–28, vs. Los Angeles Rams
10/28	**W**, 29–27, at New York Yanks
11/4	**L**, 17–24, vs. Detroit Lions
11/11	**L**, 7–28, at Pittsburgh Steelers
11/18	**L**, 13–24, at Chicago Bears
11/22	**L**, 35–52, at Detroit Lions
12/2	**L**, 28–31, vs. New York Yanks
12/9	**L**, 19–31, at San Francisco 49ers
12/16	**L**, 14–42, at Los Angeles Rams

Team Scoring

254 points scored (6th)

375 points allowed (11th)

PACKERS HEADLINE

More of the same, as seven-game season-ending losing streak leads to another 3–9 finish.

▶ 6–6   4th place ◀

Game-by-Game

9/28   **L, 14–24,**
vs. Chicago Bears

10/5   **W, 35–20,**
vs. Washington Redskins

10/12   **L, 28–30,**
vs. Los Angeles Rams

10/18   **W, 24–14, at Dallas Texans**

10/26   **L, 17–52, vs. Detroit Lions**

11/2   **W, 12–10,**
vs. Philadelphia Eagles

11/9   **W, 41–28,**
at Chicago Bears

11/16   **W, 17–3,**
at New York Giants

11/23   **W, 42–14,**
vs. Dallas Texans

11/27   **L, 24–48, at Detroit Lions**

12/7   **L, 27–45,**
at Los Angeles Rams

12/14   **L, 14–24,**
at San Francisco 49ers

Team Scoring

295 points scored (5th)

312 points allowed (10th)

Rookie receiver Billy Howton and rookie quarterback Babe Parilli help spark Green Bay passing attack and the most wins in four years.

The 1952 campaign was the beacon-of-hope season for the Green Bay Packers under coach Gene Ronzani. It wasn't a winning year, but the 6–6 record was their best since 1947. It appeared that Ronzani's rebuilding plan was working.

If Ronzani had been through a honeymoon period, in which fans squirmed as the team's record resembled the last days of Curly Lambeau, this season provided optimism. Probably the most satisfying victory was a 41–28 triumph over the Chicago Bears.

The defense remained porous, but the offense became more explosive as Ronzani focused on building a dangerous passing attack. Two new players who arrived through the draft played a big role in this. Tobin Rote was seemingly a fixture at quarterback, but rookie Vito "Babe" Parilli out of Kentucky ended up splitting the duties with the holdover.

Parilli threw for 1,416 yards and 13 touchdowns. Rote also threw for 13 touchdowns while compiling 1,268 passing yards. But there were two major differences in their stats. Parilli, the newcomer, threw 17 interceptions. Rote, the third-year man, threw only eight. Rote, who could also use his feet, rushed for 313 yards.

The Packers already had Robert Mann as a solid wide receiver, and he caught 30 balls for six touchdowns. But the new face in the receiving corps was rookie Billy Howton, a game-breaker and the finest Green Bay pass catcher since Don Hutson. Howton caught 53 passes for 13 touchdowns and averaged 23.2 yards per catch.

As a rookie in 1952, end Billy Howton recorded a league-best 1,231 receiving yards while leading Green Bay with 53 receptions. He also led all Packers with 13 touchdowns during his All-Pro campaign.
Vernon Biever/Getty Images

Billy Howton

Joining the team of all-time great receiver Don Hutson made it challenging for Billy Howton to set records, but he did occasionally break one of the marks belonging to the "Alabama Antelope." And he was certainly the best Green Bay Packers receiver of the 1950s.

The 6-foot-2, 190-pound Texan caught more passes during his 12-year career in the NFL than Hutson did in 11, but Howton did not spend all his playing days with the Packers. Howton's NFL mark of 503 receptions eclipsed Hutson's 488.

In his early days with the Packers, Howton enjoyed a reunion catching passes from college teammate Tobin Rote. After seven seasons in Green Bay, starting in 1952, Howton was traded to the Cleveland Browns for one season. He retired, but the Dallas Cowboys—who were not far from his Littlefield, Texas, home—talked him into a comeback. Howton played four seasons with Dallas.

Howton twice eclipsed 1,000 receiving yards in a season for the Packers. In 1952 he scored 13 touchdowns through the air, and in 1956 he rang up 12 touchdown receptions. When he retired in 1963, Howton held the NFL record for most receiving yards (8,459).

Howton, who relied on speed and creative moves to get free against defensive backs, said cutting across the middle was a dangerous venture.

"You might as well catch them in the middle, because they're going to hit you whether you catch the ball or not," he said.

Vernon Biever/Getty Images

Dave Hanner

While not as famous, Dave Hanner became as much of an institution in Green Bay as Curly Lambeau, and he is one of the few who could boast of a longer association with the team than its founder.

Known as "Hawg" Hanner, the beefy defensive lineman was connected to the Packers for his entire professional life. As a player, coach, and scout, Hanner drew a paycheck from the Packers for 42 years.

A University of Arkansas alum, Hanner was drafted in the fifth round in 1952. The 6-foot-2, 257-pound tackle and end played in 160 out of 164 possible games before retiring from the field in 1964. He was twice chosen All-Pro, and he played on the Green Bay title teams of the early 1960s.

Over the years, Hanner assisted Vince Lombardi, Dan Devine, and Bart Starr in different coaching roles.

Hanner broke in with the 6–6 team that gave fans hope, but one of his most memorable games was a huge disappointment that year. He got a taste of the Packers' problems when the Rams drove 92 yards for the winning touchdown in a game that Hanner felt had been won. "It was the biggest letdown I ever experienced," he said.

Renowned for his toughness and durability, Hanner missed some games in 1961 when he underwent an appendectomy. The illness ended a 109-game playing streak.

"They said I'd be out three weeks at the most," Hanner said. He sat out just one game, though he did miss teammate Max McGee's wedding reception.

MVP Books Collection

Floyd "Breezy" Reid (24) blazes around the Detroit defense during a 14–7 loss at City Stadium on October 15. Reid was the top rusher for the two-win Packers of 1953. *Vernon Biever/Getty Images*

Game-by-Game

9/27	**L**, 0–27,	vs. Cleveland Browns
10/4	**L**, 13–17,	vs. Chicago Bears
10/11	**L**, 20–38,	vs. Los Angeles Rams
10/18	**W**, 37–14,	vs. Baltimore Colts
10/24	**L**, 14–31,	at Pittsburgh Steelers
10/31	**W**, 35–24,	at Baltimore Colts
11/8	**T**, 21–21,	at Chicago Bears
11/15	**L**, 7–14, vs. Detroit Lions	
11/22	**L**, 7–37,	vs. San Francisco 49ers
11/26	**L**, 15–34,	at Detroit Lions
12/6	**L**, 14–48,	at San Francisco 49ers
12/12	**L**, 17–33,	at Los Angeles Rams

Team Scoring

200 points scored (9th)

338 points allowed (11th)

Green Bay's management and fans felt as if the team took one giant step backward in 1953. After the promising 1952 season, it was as if all hope was shattered.

The Packers lost their first three games of the season, won one, lost one, won one, and never won again. A 21–21 tie snuck in there, but as things fell apart the once-impressive offense showed little and the defense was on its way to allowing a massive 338 points.

With two games left, which included a West Coast trip to play the 49ers in San Francisco and the Rams in Los Angeles, coach Gene Ronzani was relieved of command. Strangely, he was replaced by co-coaches Ray McLean and Hugh Devore. The team lost both games in California to finish 2–9–1. Neither coach was retained the next season.

The Packers went with the two-quarterback deal again, but neither Tobin Rote nor Babe Parilli thrived in the arrangement. Both of their yardage totals were down, and their interception totals were sky-high. Rote threw 15 and Parilli 19.

Neither Billy Howton nor Robert Mann matched their pass-catching totals of the year before, and both missed games. Howton caught 25 passes but played in only eight games. Mann (23 catches) appeared in 10 games. The most reliable ballcarrier was Breezy Reid, who rushed for 492 yards and averaged 5.2 yards per carry.

One bright spot on defense was a find out of the University of Texas named Bobby Dillon, who intercepted nine passes as a rookie.

PACKERS HEADLINE

Ronzani gets the axe, but co-coaches Ray McLean and Hugh Devore don't do much better as replacements.

Jim Ringo

At 200 pounds as a rookie coming out of Syracuse in 1953, Jim Ringo was undersized for a center. Somehow, he worked his way onto the Packers' roster, and he was a veteran when coach Vince Lombardi arrived in 1959. Ringo was the center on Green Bay's first two championship teams in the early 1960s after he grew to 235 pounds.

Just 20 when he reported to his first Green Bay training camp, Ringo was discouraged by the size of the competition. He was going to quit football, but he said he wouldn't have been welcome at home. "They [his family] said, 'You should at least try.'"

Legend has it that Lombardi traded Ringo to the Philadelphia Eagles before the 1964 season because the player brought an agent with him to Lombardi's office to negotiate a new contract for a raise. The story goes that Lombardi excused himself from the meeting for five minutes and then returned to inform Ringo he had just been traded to the Eagles, and to go negotiate with them.

A 10-time Pro Bowl selection, Ringo was voted into the Pro Football Hall of Fame in 1981. He compiled a 182-game playing streak, never sitting out from 1954 to 1967.

"It was more of a fear of losing my job," Ringo said of why he persisted despite injuries. His streak ended with seven games left in his last season. He then became a longtime NFL assistant coach for several teams, but not the Packers.

JIM RINGO
CENTER   GREEN BAY PACKERS

MVP Books Collection

Enter another new head coach for the Green Bay Packers, who had managed to go through three of them in 1953. Lisle Blackbourn represented the second fresh start since Curly Lambeau took his act to the Chicago Cardinals (and by 1952, the Washington Redskins).

Blackbourn had a deep background in Wisconsin football. He played college ball at small Lawrence University in Appleton. He later became head coach at Marquette University, and wrapped around his rocky coaching career with the Packers, he coached high school ball in Wisconsin, worked on the staff at the University of Wisconsin, coached Marquette a second time, and coached another small Wisconsin school, Carroll College.

The shake-up at the top in Green Bay seemed to do the team some good during the 1954 season, though not a huge amount. It was a streaky year en route to a 4–8 finish. Blackbourn's club started poorly, with three straight losses, and then the team won three straight. Yet the season ended with a four-game losing streak.

Blackbourn was a one-quarterback man. Babe Parilli ended up with the Ottawa Roughriders for a season in Canada, and Tobin Rote blossomed as the starting quarterback. Rote completed 180 of 382 passes for 2,311 yards and 14 touchdowns. Breezy Reid led the team again in rushing with 507 yards.

But the biggest action was in the passing game. Billy Howton recovered from injury and caught 52 passes. Howie Ferguson, in his best season with the Pack, caught 41, and newcomer Max McGee, a fifth-round draft pick out of Tulane—who would play a significant role in Packers lore in later years—grabbed 36.

In his rookie season of 1954, end Max McGee was third on the team with 36 receptions, but he led the way with nine touchdowns. Here he runs the ball during a 35–17 win over the Los Angeles Rams at Milwaukee County Stadium, during which he caught one TD pass. *Vernon Biever/Getty Images*

▶ 4–8 5th place ◀

Game-by-Game

9/26	**L**, 20–21, vs. Pittsburgh Steelers
10/3	**L**, 3–10, vs. Chicago Bears
10/10	**L**, 17–23, vs. San Francisco 49ers
10/17	**W**, 35–17, vs. Los Angeles Rams
10/24	**W**, 7–6, at Baltimore Colts
10/30	**W**, 37–14, at Philadelphia Eagles
11/7	**L**, 23–28, at Chicago Bears
11/13	**W**, 24–13, vs. Baltimore Colts
11/21	**L**, 17–21, vs. Detroit Lions
11/25	**L**, 24–28, at Detroit Lions
12/5	**L**, 0–35, at San Francisco 49ers
12/12	**L**, 27–35, at Los Angeles Rams

Team Scoring

234 points scored (8th)

251 points allowed (5th)

PACKERS HEADLINE

Wisconsin native Lisle Blackbourn takes the reins as coach, brings marginal improvement in wins and losses.

1955

Game-by-Game

9/25	**W**, 20–17, vs. Detroit Lions
10/2	**W**, 24–3, vs. Chicago Bears
10/8	**L**, 20–24, vs. Baltimore Colts
10/16	**W**, 30–28, vs. Los Angeles Rams
10/23	**L**, 10–41, at Cleveland Browns
10/29	**L**, 10–14, al Baltimore Colts
11/6	**L**, 31–52, at Chicago Bears
11/13	**W**, 31–14, vs. Chicago Cardinals
11/20	**W**, 27–21, vs. San Francisco 49ers
11/24	**L**, 10–24, at Detroit Lions
12/4	**W**, 28–7, at San Francisco 49ers
12/11	**L**, 17–31, at Los Angeles Rams

Team Scoring

258 points scored (5th)

276 points allowed (10th)

PACKERS HEADLINE

Promising 3–1 start ends up as .500 finish.

Inching back to respectability, the Packers finished 6–6 in coach Lisle Blackbourn's second season. It was a nice move up from 4–8, even if the team did not crack 500.

Green Bay started out 2–0, and both games were memorable. The opener at City Stadium was against the Detroit Lions, and the Packers trailed as the clock ran down to less than a minute to go. Quarterback Tobin Rote hit newcomer Gary Knafelc with a 28-yard touchdown pass to win the game 20–17.

Knafelc, a second-year NFL player, came over from the Chicago Cardinals, and this was his introduction to Green Bay fans. They fell in love, storming the field and carrying him off on their shoulders.

The second game was a pleasing 24–3 victory over the Chicago Bears, the best defensive performance of the season. However, the defense still had its problems throughout the year.

A three-game losing streak in the middle of the season was costly, and that included a 52–31 pummeling by the Bears in Chicago. About 20 percent of the team's points allowed that year came in that game. It was the most forgettable contest of the season.

Rote, who continued to be a reliable signal-caller, could make things happen with his arm and legs. He threw for 1,977 yards and 17 touchdowns and rushed for 332 yards. Fullback Howie Ferguson emerged as a workhorse, carrying the ball for 859 yards and hauling in 22 passes. Billy Howton had a team-leading 44 catches.

Al Carmichael wraps up a reception in front of Colts defensive back Don Shula during the Packers' 24–20 loss to Baltimore on October 8. Carmichael did a little of everything for Green Bay in six seasons (1953–1958): catching passes, running the ball, and returning kicks and punts.
Vernon Biever/Getty Images

Bobby Dillon

A 6-foot-1, 180-pound defensive back from the University of Texas, Bobby Dillon is among the finest secondary men in Green Bay Packers history. In an eight-season career, he intercepted 52 passes and returned five of them for touchdowns.

On a defense that was wobbly throughout his career (1952–1959), Dillon was a reliable fixture. His performance was even more remarkable considering he had clear vision in only one eye. He had lost an eye in a childhood accident.

"I suppose it might have made a difference," Dillon said, "but I never thought about it. I'm just happy I could play as long as I did. I wish they had paid more money."

Among Dillon's accomplishments was the theft of four passes in a single game and stealing nine passes in a season three times—in 1953, 1955, and 1957.

Dillon's four-interception game came on November 26, 1953. It was Thanksgiving Day, tucked into the middle of one of the worst seasons in Packers history. Most amazingly, despite Dillon's heroics, Green Bay lost 34–15.

Dillon's victim was an old friend, Lions quarterback Bobby Layne, who had also attended Texas. "We always had a rivalry going," Dillon said. "We'd talk before the game, and he was always going to 'get' me and I was always going to 'get' him. It was just one of those days where you were in the right place at the right time. Usually, when you get that many interceptions, that many turnovers, you win."

AP Photo/Pro Football Hall of Fame

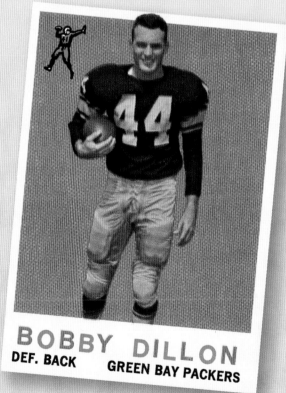

BOBBY DILLON
DEF. BACK   GREEN BAY PACKERS

MVP Books Collection

Forrest Gregg

A 6-foot-4, 250-pound slab of granite, Forrest Gregg was one of the toughest offensive linemen of his time and was a nine-time Pro Bowl selection on his way to the Pro Football Hall of Fame. Gregg was a mountain on the line for the Packers during their five title triumphs of the 1960s, and he later coached the team.

A second-round draft pick out of Southern Methodist University in 1956, Gregg played 15 seasons in the league. He viewed himself as a defensive lineman, but then—Green Bay coach Lisle Blackbourn told Gregg he wanted him on offense

at tackle. To adapt, Gregg studied film of Jim Parker and Roosevelt Brown—two of the best of all time.

"That's the only way a fellow with a little ability can become a good tackle," Gregg said, "and that is through hard work."

Gregg moved to guard after a few seasons under coach Vince Lombardi in the 1960s, and he had his greatest success in that position. He finished his playing career with the Dallas Cowboys and won a sixth championship ring.

"Moving to guard meant learning new assignments and new techniques and meeting new opponents," Gregg said. "But I welcomed the challenge just to see if I could do it."

After retirement, Gregg moved into coaching. He became head coach of the Cleveland Browns, Cincinnati Bengals, and Packers, returning to his old team as the field boss in 1984 and lasting until 1987. Gregg also worked as athletic director at SMU.

Robert Riger/Getty Images

In season with little reason to cheer, receiver Billy Howton sets new franchise record with 257 receiving yards against the Rams at home.

▶ 4–8   5th place ◀

Green Bay's most impressive victory during the 1956 season was a 42–17 decision against the Los Angeles Rams at Milwaukee. Here end Gary Knafelc (84) makes a leaping catch for a second-quarter score, one of three touchdown passes by quarterback Tobin Rote. *AP Photo*

Game-by-Game

9/30	L, 16–20, vs. Detroit Lions
10/7	L, 21–37, vs. Chicago Bears
10/14	W, 38–33, vs. Baltimore Colts
10/21	W, 42–17, vs. Los Angeles Rams
10/28	L, 21–28, at Baltimore Colts
11/4	L, 7–24, vs. Cleveland Browns
11/11	L, 14–38, at Chicago Bears
11/18	L, 16–17, vs. San Francisco 49ers
11/22	W, 24–20, at Detroit Lions
12/2	W, 24–21, at Chicago Cardinals
12/8	L, 20–38, at San Francisco 49ers
12/16	L, 21–49, at Los Angeles Rams

Team Scoring

264 points scored (5th)

342 points allowed (12th)

The big problem for coach Lisle Blackbourn in 1956 was that the Packers season more resembled 1954 than 1955. It was back to 4–8 again. This was no way to show progress.

Beginning with two straight losses, Green Bay flashed a modicum of hope with two straight wins over the Los Angeles Rams and Baltimore Colts. But that was the end of that tune. What followed were four straight losses.

There was even some internal dissension. The front office complained to Blackbourn that he wasn't playing No. 1 draft pick Jack Losch at running back enough. Losch carried the ball 19 times for 43 yards for a 2.3 yards-per-carry average. Then he gave up football and joined the Air Force. That was his only season in the NFL.

However, Losch figured in the most exciting victory of the season. When the Packers clobbered the Rams 42–17, receiver Billy Howton caught seven passes for a team-record 257 yards. Howton's mark topped Don Hutson's single-game record of 237 yards. Howton caught two touchdown passes that day, one from quarterback Tobin Rote and the other on an option from Losch.

The Packers notched another very satisfying triumph on Thanksgiving Day in the traditional holiday match with the Detroit Lions. The Packers were floundering and the Lions were trying to move into first in the division, but Green Bay won 24–20 to prevent that. Rote threw two TD passes and scored another himself.

Sitting behind Tobin on the bench in 1956 was the team's seventeenth-round pick in that year's draft: Bart Starr of Alabama. The rookie appeared in nine games and got one start, but he would get his chance to take more snaps soon enough.

1957

Game-by-Game

9/29	W, 21–17, vs. Chicago Bears
10/6	L, 14–24, vs. Detroit Lions
10/13	L, 17–45, vs. Baltimore Colts
10/20	L, 14–24, vs. San Francisco 49ers
10/27	W, 24–21, at Baltimore Colts
11/3	L, 17–31, vs. New York Giants
11/10	L, 14–21, at Chicago Bears
11/17	L, 27–31, vs. Los Angeles Rams
11/24	W, 27–10, at Pittsburgh Steelers
11/28	L, 6–18, at Detroit Lions
12/8	L, 17–42, at Los Angeles Rams
12/15	L, 20–27, at San Francisco 49ers

Team Scoring

218 points scored (8th)

311 points allowed (12th)

PACKERS HEADLINE

Second-year quarterback Bart Starr gets starting job, and rookie back Paul Hornung brings tougher running game.

The fourth year of the Lisle Blackbourn coaching era was the last year of the Lisle Blackbourn coaching era. The Packers finished 3–9, and it seemed as if the team was running in place. Dismayed directors gave up on Blackbourn after the season.

Over the preceding few years, the losing Packers had come under increasing pressure from other NFL owners to either move all of the team's home games to Milwaukee or to build a bigger stadium in Green Bay. Once again proving their love for their hometown team, the citizens voted to build a new City Stadium. The $960,000 cost was financed through municipal bonds, and the building was ready to go for the start of the 1957 season.

So was the flashy new acquisition—No. 1 draft choice Paul Hornung, the Heisman Trophy winner out of Notre Dame. Buzz was strong and optimism high with the addition of Hornung and No. 2 pick Ron Kramer, an end, plus the new stadium. Then the Packers went 5–0–1 during the exhibition season.

With Tobin Rote shipped off to Detroit, Bart Starr took over the starting quarterback role and completed 117 of 215 passes for 1,489 yards, eight touchdowns, and 10 interceptions.

Everything was grand until the season began. Although the Packers topped the Chicago Bears in the opener 21–17, with Billy Howton catching eight passes for 165 yards, Green Bay promptly lost six of its next seven games. That stretch essentially was Blackbourn's obituary as coach.

Over four seasons in charge, Blackbourn never topped the .500 mark. However, of the five coaches who bridged the gap between Curly Lambeau and Vince Lombardi, Blackbourn won the most games. After posting a 17–31 record as coach, Blackbourn continued to work as a scout for the organization.

The 1957 season was Green Bay's tenth in a row without a winning record, but rookie running back Paul Hornung—here breaking free from the Giants defense on November 3 at Lambeau Field—arrived that year as a bona fide star. *Vernon Biever/Getty Images*

Ron Kramer

In the late 1950s and early 1960s, the tight end was still mostly looked at as a guy who had to block first and was an afterthought in the passing game. That was slowly changing, and Ron Kramer was one of those who came along at the time to help broaden the role.

"You can call me a tackle who has to catch passes," said Kramer, a first-round 1957 pick out of Michigan. "The most important thing is to get off the ball quickly. Unlike the other receivers, I must get by a linebacker."

At 6-foot-3, 250 pounds, Kramer had the perfect build to perform both tasks during a 10-year NFL career, the first seven with Green Bay. Kramer caught 229 passes in his career and—when healthy and in top form with the Packers as they claimed championships—he grabbed about 35 balls a year thrown by Bart Starr.

Kramer, who died in 2011 at 75, was a member of the Packers before coach Vince Lombardi was hired. He was part of the transition from the bad days of the 1950s to the great days of the 1960s.

"Most us played together when we were horrible losers," Kramer said. "Vince Lombardi gave us the incentive to become winners. It's hard to believe we'll be losers again."

Kramer had stomach problems during his career, and he frequently skipped meals on game days. However, a teammate suggested that "he eats linebackers" during games to make up for lack of calories.

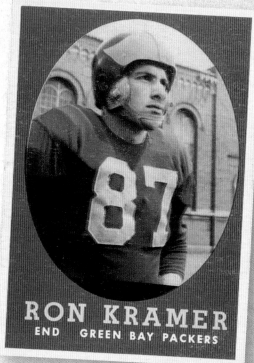

RON KRAMER
END   GREEN BAY PACKERS

MVP Books Collection

Ron Kramer in action, circa 1961. *Robert Riger/Getty Images*

New City Stadium

Tired of being accused of riding the coattails of big cities with their big payouts for large attendance at road games, and under pressure from the National Football League either to build a new stadium in Green Bay or move all home games to Milwaukee, the community's citizens took steps to ensure their hold on pro football.

On September 29, 1957, Green Bay introduced a new City Stadium to replace the old home facility for the Packers. With a party that would compare locally to the opening ceremonies of the Olympics, Green Bay threw a celebration that attracted 135,000 people to a weekend's worth of festivities. At the time, Green Bay's population was about 63,000.

The $960,000 stadium was financed by municipal bonds, and the jam-packed building for the opening game against the Chicago Bears—a victory—held 32,132 fans. Among those on the scene for the weekend activities were Vice President Richard Nixon and Miss America. Some of the activities included a farewell event at old City Stadium and a Venetian Nights boat parade on the Fox River.

When it opened in 1925, the original City Stadium attracted a little over 5,000 fans to games. It was expanded to 15,000 and ultimately to 25,000, but near the end of its run through 1956, it sorely lacked modern amenities.

The festivities so warmed the community that the *Green Bay Press-Citizen* declared that anyone not pleased "is the kind of fellow who would growl about not getting eggs in his beer."

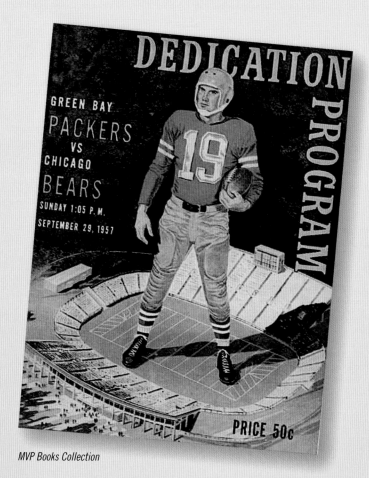

MVP Books Collection

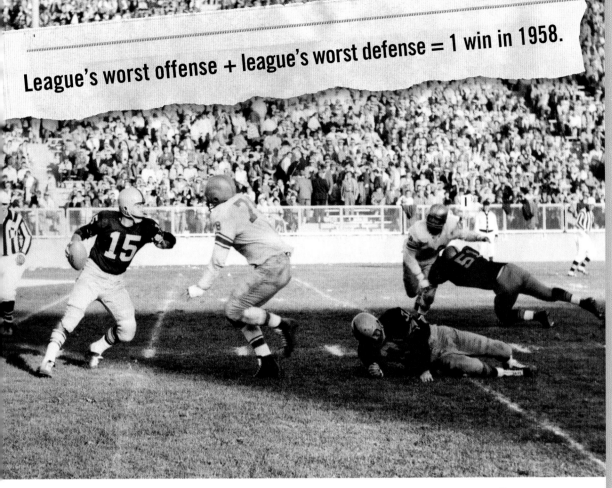

League's worst offense + league's worst defense = 1 win in 1958.

There weren't many causes for celebration during the Packers' 1–10–1 season in 1958, but the 13–13 tie with the Lions on October 5 was about as good as it got. Here Bart Starr scrambles free from the Detroit defense with his back up against his own end zone. *Vernon Biever/Getty Images*

Game-by-Game

9/28	L, 20–34,	vs. Chicago Bears
10/5	T, 13–13, vs. Detroit Lions	
10/12	L, 17–24,	vs. Baltimore Colts
10/19	L, 21–37,	at Washington Redskins
10/26	W, 38–35,	vs. Philadelphia Eagles
11/2	L, 0–56, at Baltimore Colts	
11/9	L, 10–24, at Chicago Bears	
11/16	L, 7–20,	vs. Los Angeles Rams
11/23	L, 12–33,	vs. San Francisco 49ers
11/27	L, 14–24, at Detroit Lions	
12/7	L, 21–48,	at San Francisco 49ers
12/14	L, 20–34,	at Los Angeles Rams

Team Scoring

193 points scored (12th)

382 points allowed (12th)

Obscured by a mess of a season that ended 1–10–1 and represented the one-year reign of Ray McLean, back from his hiatus after the two-game cameo as co-coach in 1953, was that the Packers were amassing young talent with potential.

Scout Jack Vainisi was finding talent all over the hinterlands, and the Packers were signing up young ballplayers with a future. However, they were too young in 1958. The players, along with the short-lived McLean and the fans in the shiny new stadium, suffered together.

The numbers were embarrassing. The team scored only 193 points, and the defense was trampled for 382 points. Although the Packers were losing, a lot of witnesses saw them up close that season, at home and on the road, with overall attendance for Green Bay games reaching 449,019.

Bart Starr was in his second year at quarterback, though he split duties with Babe Parilli, who had returned from the Canadian Football League. Paul Hornung settled in at halfback. Jim Taylor had arrived at fullback. Jim Ringo at center, Jerry Kramer at guard, and defenders such as linebackers Ray Nitschke and Bill Forester and defensive back Jesse Whittenton were on the premises. They were excellent football players who just hadn't proved it yet.

Parilli was at the helm for the one victory, a 38–35 decision over the Philadelphia Eagles. Parilli threw four touchdown passes in that game, two of them to Max McGee. Starr led Green Bay to the tie, 13–13, against the Detroit Lions.

Robert Riger/Getty Images

Paul Hornung

Nicknamed the "Golden Boy" because of his flowing blond locks and his dashing style, 6-foot-3, 215-pound halfback Paul Hornung arrived in Green Bay in 1957, and he went on to help define the era of the Vince Lombardi Packers in the 1960s. He may have been showy, but Hornung got the work done. He was a scoring machine who cranked out touchdowns, field goals, and extra points.

Hornung had been the 1956 Heisman Trophy winner as a quarterback with Notre Dame, and he was drafted with the No. 1 overall pick in 1957.

At first, Hornung didn't have a position in Green Bay. His arm was not accurate enough for him to be a pro quarterback. He wasn't sprinter fast. But once he got a chance, he proved he was simply a terrific player. Hornung

had his own doubts about going to Green Bay. He had hoped to play in Chicago because it was a fun town. "I hated Green Bay back then," Hornung said. "When I got there, Green Bay was the Siberia of sports."

Although it came in a non-championship Packers season, one number closely associated with Hornung is 176. That's the number of points he scored in the 1960 season, an NFL record that held for 46 years; he twice collected 23 points in a game that season. The following year, Hornung scored 146 while missing two games because of Army service and despite hardly ever practicing. He was unavailable to practice with the team prior to the NFL Championship Game against the Giants. But in the 37–0 Green Bay rout over New York, Hornung scored 19 points.

He was named NFL Most Valuable Player in 1961, and he promised big things for 1962.

"Something the fans haven't seen before," Hornung said. "I just can't help being dramatic."

Hornung played in just nine games the next year, however. He scored 760 points in all for Green Bay in a career that lasted from 1957 to 1966. Versatility was his strong suit. A former college quarterback, Hornung could throw the option pass. He ran for 3,711 yards (4.2 per carry) and caught 130 passes in his pro career.

Hornung missed the 1963 season when NFL Commissioner Pete Rozelle suspended him for gambling. As part of the arrangement to lift the suspension for 1964, Hornung, a native of Louisville, agreed not to attend the Kentucky Derby. Hornung believed that Lombard's lobbying of Rozelle got him reinstated for the 1964 season.

Topps card honoring Hornung's record-breaking season of 1960.
MVP Books Collection

Paul Hornung ad for Wilson footballs, circa 1961.
MVP Books Collection

"Paul is a great football player," Lombardi said.

"Everything changed when Vince Lombardi became our coach in 1959," Hornung said. "The great thing about him is discipline. Professional football is a sport where you get paid whether you win or lose. But personal pride also enters into it and the difference is happiness. It's like going first-class instead of second-class, and I have first-class tastes."

▶ 7–5   3rd place ◀

Game-by-Game

9/27	W, 9–6, vs. Chicago Bears
10/4	W, 28–10, vs. Detroit Lions
10/11	W, 21–20, vs. San Francisco 49ers
10/18	L, 6–45, vs. Los Angeles Rams
10/25	L, 21–38, at Baltimore Colts
11/1	L, 3–20, at New York Giants
11/8	L, 17–28, at Chicago Bears
11/15	L, 24–28, vs. Baltimore Colts
11/22	W, 21–0, vs. Washington Redskins
11/26	W, 24–17, at Detroit Lions
12/6	W, 38–20, at Los Angeles Rams
12/13	W, 36–14, at San Francisco 49ers

Team Scoring

248 points scored (8th)

246 points allowed (6th)

Vince Lombardi becomes new head coach.

Once again on the prowl for a new coach, the Green Bay Packers management team tried to be careful and selective. They wanted to restore the glory years of Curly Lambeau. Their research led them to a decision that finally ended the forlorn stretch of football that had lasted throughout the 1950s.

The new field boss, poised to become a legend, was Vince Lombardi. Lombardi's first Packers team began the turnaround with a 7–5 record. The Packers hadn't won seven games in a season since 1944. The fans in the league's coldest city warmed quickly to the new guy's hard-nosed leadership style.

The 1959 season was a season of extremes. The Lombardi regime began auspiciously with a 9–6 triumph over the arch rival Chicago Bears, and the Packers won their first three in a row. Faith, at that point only skin-deep, was shaken by a five-game losing streak. But when the Packers closed the season with a four-game winning streak (three of them on the road), Lombardi left his audience smiling.

A key personnel change, with long-term implications, was at the heart of the transition from the old, sad-sack Packers to the new-look Packers. The year began with veteran Lamar McHan starting at quarterback, and he held the job for seven weeks. That's when Lombardi decided to try something fresh. He made previously shaky Bart Starr the starter. Starr's ascension represented a necessary step in the creation of what became the greatest dynasty in NFL history.

There was a new man in the middle for Green Bay in 1959. In his first season as head coach, Vince Lombardi led the Packers to their first winning season since 1947. It would only get better from there. *Robert Riger/Getty Images*

Em Tunnell with Vince Lombardi, 1961. *Corbis/Bettman*

Emlen Tunnell

A Hall of Fame defensive back for his accomplishments with the New York Giants, Emlen Tunnell was brought to Green Bay by Vince Lombardi in 1959. Tunnell served as a player-coach, bringing his acumen to the secondary.

For years, Tunnell held the NFL record for most interceptions with 79, and he remains second on the all-time list. His final three seasons were with the Packers, and he played in all 12 games each season, collecting his last five interceptions with the Pack.

The 6-foot-1, 185-pound defensive maestro also excelled at running back kicks and punts. In 1951, Tunnell returned three punt returns for touchdowns. Once, he returned a kickoff 100 yards for a score.

But Lombardi wanted Tunnell to help install the Giants' defensive philosophy. At the time, Tunnell was the only African American player on the Packers. That changed swiftly.

As a member of the active roster, Tunnell was viewed more as a player than a coach, but in 1965 he became the first official African American coach in the NFL for the Giants. In 1975, Tunnell also became the first African American elected to the Pro Football Hall of Fame.

Tunnell served as a liaison between Lombardi, whom he knew well, and the younger black players, and he served as a watchdog for any racism in the community.

"Emlen would not take anything from anybody, but he could be an important mediator when tempers got out of hand," said Packers star defensive end Willie Davis.

Team Leaders

(**Boldface** indicates league leader)

Scoring Leaders (Points)
1950: Billy Grimes, 48
1951: Fred Cone, 50
1952: Bill Howton, 78
1953: Fred Cone, 74
1954: Fred Cone & Max McGee, 54
1955: Fred Cone, 78
1956: Fred Cone & Bill Howton, 72
1957: Fred Cone, 74
1958: Paul Hornung, 67
1959: Paul Hornung, **94**

Rushing Leaders (Carries / Yards / TDs)
1950: Billy Grimes, 84 / 480 / 5
1951: Tobin Rote, 76 / 523 / 3
1952: Tobin Rote, 58 / 313 / 2
1953: Breezy Reid, 95 / 492 / 3
1954: Breezy Reid, 99 / 507 / 5
1955: Howie Ferguson, 192 / 859 / 4
1956: Tobin Rote, 84 / 398 / 11
1957: Don McIlhenny, 100 / 384 / 1
1958: Paul Hornung, 69 / 310 / 2
1959: Paul Hornung, 152 / 681 / 7

Passing Leaders (Completions / Attempts / Yards)
1950: Tobin Rote, 83 / 224 / 1,231
1951: Tobin Rote, 106 / 256 / 1,540
1952: Babe Parilli, 77 / 177 / 1,416
1953: Tobin Rote, 72 / 185 / 1,005
1954: Tobin Rote, **180** / **382** / 2,311
1955: Tobin Rote, 157 / 342 / 1,977
1956: Tobin Rote, **146** / **308** / **2,203**
1957: Bart Starr, 117 / 215 / 1,489
1958: Babe Parilli, 68 / 157 / 1,068
1959: Bart Starr, 70 / 134 / 972

Receiving Leaders (Receptions / Yards / TDs)
1950: Al Baldwin, 28 / 555 / 3
1951: Bob Mann, 50 / 696 / 8
1952: Bill Howton, 53 / **1,231** / 13
1953: Bill Howton, 25 / 463 / 4
1954: Bill Howton, 52 / 768 / 2
1955: Bill Howton, 44 / 697 / 5
1956: Bill Howton, 55 / **1,188** / **12**
1957: Bill Howton, 38 / 727 / 5
1958: Max McGee, 37 / 655 / 7
1959: Boyd Dowler, 32 / 549 / 4

Interceptions (Number / Yards / TDs)
1950: Rebel Steiner, 7 / 190 / 1
1951: Jug Girard, 5 / 25 / 0
1952: Bobby Dillon, 4 / 35 / 0;
    Bob Forte, 4 / 50 / 0; Ace Loomis, 4 / 115 / 1
1953: Bobby Dillon, 9 / 112 / **1**
1954: Bobby Dillon, 7 / 111 / 1
1955: Bobby Dillon, 9 / 153 / 0
1956: Bobby Dillon, 7 / **244** / 1
1957: Bobby Dillon, 9 / 180 / 1;
    John Symank, 9 / 198 / 0
1958: Bobby Dillon, 6 / 134 / 1
1959: Bill Forester, 2 / 48 / 0;
    Bob Freeman, 2 / 22 / 0; John Symank, 2 / 46 / 0;
    Emlen Tunnell, 2 / 20 / 0

Fred Cone

BACK-PACKERS

MVP Books Collection

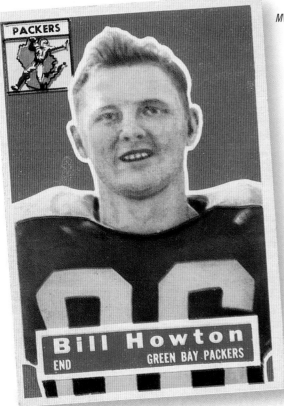

MVP Books Collection

1955: John Martinkovic, DE
1955: Roger Zatkoff, LB
1956: Bobby Dillon, DB
1956: Bill Howton, End
1956: Tobin Rote, QB
1956: Roger Zatkoff, LB
1957: Bobby Dillon, DB
1957: Bill Howton, End
1957: Jim Ringo, C
1958: Bobby Dillon, DB
1958: Jim Ringo, C
1959: Bill Forester, LB
1959: Forrest Gregg, T
1959: Paul Hornung, HB
1959: Jim Ringo, C
1959: Emlen Tunnell, DB

1st-Round Draft Picks

1950: Clayton Tonnemaker (4), C, Minnesota
1951: Bob Gain (5), OT, Minnesota
1952: Vito "Babe" Parilli (4), QB, Kentucky
1953: Al Carmichael (7), HB, Southern California
1954: Art Hunter (3), OT, Notre Dame; Veryl Switzer (4), Back, Kansas State
1955: Tom Bettis (5), LB, Purdue
1956: Jack Losch (8), HB, Miami
1957: Paul Hornung (1), HB, Notre Dame; Ron Kramer (4), End, Michigan
1958: Dan Currie (3), LB, Michigan State
1959: Randy Duncan (1), QB, Iowa

First-Team All-Pros

1954: Bobby Dillon, DB
1955: Bobby Dillon, DB
1955: Roger Zatkoff, LB
1956: Bill Howton, End
1957: Bobby Dillon, DB
1957: Bill Howton, End
1957: Jim Ringo, C
1958: Bobby Dillon, DB
1959: Jim Ringo, C

Pro Bowl Selections

1950: Billy Grimes, HB
1950: Ed Neal, C
1951: Billy Grimes, HB
1951: Dick Wildung, T
1952: Bill Howton, End
1952: Deral Teteak, LB
1952: Abner Wimberly, End
1953: Dave Hanner, DT
1953: John Martinkovic, DE
1953: Clayton Tonnemaker, LB
1954: Dave Hanner, DT
1954: John Martinkovic, DE
1954: Roger Zatkoff, LB
1955: Bobby Dillon, DB
1955: Howie Ferguson, FB
1955: Bill Howton, End

Official Program

CHICAGO BEARS
SEPTEMBER 28
GREEN BAY

WASHINGTON
OCTOBER 5
MILWAUKEE

LOS ANGELES
OCTOBER 12
MILWAUKEE

DETROIT
OCTOBER 26
GREEN BAY

PHILADELPHIA
NOVEMBER 2
MILWAUKEE

DALLAS
NOVEMBER 23
GREEN BAY

CHICAGO BEARS VS. GREEN BAY PACKERS

SUNDAY, SEPTEMBER 28, 1952
1:30 P.M.
GREEN BAY CITY STADIUM

PRICE **25¢**

THE 1960s

The 1960s were not only the best decade in Green Bay Packers history, but really in the history of any pro football franchise. The achievements of the Packers in the Vince Lombardi coaching era—five NFL titles and six NFL Championship Game appearances—exceed any run of success any other team has ever put together.

In 1960, the Packers reached the NFL Championship Game and lost to the Philadelphia Eagles. Their spirits beaten down by more than a decade of losing, Packers fans—among the most loyal and enthusiastic in the league—were delirious over simply reaching the title game. For Lombardi, who whether accurately or not has always been credited with the phrase "Winning isn't everything, it's the only thing," getting that far and losing was no reason for celebration. After the Packers fell, Lombardi said, "This is the last time we'll lose in a championship game."

By 1961, the Packers were headed into their prime years. They won their first NFL crown since 1944 after thoroughly manhandling the New York Giants 37–0 in the title game. Paul Hornung really wanted to rub it in against the helpless Giants.

"It would have been a lot worse if Lombardi hadn't called off the dogs," Hornung said. "Hell, I wanted to match the 73–0 whipping that the Bears had put on the Redskins in the 1940 title game."

In 1962, the Packers went 13–1 in the regular season and won another title. That was the '60s Packers team that Hornung believed was the best of them all. Hornung made more news by not playing in 1963. He was suspended by NFL Commissioner Pete Rozelle for gambling and associating with undesirables. The Bears beat out the Packers by one game in the standings and won the title that year.

By 1964 Hornung was back, but the Pack was not. The team endured a much shakier 8–5–1 season. Around the league, people wondered if the Packers were capable of restoring the magic of Lombardi's first years.

The answer smacked them in the face in 1965 when Green Bay finished 10–3–1 and won another championship, besting the Cleveland Browns 23–12 in the title game. There were new faces in the lineup, but the core group of stars, from Jim Taylor and Hornung to quarterback Bart Starr and guard Forrest Gregg—as well as defenders Willie Davis, Henry Jordan, Ray Nitschke, and Willie Wood—were still on the job.

In 1966, the stingy D allowed just 163 points, as it held opponents to fewer than 10 points six times. The Packers roared to a 12–2 record, defeated the Dallas Cowboys 34–27 in the NFL title game, and advanced to play in the first Super Bowl.

The Packers were symbols of the old guard. The Kansas City Chiefs represented the upstart American Football League. Green Bay wanted to send a message that it was not just the best team in the NFL but the best team in football, period. The Pack manhandled the Chiefs 35–10.

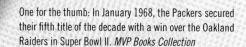

One for the thumb: In January 1968, the Packers secured their fifth title of the decade with a win over the Oakland Raiders in Super Bowl II. *MVP Books Collection*

Coach Vince Lombardi and the Packers rode to victory in the 1961 title game against the New York Giants, kicking off a decade-long dynasty that saw the team win five NFL championships. *Marvin E. Newman/Sports Illustrated/Getty Images*

World Championship Game AFL vs. NFL

JANUARY 15, 1967/LOS ANGELES COLISEUM

PRICE $1.00

A year later, the Packers did it again, capturing another Super Bowl after finishing 9–4–1. First they fell the Los Angeles Rams, and then in the NFL title game Green Bay topped the Dallas Cowboys 21–17. The December 31, 1967, game was labeled the "Ice Bowl," one of the more memorable games in NFL history. The game-time temperature was minus 13, and players fought frostbite.

The foe in the second Super Bowl was the Oakland Raiders, and Green Bay upheld league honor again. Conquering the Raiders gave the Packers a third straight championship, equaling the Packers' accomplishment of 1929–31. The victory also marked the fifth Packers title of the 1960s.

Super Bowl I game program. *MVP Books Collection*

1960

Game-by-Game

9/25	L, 14–17, vs. Chicago Bears
10/2	W, 28–9, vs. Detroit Lions
10/9	W, 35–21, vs. Baltimore Colts
10/23	W, 41–14, vs. San Francisco 49ers
10/30	W, 19–13, at Pittsburgh Steelers
11/6	L, 24–38, at Baltimore Colts
11/13	W, 41–7, vs. Dallas Cowboys
11/20	L, 31–33, vs. Los Angeles Rams
11/24	L, 10–23, at Detroit Lions
12/4	W, 41–13, at Chicago Bears
12/10	W, 13–0, at San Francisco 49ers
12/17	W, 35–21, at Los Angeles Rams

Playoffs

12/26	L, 13–17, vs. Philadelphia Eagles

Team Scoring

332 points scored (2nd)

209 points allowed (2nd)

Paul Hornung set a new NFL record with 176 points scored as Packers return to Championship Game.

Paul Hornung goes airborne over the line of scrimmage for a touchdown against the 49ers in Milwaukee on October 24, 1960. The halfback scored two touchdowns, booted two field goals, and kicked five extra points as Green Bay battered San Francisco, 41–14. *AP Photo*

It took only until the second season under Vince Lombardi for the Packers to play for a championship. Green Bay won the Western Conference crown, but it lost the NFL title game to the Philadelphia Eagles 17–13. By professional sports standards, it seemed as if the gruff coach, who had been a career assistant, had manufactured an overnight miracle.

For Packers fans, who had grown used to the team being at the bottom of the heap since the late 1940s, the 1960 season was an almost nonstop thrill machine. Halfback Paul Hornung scored a league-record 176 points, scoring via touchdowns, field goals, and extra points. When not employing his toe on behalf of the cause, the shifty Hornung, the 1956 Heisman Trophy winner at Notre Dame, piled up 671 yards rushing.

Hornung, a.k.a. the "Golden Boy" because of his ground-gaining prowess (13 touchdowns, too) and his blond locks, was only the Packers' second most dangerous running option. Jim Taylor, the fullback, was the man who ran through defenders, leading with his shoulder, while Hornung busied himself running around them.

Taylor wore his hair closely cropped. He had a look about him that suggested if you messed with the cattle on his ranch, he was going to brand *you*. He was 6 feet tall and weighed 215 pounds. A human battering ram, Taylor rushed for 1,101 yards and scored 11 touchdowns. Taylor and Hornung complemented one another perfectly in the backfield beside quarterback Bart Starr.

1960 Championship Game

In 1960, in only their second season under coach Vince Lombardi, the Green Bay Packers advanced to the NFL Championship Game for the first time in 16 years. The Packers lost 17–13 to the Philadelphia Eagles, but Lombardi promised that his team would be back.

To win the 1960 Western Division title, the Packers needed a victory in the last regular-season game over the Los Angeles Rams, and they prevailed, 35–21. After the win, the team was greeted at the Green Bay airport by 10,000 fans.

The Eagles were led by quarterback Norm Van Brocklin, in the last game of his storied career, and Philadelphia had to come from behind. Green Bay's Paul Hornung, who played multiple roles for the team while scoring an NFL-record

176 points in 1960, started the scoring in the title game in Philadelphia with a 20-yard field goal. Hornung followed with a second 20-yard boot.

In the second quarter, Van Brocklin hit Tommy McDonald for a 35-yard touchdown pass, and when Bobby Walston kicked the extra point, Philadelphia led 7–6. Walston added a 15-yard field goal, and the Eagles led 10–6 at halftime.

The Packers scored their only touchdown of the game in the fourth quarter when quarterback Bart Starr completed a seven-yard touchdown pass to Max McGee. Hornung kicked the extra point for a 13–10 lead. But the Packers couldn't hold it. The Eagles got the winning score on a five-yard run by Ted Dean followed by a Walston extra point.

MVP Books Collection

Max McGee makes a leaping catch during the NFL Championship Game in Philadelphia on December 26, 1960. *Herb Scharfman/Sports Imagery/Getty Images*

Vince Lombardi

It was the chance Vince Lombardi had been waiting for come true when the Green Bay Packers offered him the head coaching job. No one imagined how mutually beneficial the relationship would be.

The Packers had been stumbling around the NFL desert for a decade when Lombardi was hired to start the 1959 season and hopefully breathe life into the franchise. He succeeded so stunningly that in Green Bay, more than 40 years after his death, Lombardi is spoken of with the same awe and admiration as the saints in church.

A longtime assistant coach in college and the former offensive coordinator of the New York Giants, Lombardi joined the Packers at age 46. He had a reputation as a great Xs and Os man, but he wanted to prove he could run his own show.

The challenge couldn't have been mightier. The proud Packers, owners of six championships under Curly Lambeau, hadn't been any good at all for a decade. Lombardi had a winning season his first year and took his team to the NFL Championship Game in 1960. Then he presided over the capture of five NFL titles during the '60s.

Lombardi drilled his players hard, always demanding a lot. He could be aloof but witty, charming but harsh, and very Catholic. He was not the players' big brother, but their leader. And while he knew there was no such thing as perfection on the football field, he pursued it.

Lombardi had played high school football and college ball at Fordham. He coached high school football and then worked as an assistant coach in college and the pros. When the Packers gave him the keys to the car, he proved to be the greatest pro football coach of all time.

When the new coach first greeted the Packers in the locker room, he told them what he expected.

"I have never been on a losing team, gentlemen," Lombardi said, "and I do not intend to start now!"

Over time, Lombardi became associated with the statement "Winning isn't everything, it's the only thing." Whether he truly uttered those words or not, they are part of the Lombardi legend. That seemed to be how he thought anyway. "As a person, I am not well enough adjusted to accept a defeat," Lombardi said. "The trouble with me is that my ego just cannot accept a loss."

Shutterstock.com

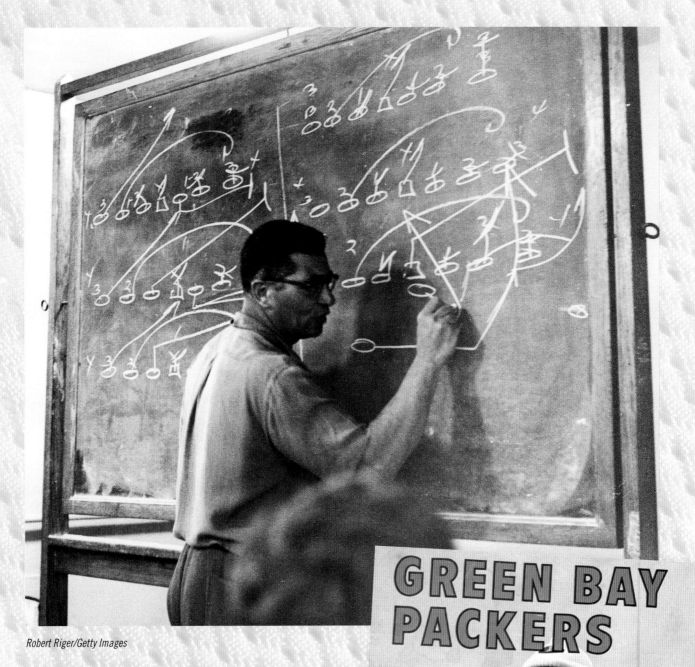

Robert Riger/Getty Images

Lombardi was known as a disciplinarian. He wanted players who would listen and execute. He did not tolerate goofing off.

"All your efforts in any business should be directed to taking the risks out of it," he said. "The satisfactions are few for perfectionists, but I have never known a good coach who wasn't one. This is a game for madmen. In football, we're all mad. I have been called a tyrant, but I have also been called the coach of the simplest system in football and I suppose there is some truth in both of those."

GREEN BAY PACKERS

1962 YEAR BOOK
ONE DOLLAR

MVP Books Collection

1961

▶ 11–3   1st place ◀

Game-by-Game

9/17	**L**, 13–17, vs. Detroit Lions
9/24	**W**, 30–10, vs. San Francisco 49ers
10/1	**W**, 24–0, vs. Chicago Bears
10/8	**W**, 45–7, vs. Baltimore Colts
10/15	**W**, 49–17, at Cleveland Browns
10/22	**W**, 33–7, at Minnesota Vikings
10/29	**W**, 28–10, vs. Minnesota Vikings
11/5	**L**, 21–45, at Baltimore Colts
11/12	**W**, 31–28, at Chicago Bears
11/19	**W**, 35–17, vs. Los Angeles Rams
11/23	**W**, 17–9, at Detroit Lions
12/3	**W**, 20–17, vs. New York Giants
12/10	**L**, 21–22, at San Francisco 49ers
12/17	**W**, 24–17, at Los Angeles Rams

Playoffs

| 12/31 | **W**, 37–0, vs. New York Giants |

Team Scoring

391 points scored (1st)

223 points allowed (2nd)

Jim Taylor and Paul Hornung lead the Pack to an NFL-best 2,350 rushing yards and, more importantly, an NFL title.

When looking back at the Packers of the 1960s, the glamour boys of the offense are bathed in the glow of bright spotlights. But by his second season, coach Vince Lombardi established his team's identity through intimidating defense.

In 1961, the Packers galloped to the NFL title, compiling an 11–3 record and overwhelming the New York Giants 37–0 in the title game.

An early highlight in the season was shutting out the Bears, 24–0. A later highlight was beating Chicago a second time, 31–28. The biggest highlight was crushing the Giants for the franchise's first NFL crown since 1944. To that point, it was the seventh championship in team history. The team scored 391 points and permitted just 223.

Jim Taylor ran for 1,307 yards and scored 15 touchdowns. Hornung again led the NFL in scoring with 146 points. But the tenacity of the defense was breathtaking. The Packers intercepted 29 passes. Four different defensive backs—John Symank, Jesse Whittenton, Willie Wood, and Hank Gremminger—each made five picks.

For the first time in his pro career, quarterback Bart Starr didn't share the job. By completing 58.3 percent of his passes, 16 of them for touchdowns, Starr made sure that job would stay his.

When the Packers thumped the Giants, it was a symbolic triumph for small-town America over sophisticated America. In the locker room, Lombardi told his players they were not only the best team in the league that year, but the best in NFL history.

Tight end Ron Kramer goes up between New York defenders to pull in one of his four catches during the 1961 Championship Game against the Giants. Kramer's two touchdown grabs helped propel the Packers to a resounding 37–0 win for the title. *Vernon Biever/Getty Images*

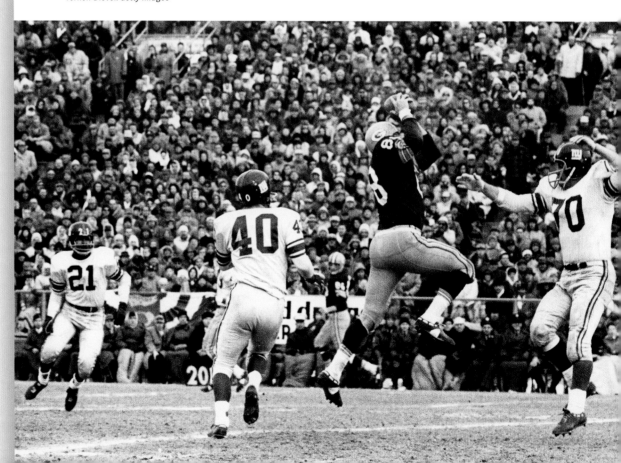

1961 Championship Game

Paul Hornung, Green Bay's star halfback, was on leave from Army duty when the Packers faced off against the New York Giants in the NFL Championship Game on December 31, 1961. The Hall of Fame back scored 19 points in the game, and his teammates kept pace as Green Bay won its first NFL championship since 1944 by demolishing the Giants 37–0.

Nothing was close about the game except the first quarter, when it was 0–0. After that it was all Packers, who rolled up a 24–0 lead by halftime. When it was over, Lombardi told his team they were "the greatest in the history of the NFL. I had no idea it would end like this."

Hornung scored a touchdown, kicked four extra points and three field goals, and also rushed for 89 yards. "Paul sure had a great day," said fullback Jim Taylor. "We planned to use him and hoped they were waiting for me. I guess that's what happened."

Quarterback Bart Starr threw three touchdown passes. Still, it was the Packers defense that humbled the Giants, chasing their star quarterback, Y. A. Tittle, all over the lot. Tittle threw four interceptions.

"We couldn't have won with 22 men on the field at once," Tittle said.

The game did have that look about it. Veteran Packers center Jim Ringo said the credit belonged to Lombardi, who molded the team. "Everything he told us came true," Ringo said. "He said, 'Work hard, give me 100 percent, and someday you are going to be the champions.'"

A year later, Lombardi's advice would prove true again, against the same foe.

Game program to the 1961 NFL Championship Game. *MVP Books Collection*

A fellow Wisconsin institution offers congratulations to the 1961 champs. *MVP Books Collection*

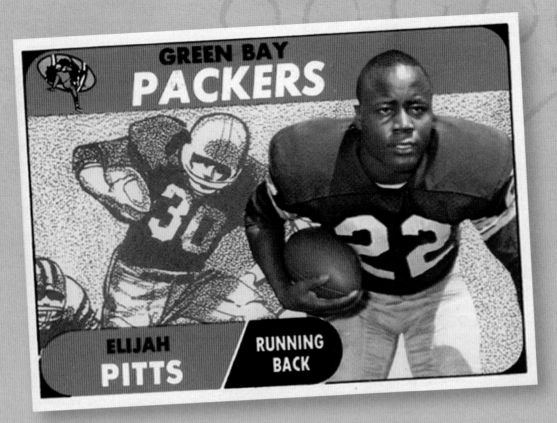

MVP Books Collection

Elijah Pitts

The steady halfback who played college ball for tiny Philander Smith was a Packers find. Elijah Pitts was chosen in the thirteenth round of the NFL draft in 1961, No. 180 overall, but he was a member of all of Green Bay's title teams of the 1960s before wrapping up a solid career with other teams.

Initially, Pitts was a backup back, serving behind Paul Hornung, and although he never became a starter, the importance of his role increased over the years. Pitts was a valuable to the Packers as a punt and kickoff return man. But the 6-foot-1, 204-pounder also had his moments running from scrimmage.

"I've found the quicker I can get to a hole," said Pitts, who was from Mayflower, Arkansas, "the better off I'll be. You can't hold out those big monsters forever."

Though technically always second on the depth chart, Pitts had coach Vince Lombardi's trust in key situations. "You've got to think of him like a first-stringer," Lombardi said.

Pitts tallied 28 rushing touchdowns in his career and, with limited carries, rushed for nearly 2,000 yards. He added another seven TDs via receptions. During the 1966 season against the Detroit Lions, Pitts rushed for 99 yards and three touchdowns, coming through when needed. That season, Pitts scored 10 touchdowns, rushing and receiving combined.

"When we were winning, I never thought it would end," Pitts said. "I went from one season to the next expecting to win. I never imagined losing."

Jim Taylor

A bulldog in cleats, Jim Taylor ran through people and over people who tried to tackle him during his tenure as Green Bay's fullback during the Vince Lombardi era. Taylor was tougher than he was big at 6-foot and 215 pounds, but in his NFL career he produced 93 touchdowns and 8,597 yards rushing, mostly with the Packers.

Not as flashy as backfield running mate Paul Hornung, Taylor was perfectly suited for a cold-weather team that ground out yardage. Lombardi knew what he had: a player capable of carrying would-be tacklers on his back. He referred to Taylor as "the most determined runner I've ever seen."

Taylor recorded five 1,000-yard rushing seasons for the Packers and was chosen All-Pro six times. Four times he helped lead the Packers to championships. The biggest obstacle in Taylor gaining recognition was the overlap of his career with that of Jim Brown, who set NFL career records for rushing yards and touchdowns during his playing days with the Cleveland Browns.

A highly lauded All-American at Louisiana State, Taylor was a second-round pick for the Packers in 1958. The hard-running back led the NFL in rushing in 1962, and that season he scored the Packers' only touchdown in their 16–7 title win over the New York Giants.

Although receiving was not his primary role with the Packers, Taylor also caught 225 passes and accounted for 10 of his touchdowns through the air. A physical player, like everyone else in Lombardi's system, Taylor was counted on to block, too.

"Blocking is making your mind up to get the job done," Taylor said. "You can't figure on saving yourself for the run. When the play calls for a block, you gotta block."

Taylor played in an era when any trash talking between players on opposing teams stayed on the field and was not publicized. New York Giants linebacker Sam Huff recalled Taylor giving him the business after tackles. "Is that the hardest you can hit?" Taylor would say.

The first Packers player from the '60s glory days to be inducted into the Hall of Fame (in 1976), Taylor prided himself on his toughness. He sometimes used his knees as weapons on tacklers, and he frequently struck out at them with his arm.

"They don't tackle real low anyway, so the arm helps," Taylor said. "You get a man who's not real aggressive and the arm helps. Maybe you'll get an extra yard or two. Sometimes you have to run over a man when it seems that you can run around him. I figure if you give a guy a little blast, the next time he won't be so eager."

Taylor, who won the NFL's MVP Award in 1962, is a member of the Packers Hall of Fame and the Wisconsin Athletic Hall of Fame in addition to being enshrined in Canton, Ohio.

Focus on Sport/Getty Images

1962

▶ 13–1   1st place ◀

Game-by-Game

9/16	W, 34–7, vs. Minnesota Vikings
9/23	W, 17–0, vs. St. Louis Cardinals
9/30	W, 49–0, vs. Chicago Bears
10/7	W, 9–7, vs. Detroit Lions
10/14	W, 48–21, at Minnesota Vikings
10/21	W, 31–13, vs. San Francisco 49ers
10/28	W, 17–6, at Baltimore Colts
11/4	W, 38–7, at Chicago Bears
11/11	W, 49–0, at Philadelphia Eagles
11/18	W, 17–13, vs. Baltimore Colts
11/22	L, 14–26, at Detroit Lions
12/2	W, 41–10, vs. Los Angeles Rams
12/9	W, 31–21, at San Francisco 49ers
12/16	W, 20–17, at Los Angeles Rams

Playoffs

12/30	W, 16–7, at New York Giants

Team Scoring

415 points scored (1st)

148 points allowed (1st)

PACKERS HEADLINE

Packers repeat as champions by dominating on offense and defense.

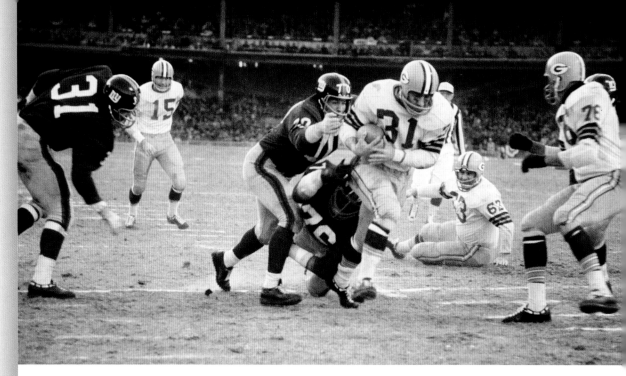

Jim Taylor breaks through the tackles of New York Giants linebacker Sam Huff (70) and defensive tackle Rosey Grier (76) during the 1962 NFL Championship Game. Taylor scored once and ran for a game-high 85 yards in the 16–7 Packers win on December 30 at Yankee Stadium. *Vernon Biever/Getty Images*

When the Green Bay Packers won the NFL championship a second year in a row in 1962, it was an uncommon feat. At that point in league history, only one team had ever won three straight crowns—the Packers of 1929, 1930, and 1931.

It is often said in sports that repeating a championship is tougher than winning one, but Vince Lombardi's Packers of the early 1960s were built for the long run, and they were still peaking after the 1961 title. Lombardi signed off the 1961 season by saying his team may have played the greatest ever on the day it wiped out the New York Giants, but the Packers were even better week in and week out the next year.

In 1962, the Packers finished 13–1. The team scored 415 points and allowed just 148, fewer than the year before. Green Bay shut out three opponents and beat eight teams by at least 17 points.

Jim Taylor had his career high with 1,474 rushing yards, and he scored 19 touchdowns. Paul Hornung was injured for part of the season, though he still scored 74 points. Bart Starr completed 62.5 percent of his passes, astonishing for a time when many quarterbacks barely completed 50 percent. Willie Wood emerged in the secondary with nine interceptions.

The one team capable of tackling the Packers was Western Conference foe Detroit. Green Bay eked out a 9–7 win. The second showdown would become famous in both cities. In a nationally televised Thanksgiving Day game, the Lions throttled the Packers 26–14.

"This one game, [Lions defensive tackle] Roger Brown sacked Bart about six times," Hornung said. "It got to be a joke. The Lions had a helluva defensive team. It was always knock-down, drag-out when we played. In those years, the Packers and the Lions were always 1-2 in the league, and the Lions hated us because they were always No. 2."

Hornung's "always" part was a bit of an exaggeration. In those days, there were no rounds of playoffs. The winner of the West and the winner of the East met in the championship game. The Thanksgiving licking was humbling, but the Packers won their remaining three regular-season games and faced the Giants in the NFL Championship Game for the second year in a row.

1962 Championship Game

A year had passed since the Green Bay Packers and New York Giants met to decide the 1961 NFL title, and the Giants, 12–2 in 1962, had not lived down the humiliating Packers decimation. Rarely had any team been fueled with so much motivation for revenge.

Round two of Packers vs. Giants was much closer than the previous year's had been, and it was a struggle all the way.

"Taylor and I later agreed that we had never been hit as hard as we were that day," Hornung said.

But the Packers hit the Giants harder and earned their repeat.

Played in 17-degree temperatures at Yankee Stadium, it was Green Bay weather in New York for the 1962 Championship Game. Years later, Jerry Kramer remembered the wind vividly. "The wind was blowing so hard that it actually blew the benches over at halftime," he said, "and blew them onto the field, maybe 10 yards from the sidelines."

The game had been touted as a showdown between Green Bay's defense and New York's offense. During the regular season, the Packers led the league in four defensive categories, including fewest points allowed (148) and most interceptions (31). The Giants led the NFL in total offense and touchdown passes, among other stats.

In the end, it was Green Bay's defense that excelled—forcing three fumbles and one interception—and ill-timed penalties hurt New York. The only Packers touchdown in their 16–7 victory was scored on a seven-yard run by fullback Jim Taylor, who battled for 85 rushing yards on 31 carries. Green Bay's Jerry Kramer nailed field goals of 26, 29, and 30 yards.

The Packers scored in every quarter, while the Giants couldn't convert in close. Their only score was a touchdown in the third quarter. New York blocked a Max McGee punt in the end zone, and Jim Collier recovered it for six points.

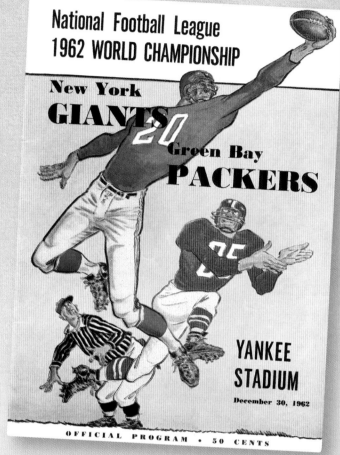

MVP Books Collection

Nearly 65,000 fans at Yankee Stadium chanted "Beat Green Bay!" all afternoon, but the Giants couldn't. For the second straight title game, Y. A. Tittle had a miserable afternoon in the inhospitable conditions, going 18-for-41.

The Giants were once again disappointed. "I never before saw a team that tried so hard and lost," said New York receiver Kyle Rote.

Ray Nitschke

Ray Nitschke played his 15 years for the Green Bay Packers during the true golden era of pure middle linebackers. Overlapping with Bill George, Sam Huff, Joe Schmidt, Les Richter, Dick Butkus, and Chuck Bednarik, the 6-foot-3, 235-pound Nitschke was as honored as any of them.

Coming out of the University of Illinois, Nitschke played for the Packers from 1958 to 1972, was a first- or second-team All-Pro seven times, was chosen for the NFL's fiftieth anniversary team and its seventy-fifth anniversary team, and—in a rarity as a defensive player—was named the Most Valuable Player of the 1962 championship game. In 1978, Nitschke was elected to the Pro Football Hall of Fame.

The common quality between Nitschke and all of those other high-profile linebackers was that they seemed to be the toughest, meanest men on the field every Sunday.

Nitschke, a member of all the Packers' '60s title teams, intercepted 25 passes in his career and scored two touchdowns. Revered among Green Bay fans, the unpretentious Nitschke maintained a listed phone number in the telephone book after his retirement until he died at age 61 in 1998. The community subsequently named a bridge after him.

Although not as publicized as some other middle linebackers, Nitschke believed he was better than any of them. "I've always thought I was the best middle linebacker in professional football," he said. "Whenever I went onto that field, I was the best middle linebacker. I had to be. Otherwise it wouldn't have been fair because that center who was trying to block me thought he was the best center who ever lived."

Nitschke had the unfortunate timing of being a rookie on the terrible Packers team of 1958, the team that finished 1–10–1. But he also had the good fortune to be a member of the Packers when coach Vince Lombardi assumed command.

"When Vince Lombardi took over the team for the 1959 season, he brought us together," Nitschke said. "Lombardi made everybody on his team feel like part of one family. We'd work together, play together. There weren't different factions creating problems. His special asset was his ability to handle men."

Nitschke believed early on that Lombardi was convinced he was a tough guy because of a practice-field incident. One day, the Packers were working out and a storm blew in. The winds were so strong that they knocked down a metal tower—right onto Nitschke. Even though he was lying flat on the ground, he bounced back up to resume practice. "Apparently, the coach felt that it would take more than half a ton of steel to dent my head," Nitschke said.

In the tight, 16–7 championship game victory over the New York Giants in 1962, Nitschke recovered two fumbles and earned the MVP Award, with the prize being a new Corvette.

"It was a great satisfaction to know that a defensive man was getting some credit for a change," he said.

Vernon Biever/Getty Images

Star halfback Paul Hornung suspended by league for gambling, but team still defeats every opponent except the Bears.

The biggest impediment to Green Bay winning a third straight title occurred months before the season began, when star halfback Paul Hornung was suspended for the year by Commissioner Pete Rozelle for gambling on football games.

It was like absorbing a season-ending injury. The Packers seemingly played well enough to win another title, finishing 11–2–1, but there was just one problem. This year, the Chicago Bears were just a little bit better. The Bears handed the Packers their only two losses, and that was the difference in the final standings. It was the Bears, not the Packers, who won it all in 1963.

That was despite Green Bay outscoring teams 369–206 and with the Packers winning the same number of games as the Bears. Green Bay spent the entire season chasing Chicago after an opening-day 10–3 loss. The season actually came down to a November 17 game in Chicago, in which the Bears triumphed 26–7. If the final score had been reversed that day and everything else remained the same, Green Bay would have won the Western Division. In the modern NFL, the Packers would have reached the playoffs, but during this period only first place counted.

Fullback Jim Taylor led the team in rushing, as usual, with 1,018 yards. Tom Moore filled in for Hornung at halfback and rushed for 658 yards. Jerry Kramer handled Hornung's placekicking job, making 43 extra points and 16 field goals. The Packers were so good that 14 players received some kind of postseason All-NFL recognition, including backup Moore.

Game-by-Game

9/15	L, 3–10, vs. Chicago Bears
9/22	W, 31–10, vs. Detroit Lions
9/29	W, 31–20, vs. Baltimore Colts
10/6	W, 42–10, vs. Los Angeles Rams
10/13	W, 37–28, at Minnesota Vikings
10/20	W, 30–7, at St. Louis Cardinals
10/27	W, 34–20, at Baltimore Colts
11/3	W, 33–14, vs. Pittsburgh Steelers
11/10	W, 28–7, vs. Minnesota Vikings
11/17	L, 7–26, at Chicago Bears
11/24	W, 28–10, vs. San Francisco 49ers
11/28	T, 13–13, at Detroit Lions
12/7	W, 31–14, at Los Angeles Rams
12/14	W, 21–17, at San Francisco 49ers

Team Scoring

369 points scored (2nd)

206 points allowed (2nd)

Halfback Tom Moore (25) plows ahead into Detroit defense during the Packers' 31–10 win over the Lions on September 22 at Milwaukee County Stadium. Moore gained 122 yards and scored two touchdowns in the effort. *Vernon Biever/Getty Images*

1964

Game-by-Game

9/13	**W**, 23–12,	vs. Chicago Bears
9/20	**L**, 20–21,	vs. Baltimore Colts
9/28	**W**, 14–10,	at Detroit Lions
10/4	**L**, 23–24,	vs. Minnesota Vikings
10/11	**W**, 24–14,	vs. San Francisco 49ers
10/18	**L**, 21–24,	at Baltimore Colts
10/25	**L**, 17–27,	vs. Los Angeles Rams
11/1	**W**, 42–13,	at Minnesota Vikings
11/8	**W**, 30–7,	vs. Detroit Lions
11/15	**L**, 14–24,	at San Francisco 49ers
11/22	**W**, 28–21,	vs. Cleveland Browns
11/29	**W**, 45–21,	at Dallas Cowboys
12/5	**W**, 17–3,	at Chicago Bears
12/13	**T**, 24–24,	at Los Angeles Rams

Team Scoring

342 points scored (5th)

245 points allowed (2nd)

PACKERS HEADLINE

Injuries and early season struggles keep Packers out of the postseason for second year in a row.

After missing the entire 1963 season due to suspension, Paul Hornung was back at the center of the Packers offense in 1964. In the 17–3 victory over the Bears on December 5, the Hall of Famer ran for one touchdown, kicked one field goal, and kicked two extra points. *Vernon Biever/Getty Images*

For the first time under coach Vince Lombardi, the Packers showed signs of slippage. Although halfback Paul Hornung earned a reprieve after his one-year suspension for gambling and returned, and the core of the team was solid, the Packers looked more human than superhuman in 1964.

The final record was 8–5–1. Not so many years earlier, that would have been very pleasing for Green Bay fans. But after the previous three seasons, the record elicited more of a "What's wrong with the Packers?" response.

A number of injuries contributed to a slow start, and it was possible that the shortage of new blood did, too, since three of the team's top four draft choices signed with the competing American Football League. Despite beating the Chicago Bears twice, the main difference between being a good team and a great team for the Packers was losing the close ones. They lost 21–20 to the Baltimore Colts, 24–23 to the Minnesota Vikings, and 24–21 to the Colts a second time. That was the season in a nutshell.

Hornung returned and scored 107 points while rushing for 419 yards. Jim Taylor topped 1,000 yards again, with 1,169. And quarterback Bart Starr was never better. Starr threw for 2,144 yards while completing 163 out of 272 pass attempts, a completion percentage that was just a hair under 60. He threw for 15 touchdowns with only four interceptions.

However, after the 3–4 start, the Packers closed with a 5–1–1 rush, giving hope for a comeback season in 1965.

Dave Robinson

Linebacker Dave Robinson came along early enough in the 1960s to share the glory as part of three Green Bay Packers championship teams. But he stayed around long enough to suffer in the '70s, when things went sour and every win became especially precious.

Robinson grew up in southern New Jersey's suburbs of Philadelphia and played college ball at Penn State. He was drafted in 1963 and, as older Packers retired and he got to play more, became a three-time Pro Bowler.

Before sportswriters overused the phrase, Robinson described himself as "a guided missile" on the field. The 6-foot-3, 245-pound hard hitter loved contact and was very proprietary of his territory.

Robinson described how he sought out the opposing ballcarrier.

"All the keys are the science, and they're designed to get me close enough to play the football," Robinson said. "Then it's seek and destroy. You have to like to hit. I think you could take almost anybody and teach them to react properly. After that it's all from within."

Robinson played with the Packers from 1963 to 1972 and then spent two years with the Washington Redskins. Robinson never wanted to leave Green Bay, but he became disenchanted playing for coach Dan Devine and almost quit instead of reporting to Washington. He finished with 27 interceptions and 12 fumble recoveries.

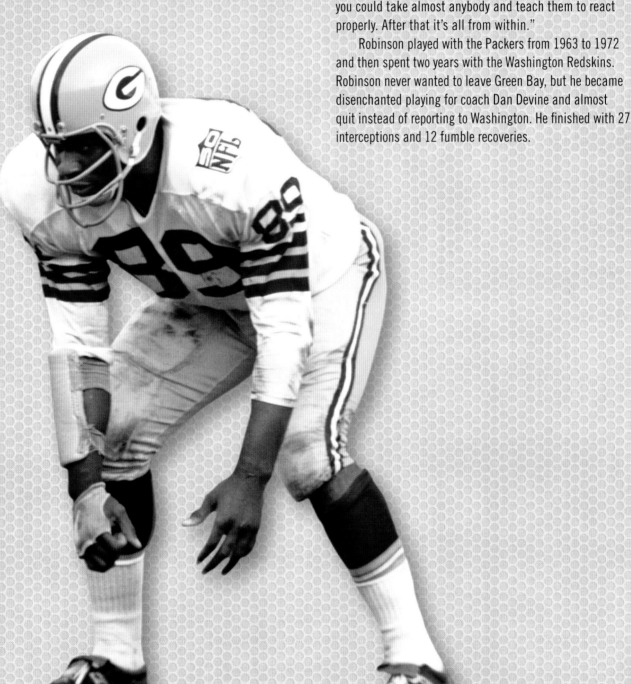

Tony Tomsic/Getty Images

Linemen Henry Jordan (left) and Willie Davis (right) were cornerstones of Green Bay's defense throughout the 1960s. *Vernon Biever/Getty Images*

Henry Jordan

A seven-time All-Pro defensive tackle, Henry Jordan began his NFL career with the Cleveland Browns. After being acquired by the Packers two years later, he became an immovable object on the front line as Green Bay won five titles in the 1960s.

When he came out of the University of Virginia, Jordan stood 6-foot-3 and weighed 240 pounds. Prematurely balding, Jordan looked older than he was. He was a tough guy on the field and something of a comedian off of it, which helped to keep his teammates loose.

A Packer who lived in the community, Jordan was so popular that little kids would knock on his door and ask if he could come out and play, which he did.

When he was well into his career, Jordan said he wasn't contemplating retirement. "Playing for the Packers is a way of life," Jordan said. "I'll keep playing until Lombardi tells me to stop."

Lombardi actually gave up coaching the Packers before Jordan gave up playing for the team. Jordan felt that Lombardi was a master of psychology and that his methods kept Green Bay's players hungry and chasing more titles instead of letting down.

"I think normally human nature would make it so, but Coach Lombardi won't let us relax in this respect," Jordan said. "We've got the winning habit. Got to keep it going."

Jordan was only 42 when he died of a heart attack in 1977. In 1995, he was elected to the Pro Football Hall of Fame.

MVP Books Collection

HENRY JORDAN
GREEN BAY PACKERS   TACKLE

Willie Davis

At 6-foot-3 and 245 pounds, Willie Davis was a small defensive end compared to those playing today, but he loomed big for any ballcarrier and quarterback who had to face him in the 1960s.

A seventeenth-round draft pick out of Grambling in 1958, Davis was tried as an offensive tackle by the Cleveland Browns. After two seasons with Cleveland, he went to Green Bay, where he blossomed into a star on the other side of the line of scrimmage. A six-time All-Pro, Davis won five championships with the Packers and was inducted into the Pro Football Hall of Fame in 1981.

Green Bay coach Vince Lombardi was looking for speed, agility, and size in his linemen, and he found those attributes in Davis, who played in 162 consecutive games during his career and recovered 21 fumbles.

"Give a man any two of those dimensions and he'll do okay," Lombardi said. "Give him all three and he'll be a great football player."

Besides those on-field skills, one of Davis' well-known trademarks was gold teeth, though later in his career he got them replaced. Attitude and never taking a play off helped define Davis' success.

"You're less than a man if you let this guy win a battle when he shouldn't," Davis said of his across-the-line foes. "Each man has got to show individual pride."

Following retirement, Davis did TV commentary and became a very successful businessman. He was the president of a chain of radio stations.

MVP Books Collection

111

1965

▶ 10–3–1   1st place ◀

Game-by-Game

9/19	**W**, 41–9, at Pittsburgh Steelers	
9/26	**W**, 20–17, vs. Baltimore Colts	
10/3	**W**, 23–14, vs. Chicago Bears	
10/10	**W**, 27–10, vs. San Francisco 49ers	
10/17	**W**, 31–21, at Detroit Lions	
10/24	**W**, 13–3, vs. Dallas Cowboys	
10/31	**L**, 10–31, at Chicago Bears	
11/7	**L**, 7–12, vs. Detroit Lions	
11/14	**W**, 6–3, vs. Los Angeles Rams	
11/21	**W**, 38–13, at Minnesota Vikings	
11/28	**L**, 10–21, at Los Angeles Rams	
12/5	**W**, 24–19, vs. Minnesota Vikings	
12/12	**W**, 42–27, at Baltimore Colts	
12/19	**T**, 24–24, at San Francisco 49ers	

Playoffs

12/26	**W**, 13–10 (OT), vs. Baltimore Colts
1/2/66	**W**, 23–12, vs. Cleveland Browns

Team Scoring

316 points scored (8th)

224 points allowed (1st)

Packers advance to NFL Championship Game after defeating Colts in divisional playoff and come away with a third title under Lombardi.

It was title time again. Bouncing back after the so-so 1964 season, the Packers tied for first with the Baltimore Colts atop the Western Division with a 10–3–1 record and then outlasted the Colts, 13–10 in overtime, to reach the NFL Championship Game. Green Bay topped the Cleveland Browns 23–12 for the crown, the third under coach Vince Lombardi.

Taking two from the Colts was critical, and the defense did more than its share to carry the Packers back to the top. Defensive backs Herb Adderley and Willie Wood and defensive end Willie Davis were all named First-Team All-Pro.

Despite besting Baltimore twice in the regular season, a rare playoff game was necessitated by the tie in the standings. The Packers and Colts met on December 26 before 50,484 fans at City Stadium. The game was deadlocked at 10–10 at the conclusion of regulation, after kicker Don Chandler hit a field goal. The Packers won in overtime on a 25-yard boot from Chandler.

The title game was played on a snowy day in Green Bay on January 2, 1966, and the Packers controlled the tempo with a running attack that saw halfback Paul Hornung gain 105 yards and fullback Jim Taylor gain 96.

"This is the best win I ever had," Lombardi said. "It came so hard all year long. Everything was hard. The season. The playoff. Everything. I never worked harder in my life for anything."

Off the field, the Packers family was saddened by the news that team founder and longtime coach Curly Lambeau had died in June 1965 while in Sturgeon Bay, Wisconsin, conversing with a neighbor. Lambeau, who coached the team from its inception in 1919 through the 1949 season, passed away abruptly from a heart attack at age 67.

After leaving the Packers following the 1949 season, Lambeau had coached the Chicago Cardinals (1950–1951) and then the Washington Redskins (1952–1953). His lifetime coaching record was 229–134–22, and the Packers won six National Football League titles with Lambeau as boss.

The 1965 Playoffs

In 1965, the Green Bay Packers won their third NFL championship under coach Vince Lombardi. The Packers defeated the Cleveland Browns 23–12 for the title, one week after winning a tough playoff game.

The Packers and Baltimore Colts had tied for the Western Division title by going 10–3–1, forcing a playoff in Green Bay. The Pack barely survived, 13–10, on a field goal in overtime in the epic game.

The teams battled to a 10–10 score at the end of regulation in the playoff, triggering the first sudden-death overtime game in Packers history. Baltimore played without injured quarterbacks Johnny Unitas and Gary Cuozzo and started halfback Tom Matte at quarterback.

Green Bay's defense contained Matte, but Baltimore contained the Packers. With less than two minutes to go, Don Chandler kicked a field goal to send the game into overtime. Baltimore complained that Chandler had missed.

"I did have some doubts," said Chandler, who didn't see the ball go through the uprights because he had his head down. Chandler's next field goal won the game after almost 14 minutes of overtime.

The title game was played in a mixture of mud and snow, and Chandler's foot was key. He booted three field goals, and the Packers defense held the great Jim Brown to 50 yards rushing. Chandler, who scored 11 points, said he had no trouble adjusting to the soggy field but was surprised to be knocked down punting.

"That's the first time in five years my uniform's been dirty," Chandler said.

MVP Books Collection

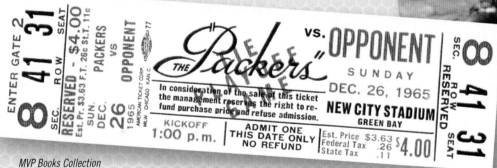

MVP Books Collection

Opposite: Jim Taylor finds a hole in the Browns defense after receiving the handoff from Bart Starr in Green Bay's 23–12 win over Cleveland in the 1965 NFL Championship Game on January 2, 1966. Taylor ran for 96 yards at muddy Lambeau Field, while fellow back Paul Hornung contributed 105 yards on the ground. *Vernon Biever/Getty Images*

Boyd Dowler

He may not have been as flashy as some famous wide receivers, but Boyd Dowler got the job done. He twice was chosen as an All-Pro, as he contributed to five Packers championships in the 1960s.

In an 11-year NFL career—10 of them with Green Bay—Dowler caught 471 passes for 7,270 yards and 40 touchdowns. He averaged 15.3 yards per reception.

The rangy Dowler, who stood 6-foot-5, initially played as a flanker. He got stronger the longer he played with the Packers, getting up to a sturdy 225 pounds.

"I kept getting bigger as I went along," said Dowler, who had played his college ball at Colorado. "I was not really grown, even when I got out of college."

Dowler was a third-round pick in 1959 and got paid just $6,000. He surprised people by winning the NFL's Rookie of the Year Award, but he said he got only a $2,000 raise out of the honor.

Dowler was a very steady contributor to the Packers' offense. In 1967, he set a personal mark for catches in a season with 54, topping his previous high of 53 in 1963. Dowler also punted for the Packers for four seasons, averaging 42.9 yards per boot for his career. One of Dowler's most memorable plays was grabbing a 62-yard touchdown pass in Super Bowl II.

AP Photo

AP Photo/NFL Photos

Max McGee

When he retired from football in 1967, Max McGee had one of the most spectacular jewelry collections around. The Packers wide receiver was part of all six Green Bay championship game appearances of the 1960s, which included five wins and one loss.

McGee, who caught 345 passes for 6,346 yards and 50 touchdowns, had his greatest moment of Packers glory in Super Bowl I. Not expecting to play because he was second-string behind Boyd Dowler, McGee went out on the town the night before the Green Bay–Kansas City Chiefs game. But pressed into action because of injury, he became the star of the game with two touchdown catches and seven receptions in all.

"I can't remember when I caught so many passes or ran so much," McGee said.

On the bus on the way to the Los Angeles Coliseum, McGee announced as a joke to his teammates, "I'm the super end and I'm on my way to play in the super game." A voice from the back of the bus replied, "Shut up, you're just a super benchwarmer." McGee got the last laugh.

That super Super Bowl showing was the final game of McGee's career. He knew he was retiring going into it.

McGee liked to get more enjoyment out of extracurricular activities than coach Vince Lombardi tolerated. "I like to have fun," McGee said. "But Lombardi doesn't like you to have too much fun. I've been fined a lot by Lombardi, but all of it in training camp."

Jim Grabowski

Although he would not have a great career replacing Jim Taylor as the Packers' fullback, Jim Grabowski made coach-general manager Vince Lombardi open his wallet when he was a rookie coming out of Illinois, where he broke Red Grange's Big Ten rushing record.

Lombardi was scared that Grabowski would take his talents to the American Football League, so he dished out big bucks, reportedly around $300,000 as a bonus, for his No. 1 draft pick in 1966.

The 6-foot-2, 220-pound power back spent five years with the Packers and was slowed by injuries. His best season was 1968, when he rushed for 518 yards.

Early in his career, Grabowski had a 123-yard rushing game against the New York Giants, and Lombardi paid him a great compliment. "He looked like Jimmy Taylor today, didn't he?" Lombardi said.

Grabowski was waived in 1971 following a knee injury.

Donny Anderson

Donny Anderson was a statement signing by Packers coach Vince Lombardi. No matter how much it cost Green Bay, the Pack was going to compete for talent against the American Football League. In 1966, Donny Anderson was drafted in the first round, along with Jim Grabowski, to become part of the Packers' backfield of the future.

Anderson was a 6-foot-2, 215-pound All-American halfback from Texas Tech. The object of a bidding war with the Houston Oilers, Anderson chose the Packers after being offered $600,000, then a rookie record.

Never a star of the magnitude of predecessor Paul Hornung, Anderson played nine years in the NFL, the first six with Green Bay. Anderson, who was also an excellent punter who helped develop the strategy of hang time, had three standout rushing years for Green Bay. He rushed for 761 yards in 1968, 853 yards in 1970, and 757 yards in 1971.

Jim Grabowski (33) and Donny Anderson (44) at training camp, 1966. *Art Shay /Sports Illustrated/Getty Images*

Packers defeat Chiefs in first-ever Super Bowl.

It was a whole new world in professional football in 1966. Peace was declared between the National Football League and the American Football League. Not only did that mean the end to raiding the other league's players, for the first time there was a season-ending title game between the champs of both leagues.

Called the AFL-NFL World Championship, the annual game would soon become known as the Super Bowl. Feeding off their hard-won championship of 1965, the Packers stormed through the regular season 12–2, overcame the Dallas Cowboys 34–27, and then faced the Kansas City Chiefs on January 15, 1967, at a neutral site in Los Angeles.

Before the leagues' settlement, Packers coach Vince Lombardi loosened the franchise purse strings and invested hundreds of thousands of dollars in long-term contracts for running backs Jim Grabowski and Donny Anderson to avoid losing his top draft picks. Also, to honor Curly Lambeau, who died in 1965, the Packers renamed City Stadium, calling it Lambeau Field.

Quarterback Bart Starr remained the rock in the pocket, completing 62.2 percent of his passes for 14 touchdowns with only three interceptions, but fullback Jim Taylor rushed for just 705 yards. The defense held six opponents to fewer than 10 points.

The Packers believed it was their responsibility to uphold the honor of the NFL in the Super Bowl. They handled the Chiefs at will, winning the trophy that would later be named after Lombardi with a 35–10 thumping.

This marked the fourth championship under Lombardi.

Hall of Famer Jim Taylor heads up field after making a catch during the NFL Championship Game against the Cowboys on January 1, 1967. The Packers' 34–27 triumph sent them to the first Super Bowl. *AP Photo*

Game-by-Game

9/10	W, 24–3, vs. Baltimore Colts
9/18	W, 21–20, at Cleveland Browns
9/25	W, 24–13, vs. Los Angeles Rams
10/2	W, 23–14, vs. Detroit Lions
10/9	L, 20–21, at San Francisco 49ers
10/16	W, 17–0, at Chicago Bears
10/23	W, 56–3, vs. Atlanta Falcons
10/30	W, 31–7, at Detroit Lions
11/6	L, 17–20, vs. Minnesota Vikings
11/20	W, 13–6, vs. Chicago Bears
11/27	W, 28–16, at Minnesota Vikings
12/4	W, 20–7, vs. San Francisco 49ers
12/10	W, 14–10, at Baltimore Colts
12/18	W, 27–23, at Los Angeles Rams

Playoffs

1/1/67	W, 34–27, at Dallas Cowboys
1/15/67	W, 35–10, vs. Kansas City Chiefs

Team Scoring

335 points scored (4th)

163 points allowed (1st)

A Fourth Title in 1966

Not only did the Green Bay Packers tough it out in a 34–27 victory over the Dallas Cowboys to win another NFL crown after a 12–2 1966 regular season, but they represented the league in the first Super Bowl in California and thrashed the Kansas City Chiefs 35–10.

The Dallas Cowboys were on their rise to prominence under coach Tom Landry, who had once been a coaching partner of Vince Lombardi with the New York Giants.

Playing boldly, with quarterback Don Meredith throwing deep, the Cowboys threw a scare into the Packers, fighting back from deficits until time ran out. Some suggested that the Packers were going to steamroll right to the Super Bowl, but they didn't make the mistake of looking ahead.

"This game will prove for all time, for all history, the greatness of my teammates," said Packers guard Fred Thurston.

The Chiefs won the AFL title by smothering the Buffalo Bills, and coach Hank Stram said his club would "tear apart the NFL" in the first interleague championship game. It didn't work out that way. The Packers dominated the Chiefs the same way they had been dominating the NFL in recent years.

Considerable pride was at stake for the teams representing each league. The NFL-AFL war had raged since 1960, and although the grudges seemed mostly held among those with higher ranks—the commissioners, team presidents, general managers, and coaches—the players wanted to prove who was best.

Kansas City displayed the hunger of the underdog and trailed just 14–10 in the first half. But the favorite had considerable emotion and motivation on its side, too. The Packers felt they had already validated their greatness against NFL teams, and they didn't want that image tarnished.

The unlikely player who became the biggest star in the first Super Bowl was a man who didn't expect to play at all. End Max McGee was nearing the end of his pro career as a backup to Boyd Dowler, and the night before the game at the Los Angeles Coliseum, McGee went out drinking and partying. He barely had any sleep. It wasn't until game day that he was told that Dowler couldn't play because of injury.

Though a little bit woozy, McGee didn't let anything affect his play, and he scored the first Super Bowl touchdown on a 37-yard pass from Bart Starr by making a one-handed grab. McGee caught a second TD throw from Starr on a 13-yard pass. Halfback Elijah Pitts also scored two touchdowns, both on runs. Starr won the MVP Award, completing 16 of 23 passes for 250 yards and two touchdowns.

The Packers were very conscious of their role in history.

"If we lose this game," Green Bay defensive back Tom Brown said, "the season won't mean anything. No one will remember that. You know what they will remember? That the Green Bay Packers were the NFL team that lost to Kansas City in the first game played between the leagues."

MVP Books Collection

Elijah Pitts scrambles into the end zone for one of his two touchdowns in Super Bowl I against the Chiefs at the Memorial Coliseum in Los Angeles. *Focus on Sport/Getty Images*

Bart Starr

The perfect leader for the 1960s Green Bay Packers, Bart Starr was an intelligent quarterback who meshed ideally with coach Vince Lombardi.

Lombardi didn't initially believe that the former Alabama standout could do the job. It wasn't until Starr got more opportunity to play over the first couple of seasons under Lombardi, and edged out challenger Lamar McHan, that he became the main man at quarterback and gained Lombardi's confidence.

There is an oft-repeated story about Starr: As soon as he met Lombardi and heard him speak, he ran to a payphone, called his wife, and told her that this guy was going to make the team a winner. Starr's first impression of the coach was clearly stronger than the impression he made on Lombardi.

Starr recognized Lombardi could make him and the team better, that he could harness and focus their talent. In return, they had to put up with a man who was incredibly intense and demanding.

"Vince Lombardi was a tough and mercurial drillmaster," Starr said. "People have often asked me whether it was difficult to tolerate his tirades, mood swings, and criticism. When I tell them it was not, they raise their eyebrows as if to say, 'You must be kidding.'"

That's because Starr was used to such treatment growing up. His father was a real, live master sergeant.

It took time for Lombardi to realize what he had in Starr, probably because he was not only inexperienced, but he didn't have the cannon arm of some other quarterbacks, such as Joe Namath. Starr was known mostly for his accuracy. Once he grabbed hold of the signal-caller's role, he wouldn't let it go. Starr was at the controls for all five of the Packers' championships during the Lombardi reign.

Focus on Sport/Getty Images

Being cool under fire, rather than resorting to rah-rah leadership, also endeared Starr to his teammates. He showed no fear in the pocket, and he had a knack for driving the team downfield when it needed a critical score. By current quarterback standards, Starr was not a large player. He stood 6-foot-1 and weighed slightly less than 200 pounds. Yet he had a presence, and it was always clear who was in charge in the huddle.

Starr played his entire NFL career for the Packers, from 1956 to 1971, and threw 152 touchdown passes. Three times he led the league in completion percentage, and four times he completed more than 62 percent of his attempts. Starr was the 1966 NFL MVP. He coached the Packers from 1975 to 1983, but he ended up with a losing record.

The Packers destroyed the New York Giants in the 1961 title game, but Starr believed the margin could have been even larger. "The 37–0 final score was not indicative of how thoroughly we dominated," Starr said, "how precisely we executed, how emotionally we played."

MVP Books Collection

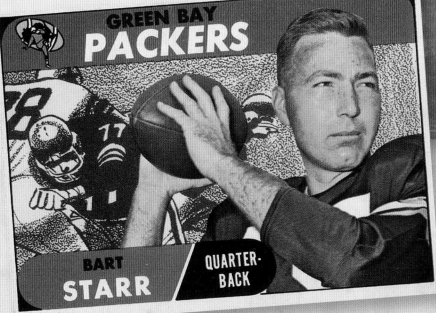

MVP Books Collection

1967

▶ 9–4–1   1st place ◀

Game-by-Game

9/17   T, 17–17, vs. Detroit Lions

9/24   W, 13–10,
        vs. Chicago Bears

10/1   W, 23–0,
        vs. Atlanta Falcons

10/8   W, 27–17, at Detroit Lions

10/15   L, 7–10,
        vs. Minnesota Vikings

10/22   W, 48–21,
        at New York Giants

10/30   W, 31–23,
        at St. Louis Cardinals

11/5   L, 10–13,
        at Baltimore Colts

11/12   W, 55–7,
        vs. Cleveland Browns

11/19   W, 13–0,
        vs. San Francisco 49ers

11/26   W, 17–13,
        at Chicago Bears

12/3   W, 30–27,
        at Minnesota Vikings

12/10   L, 24–27,
        at Los Angeles Rams

12/17   L, 17–24,
        vs. Pittsburgh Steelers

Playoffs

12/23   W, 28–7,
        vs. Los Angeles Rams

12/31   W, 21–17,
        vs. Dallas Cowboys

1/14/68 W, 33–14,
        vs. Oakland Raiders

Team Scoring

332 points scored (9th)

209 points allowed (3rd)

Green Bay gets through historic "Ice Bowl" before capturing a fifth title under Lombardi with a win in Super Bowl II.

A season that began with a nondescript tie against the Detroit Lions ended with a dramatic playoff sweep and the Packers' second straight Super Bowl championship. After finishing 9–4–1, Green Bay bested the Los Angeles Rams 28–7 to win the Western Conference championship after a league realignment created more divisions. Then, in one of the most compelling and best-remembered games in NFL history, Green Bay won the "Ice Bowl" over the Dallas Cowboys. The Packers completed the campaign with a 33–14 Super Bowl II victory against the Oakland Raiders.

Don Chandler was still in there kicking (96 points), and Bart Starr was still in there throwing, though it was an off-year and he missed two games with injury. The running attack was three-pronged and brand new, with Jim Grabowski (466 yards), Ben Wilson (453), and Donny Anderson (402) splitting the work.

Rookie kick returner Travis Williams out of Arizona State proved to be a tremendous weapon. Williams set the NFL single-season kickoff record by averaging 41.1 yards per return and running back four kickoffs for touchdowns.

The Packers of the 1960s were five-time champions and had been to six title games under coach Vince Lombardi. Most of the players besides Starr from the original group of title-holders were gone due to age, with Max McGee following them after the Super Bowl.

But the biggest shock came when Lombardi announced that he was stepping down as coach. He stayed on as general manager, and he orchestrated the promotion of longtime assistant Phil Bengston to head man.

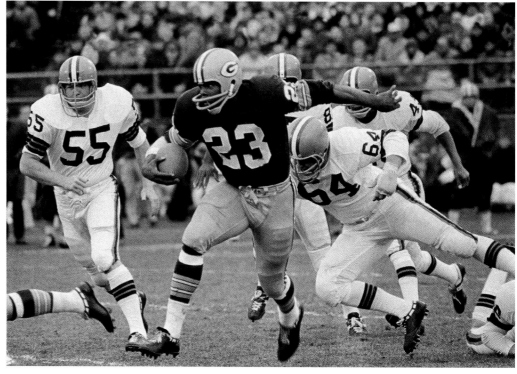

Travis Williams breaks through the Cleveland Browns defense to score on an 87-yard opening kickoff return at Milwaukee Stadium, November 12. It was one of two kickoffs the rookie returner ran back for touchdowns in the game.
AP Photo/Paul Shane

The Ice Bowl

Alaska cold. That's what the weatherman delivered to Lambeau on December 31, 1967. The 50,861 fans brought their blankets, scarves, fur-lined boots, those goofy earflapped hats, mittens, and bottles of Old Homicide in the side pockets of their coats. They were ready for the Iditarod, but they were watching football.

No matter how passionate Texas fans were about the Dallas Cowboys in this NFL Championship Game, they probably frantically flipped pages of the rulebook to see if there was some kind of regulation calling for postponement when the mercury dropped to minus 13.

If you were going to play late-December games in northern Wisconsin, there was a chance that the weather would be more suitable for snowmobiling. The winner of this game would earn a place in the second Super Bowl against the American Football League's Oakland Raiders.

It seemed logical that this game would be settled by brute strength in the trenches, and that the skill players wouldn't be able get a thing done because they were too cold to hang onto the ball. But it didn't work out that way. There were 38 points scored in the game, 21 of them by Green Bay.

Packers defensive back Willie Wood, whose car battery had died, almost didn't make it to the stadium. Referee Norm Schachter made the mistake of not stopping at a Woolworth's to buy a plastic whistle, and instead his metal whistle froze to his lips. It was so cold that broadcaster Frank Gifford was heard saying on air, "I'm going to take a bite out of my coffee."

Packers players were not as warmly dressed as the spectators. Coach Vince Lombardi didn't want any kind of psychological edge tipping to the Cowboys (not likely), so he didn't want his guys wearing gloves or other accessories.

"Once you're cold, you're cold," said Green Bay linebacker Jim Flanigan. "We'd come back to the sidelines and warm up by the space heaters. But I've never been through anything like it."

There was not a lot of offense in terms of yardage. Green Bay quarterback Bart Starr threw for 191 yards and two touchdowns (8 yards and 46 yards to flanker Boyd Dowler). Dallas quarterback Don Meredith threw for only 59 yards total that day. Dan Reeves gave the Cowboys a 17–14 third-quarter lead with a halfback-option pass to Lance Rentzel that fooled the Packers for a 50-yard score. A George Andrie seven-yard fumble return for a TD also boosted Dallas.

Despite the bitter cold weather, Green Bay fans are exuberant following the Packers' victory over Dallas Cowboys in the NFL Championship Game on December 31, 1967. *Vernon Biever/Getty Images*

As the game progressed, the temperature dropped to minus 20 and the wind swirled, creating a minus-70 windchill factor. Dallas clung to its lead, and four minutes, 50 seconds were left when the Packers got the ball back in the fourth quarter. They then began the drive that won the game.

The winning score came on the simplest of plays, when Packers quarterback Bart Starr plunged over the goal line from the one-yard line on a quarterback sneak.

"We had run out of ideas," Starr said after he scored with 13 seconds left for the victory. "The footing was real poor, and we were stumped for something to do." Guard Jerry Kramer made the block to spring Starr.

The Packers went for the touchdown instead of trying to tie the game by kicking a field goal; it was so cold, no one wanted overtime. "It was a little bit of a gamble we took," Lombardi said.

As the weary Packers celebrated, Lombardi was informed that some players might have frostbite. In typical, grand Lombardi style, he said, "Losers get frostbite."

Boyd Dowler is off to the races with a 62-yard touchdown play in the second quarter of Super Bowl II. *AP Photo*

A Ring for Every Finger

MVP Books Collection

The fifth Green Bay Packers championship under Vince Lombardi was recorded during the 1967 season when the defeated the Oakland Raiders, 33–14, in the second Super Bowl, played on January 14, 1968.

After the brutal conditions in Green Bay for the NFL Championship Game against the Dallas Cowboys, temperatures were considerably more comfortable for the Super Bowl held in Miami. Although the Raiders finished 13–1, the Packers had too much firepower, and the result was similar to the year before when the Pack topped the Chiefs.

The Packers did not think they played especially well, but Oakland got their respect.

"They're getting better," said Packers defensive tackle Henry Jordan about the AFL. "If they improve as much each year, they'll be on par with us soon. I think this was a tougher team than Kansas City, especially on defense."

Both of the Raiders' scores came on touchdown passes from Daryle Lamonica. Green Bay scored in several creative ways. Herb Adderley ran an interception back 60 yards for a touchdown. Don Chandler kicked four field goals. Boyd Dowler caught a 62-yard pass from Bart Starr, who was the MVP of the Super Bowl for the second straight year. And Donny Anderson scored on a two-yard run.

Dowler's catch was the big play. He beat Raiders defensive back Kent McCloughan.

"He was playing me tight and he bumped me, and I ran through him," Dowler said. "It was a little post pattern, and when I got by no one was left."

The overall yardage differential was inconsequential. The Packers gained 322 yards to the Raiders' 293, but Green Bay had the edge in other areas. The Packers were called for just one penalty. The Raiders fumbled three times and lost two, and Green Bay had no interceptions.

It was 16–7 at intermission, but the Packers pulled away in the second half.

"Some of us old heads got together," Kramer said. "We decided we'd play the last 30 minutes for the old man. I wouldn't be surprised if Lombardi retires before too long, and all of us love him. We didn't want to let him down."

MVP Books Collection

▶ 6–7–1   3rd place ◀

Game-by-Game

9/15	**W, 30–13,**	vs. Philadelphia Eagles
9/22	**L,** 13–26,	vs. Minnesota Vikings
9/29	**L,** 17–23, vs. Detroit Lions	
10/6	**W,** 38–7, at Atlanta Falcons	
10/13	**L,** 14–16,	vs. Los Angeles Rams
10/20	**T,** 14–14, at Detroit Lions	
10/28	**W,** 28–17,	at Dallas Cowboys
11/3	**L,** 10–13,	vs. Chicago Bears
11/10	**L,** 10–14,	at Minnesota Vikings
11/17	**W,** 29–7,	vs. New Orleans Saints
11/24	**W,** 27–7,	at Washington Redskins
12/1	**L,** 20–27,	at San Francisco 49ers
12/7	**L,** 3–16, vs. Baltimore Colts	
12/15	**W,** 28–27,	at Chicago Bears

Team Scoring

281 points scored (9th)

227 points allowed (4th)

PACKERS HEADLINE

First post-Lombardi season results in first losing campaign since 1958.

This was the season of the big thud in Green Bay. If anyone ever wondered what life would be like without Vince Lombardi as head coach, they found out that it could be very much like what it was for the Packers before Lombardi became the coach. And that was not a pretty picture. New coach Phil Bengston, Lombardi's handpicked successor, led the team to a 6–7–1 record in 1968, the 50th season of play for the franchise.

Defensively, the Packers were almost as good in terms of points allowed compared to the Super Bowl champions of the previous year, but the turnover ratio was almost even. Bengston gained his promotion after leading the superb defense under Lombardi during the glory years. Scoring was also down, and several close games were dropped, as Lombardi watched from upstairs in the front office. The Pack lost five games by a touchdown or less.

The killer instinct seemed missing, although quarterback Bart Starr was brilliant—when he was healthy—completing 63.7 percent of his pass attempts for 15 touchdowns with only eight interceptions. However, backup Zeke Bratkowski started five games. He completed 54.0 percent of his throws, but he threw just three touchdowns along with seven interceptions.

Third-year man Donny Anderson emerged as the leading ballcarrier, with 170 carries for 761 yards. The seventh overall pick in 1966, he had signed with the Packers for $600,000 after Lombardi got in a bidding war with the Houston Oilers of the American Football League. Anderson remained with Packers through the 1971 season, serving as the team's punter as well as running back.

Fred Carr, a linebacker out of Texas-El Paso, was the team's first-round draft choice in 1968. He was a starter for most of his 10-year career in Green Bay, earning three trips to the Pro Bowl.

Leading the way for the Packers' potent running game were guards Jerry Kramer (64) and Gale Gillingham (68). Here they provide blocking for the patented Packers sweep during a 29–7 victory over the Saints on November 17 at Milwaukee County Stadium. *Vernon Biever/Getty Images*

"Fuzzy" Thurston

A guard who was part of the five Green Bay titles of the 1960s, Fred "Fuzzy" Thurston had already earned a championship ring with the Baltimore Colts in 1958 before joining the Pack.

Thurston was a key factor in opening holes for the Packers' ground game, and he also helped keep things loose in the locker room. The 6-foot-1, 245-pounder was always very popular with the fans. He had attended Valparaiso in Indiana, but once Thurston joined the Packers, he never left town.

Twice All-Pro, Thurston opened a bar named Fuzzy's near Lambeau Field and has owned it ever since. Fittingly, when Thurston was asked how he stayed warm during Green Bay's famous Ice Bowl victories over the Dallas Cowboys, he said he drank "about 10 vodkas." In 2011, a Thurston Super Bowl ring sold for $50,000. He had to auction it because of a tax debt.

MVP Books Collection

Robert Riger/Getty Images

Jerry Kramer

The way it turned out, quiet offensive guard Jerry Kramer became the chronicler of the great Green Bay Packers teams of the 1960s by writing two books with well-known sports journalist Dick Schaap. Kramer wrote *Instant Replay* and then *Distant Replay* about his 11-year career.

Kramer, a five-time All-Pro, was a member of all five Packers championship squads of the '60s, though his body paid the price with nearly two dozen surgeries. Kramer became a member of the Packers in 1958, a year before Vince Lombardi took over as coach, and he stayed for Lombardi's entire tenure.

After one surgery, a rumor shot around Green Bay that Kramer had died. He was answering the phone at his doctor's office at the time. Then he showed up at his barbershop, where he was informed, "Fifteen minutes ago you were a helluva guy. Now you're an SOB again."

Kramer wrote about visiting Lombardi in the hospital when his old coach was dying of cancer. "For a long time I thought that Vince Lombardi was born at the age of 45, grinning and growling, demanding perfection," Kramer said. "No coach ever stamped himself so clearly upon a team. I knew I was his creation and we were his creation."

Kramer said he retired when he did because during a game he looked up at the press box and saw several of his former teammates as spectators. "I'm not sure I'm strong enough to stay out of football," Kramer said.

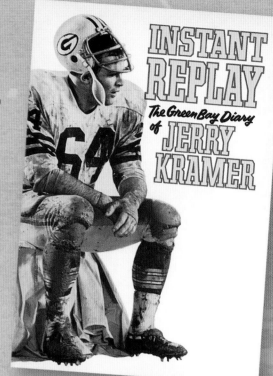

INSTANT REPLAY
The Green Bay Diary of JERRY KRAMER

MVP Books Collection

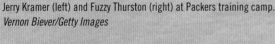

Jerry Kramer (left) and Fuzzy Thurston (right) at Packers training camp.
Vernon Biever/Getty Images

Speed made receiver Carroll Dale a big playmaker, and he gained an average of nearly 20 yards per catch during his eight-year Packers career, tops in franchise history. *AP Photo/JMC*

Game-by-Game

9/21	W, 17–0, vs. Chicago Bears	
9/28	W, 14–7, vs. San Francisco 49ers	
10/5	L, 7–19, at Minnesota Vikings	
10/12	W, 28–17, at Detroit Lions	
10/19	L, 21–34, at Los Angeles Rams	
10/26	W, 28–10, vs. Atlanta Falcons	
11/2	W, 38–34, at Pittsburgh Steelers	
11/9	L, 6–14, at Baltimore Colts	
11/16	L, 7–9, vs. Minnesota Vikings	
11/23	L, 10–16, vs. Detroit Lions	
11/30	W, 20–10, vs. New York Giants	
12/7	L, 7–20, at Cleveland Browns	
12/14	W, 21–3, at Chicago Bears	
12/21	W, 45–28, vs. St. Louis Cardinals	

Team Scoring

269 points scored (12th)

221 points allowed (3rd)

njuries and age cost the Packers during the 1969 season, yet Green Bay still posted an 8–6 record. It was the second season under head coach Phil Bengston, and it was difficult following a legend, especially when the legend was still around as general manager. The Packers touted the season with a "The Pack Is Back" theme, flooding the city with bumper stickers.

Bengston and Vince Lombardi disagreed about who should be the Packers' No. 1 draft pick. Bengston got his way, and he was wrong in the selection of 6-foot-8, 280-pound Rich Moore, a defensive tackle out of Villanova. Moore never started and never collected a sack. Once the draft ended, Lombardi issued another shocker. He was leaving as GM to become general manager and coach of the Washington Redskins.

The Packers started the season 5–2, but they faded in the late going. One by one, the stars of the championship era were retiring and Bengston had to scramble to replace several starters simultaneously. Travis Williams, the kickoff return sensation of the previous year, became the starter at halfback and rushed for 536 yards.

Quarterback Bart Starr ended up splitting time with young Don Horn. Veteran Carroll Dale was the top receiver with 45 catches and 879 receiving yards, the latter a career high. Dale, who still had his speed, averaged 19.8 yards per grab. The new kicker was Mike Mercer, who in his exhibition debut for the Packers booted five field goals. However, he hit only five out of 17 tries during the regular season.

PACKERS HEADLINE

Offense struggles as age and injuries take their toll as team closes decade with another missed postseason.

Willie Wood

Not drafted coming out of the University of Southern California, Willie Wood became one of the biggest bargain signings in the history of the NFL. Wood joined the Packers in 1960, and in a 12-year pro career the safety intercepted 48 passes and earned five championship rings on his way to the Pro Football Hall of Fame.

Wood, a 6-foot, 190-pounder, was a ferocious tackler who liked contact.

"It may be the most natural reaction for a big guy to think he can run over a smaller guy," Wood said. "But I can't recall one incident when this was the case. I've always enjoyed tackling. You've got to accept the punishment. That's the name of the game."

When Wood was overlooked, he wrote letters to every NFL team asking for a tryout, and Green Bay was the first to write back.

"I didn't know anything about defense until I came here," Wood said of Green Bay. "I was put on defense right away because the Packers considered me too small for offense."

Wood played in eight Pro Bowls, and after retirement in 1971 he became the first African American to lead a professional team on the field when he took over the Philadelphia Bell of the World Football League in 1973. Wood also became the first black head coach in the Canadian Football League when he was hired to run the Toronto Argonauts in 1980.

Wood sought a head coaching job in the NFL, but he couldn't get serious interviews. In terms of the league's outlook, it seemed the NFL was not ready to hire a black head coach.

"If you've ever had the run-around," Wood said, "it's a strange kind feeling. You know when it's happening to you."

Wood had his finest season in the secondary when he intercepted nine passes in 1962. A regular at returning kicks, Wood led the NFL in yards per punt return in 1961, and during his career he brought back two for touchdowns. Wood scored twice on interception returns, too.

Regarded as a fearless player, and one unwilling to come out of games sometimes even when hurt, Wood earned plenty of admiration from teammates. Packers defensive tackle Henry Jordan recounted: "He hurt his shoulder and he almost had tears in his eyes during a timeout. Some of us said, 'Willie, why don't you go to the bench for a while if your shoulder hurts that much?'" Wood replied, "No, I'm all right. I'll play. I've got another shoulder."

An illustration of how Wood could aid his team occurred during a 17–3 victory over the Chicago Bears, when he set up both Packers touchdowns with long punt returns and intercepted a pass. His teammates gave Wood the game ball.

"That's the first one I ever got," he said.

Wood has a section of a street named after him in Washington, D.C., where he grew up and returned after his football days ended.

Vernon Biever/Getty Images

Herb Adderley

For a guy who had played offense at Michigan State and started his NFL career on that side of the ball, Herb Adderley fared rather well on defense. In a 12-year career, mostly with the Packers but also with the Dallas Cowboys, Adderley was a member of six championship teams.

Adderley intercepted 48 passes and ran back seven for touchdowns while being named to the Pro Bowl five times. He was inducted into the Pro Football Hall of Fame in 1980.

The 6-foot-1, 200-pound Adderley was a Packers No. 1 pick in 1961 and was tried on offense for a while. But when it became clear he was not going to supplant Paul Hornung, coach Vince Lombardi tried him on defense. "I was too stubborn to switch him to defense until I had to," Lombardi said.

Adderley shined right away. He was also an excellent kickoff return man, averaging 25.7 yards per runback and recording a 103-yard kick return in 1962. Adderley also had a 98-yard return.

After a short trial on defense, Adderley discovered he loved it. "Defense is in my blood now," he said, "and nothing could make me want to go back to offense."

Adderley quickly learned that amnesia is an important trait to have for a defensive back. "You have to recognize that you're going to get beaten once in a while," he said. "You just can't dwell on it. You just have to concentrate on not letting the same man beat you again."

Vernon Biever/Getty Images

THE 1960s RECORD BOOK

Team Leaders

(**Boldface** indicates league leader)

Scoring Leaders (Points)

1960: Paul Hornung, **176**
1961: Paul Hornung, **146**
1962: Jim Taylor, **114**
1963: Jerry Kramer, 91
1964: Paul Hornung, 107
1965: Don Chandler, 88
1966: Don Chandler, 77
1967: Don Chandler, 96
1968: Carroll Dale, 48
1969: Travis Williams, 54

Rushing Leaders (Carries / Yards / TDs)

1960: Jim Taylor, **230** / 1,101 / 11
1961: Jim Taylor, 243 / 1,307 / **15**
1962: Jim Taylor, **272** / 1,474 / **19**
1963: Jim Taylor, 248 / 1,018 / 9
1964: Jim Taylor, 235 / 1,169 / 12
1965: Jim Taylor, 207 / 734 / 4
1966: Jim Taylor, 204 / 705 / 4
1967: Jim Grabowski, 120 / 466 / 2
1968: Donny Anderson, 170 / 761 / 5
1969: Travis Williams, 129 / 536 / 4

Passing Leaders (Completions / Attempts / Yards)

1960: Bart Starr, 98 / 172 / 1,358
1961: Bart Starr, 172 / 295 / 2,418
1962: Bart Starr, 178 / 285 / 2,438
1963: Bart Starr, 132 / 244 / 1,855
1964: Bart Starr, 163 / 272 / 2,144
1965: Bart Starr, 140 / 251 / 2,055
1966: Bart Starr, 156 / 251 / 2,257
1967: Bart Starr, 115 / 210 / 1,823
1968: Bart Starr, 109 / 171 / 1,617
1969: Don Horn, 89 / 168 / 1,505

Receiving Leaders (Receptions / Yards / TDs)

1960: Max McGee, 38 / 787 / 4
1961: Max McGee, 51 / 883 / 7
1962: Boyd Dowler, 49 / 724 / 2;
　　　　Max McGee, 49 / 820 / 3
1963: Boyd Dowler, 53 / 901 / 6
1964: Boyd Dowler, 45 / 623 / 5
1965: Boyd Dowler, 44 / 610 / 4
1966: Jim Taylor, 41 / 331 / 2
1967: Boyd Dowler, 54 / 836 / 4
1968: Boyd Dowler, 45 / 668 / 6
1969: Carroll Dale, 45 / 879 / 6

Interceptions (Number / Yards / TDs)

1960: Jess Whittenton, 6 / 101 / 0
1961: Hank Gremminger, 5 / 54 / 0;
　　　　John Symank, 5 / 99 / 0;
　　　　Jess Whittenton, 5 / 98 / 1;
　　　　Willie Wood, 5 / 52 / 0
1962: Willie Wood, 9 / 132 / 0
1963: Herb Adderley, 5 / 86 / 0;
　　　　Willie Wood, 5 / 67 / 0
1964: Herb Adderley, 4 / 56 / 0
1965: Herb Adderley, 6 / 175 / 3;
　　　　Willie Wood, 6 / 65 / 0
1966: Bob Jeter, 5 / 142 / 2;
　　　　Dave Robinson, 5 / 60 / 0
1967: Bob Jeter, 8 / 78 / 0
1968: Tom Brown, 4 / 66 / 0
1969: Herb Adderley, 5 / 169 / 1

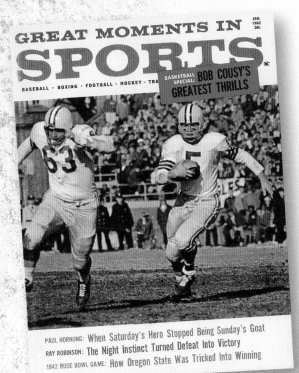

GREAT MOMENTS IN SPORTS

BASEBALL · BOXING · FOOTBALL · HOCKEY · TRA...

BASKETBALL SPECIAL: BOB COUSY'S GREATEST THRILLS

PAUL HORNUNG: When Saturday's Hero Stopped Being Sunday's Goat
RAY ROBINSON: The Night Instinct Turned Defeat Into Victory
1942 ROSE BOWL GAME: How Oregon State Was Tricked Into Winning

the Record Book

First-Team All-Pros

1960: Bill Forester, LB
1960: Forrest Gregg, T
1960: Paul Hornung, RB
1960: Henry Jordan, DT
1960: Jerry Kramer, G
1960: Jim Ringo, C
1961: Bill Forester, LB
1961: Paul Hornung, RB
1961: Henry Jordan, DT
1961: Jim Ringo, C
1961: Fuzzy Thurston, G
1961: Jesse Whittenton, CB
1962: Herb Adderley, CB
1962: Dan Currie, LB
1962: Willie Davis, DE
1962: Bill Forester, LB
1962: Forrest Gregg, T
1962: Henry Jordan, DT
1962: Jerry Kramer, G
1962: Ron Kramer, TE
1962: Jim Ringo, C
1962: Jim Taylor, RB
1963: Herb Adderley, CB
1963: Forrest Gregg, T
1963: Henry Jordan, DT
1963: Jerry Kramer, G
1963: Jim Ringo, C
1964: Willie Davis, DE
1964: Forrest Gregg, T
1964: Henry Jordan, DT
1964: Ray Nitschke, LB
1964: Willie Wood, S
1965: Herb Adderley, CB
1965: Willie Davis, DE
1965: Forrest Gregg, T
1965: Willie Wood, S
1966: Herb Adderley, CB
1966: Lee Roy Caffey, LB
1966: Willie Davis, DE
1966: Forrest Gregg, T
1966: Jerry Kramer, G
1966: Ray Nitschke, LB
1966: Bart Starr, QB
1966: Willie Wood, S
1967: Willie Davis, DE
1967: Forrest Gregg, T
1967: Bob Jeter, DB

1967: Jerry Kramer, G
1967: Dave Robinson, LB
1967: Willie Wood, S
1968: Willie Wood, S
1969: Gale Gillingham, G
1969: Willie Wood, S

Pro Bowl Selections

1960: Dan Currie, LB
1960: Bill Forester, LB
1960: Forrest Gregg, T
1960: Paul Hornung, RB
1960: Henry Jordan, DT
1960: Jim Ringo, C
1960: Bart Starr, QB
1960: Jim Taylor, FB
1961: Bill Forester, LB
1961: Forrest Gregg, T
1961: Henry Jordan, DT
1961: Max McGee, WR
1961: Jim Ringo, C
1961: Bart Starr, QB
1961: Jim Taylor, FB
1961: Jesse Whittenton, DB
1962: Bill Forester, LB
1962: Forrest Gregg, T
1962: Jerry Kramer, G
1962: Ron Kramer, TE
1962: Tom Moore, FB
1962: Jim Ringo, C
1962: Bart Starr, QB
1962: Jim Taylor, FB
1962: Willie Wood, S
1963: Herb Adderley, CB
1963: Willie Davis, DE
1963: Forrest Gregg, T
1963: Henry Jordan, DT
1963: Jerry Kramer, G
1963: Jim Ringo, C
1963: Jim Taylor, FB
1963: Jesse Whittenton, DB
1964: Herb Adderley, CB
1964: Willie Davis, DE
1964: Forrest Gregg, T
1964: Ray Nitschke, LB
1964: Jim Taylor, FB
1964: Willie Wood, S
1965: Herb Adderley, CB

1965: Lee Roy Caffey, LB
1965: Willie Davis, DE
1965: Boyd Dowler, WR
1965: Willie Wood, S
1966: Herb Adderley, CB
1966: Willie Davis, DE
1966: Forrest Gregg, T
1966: Henry Jordan, DT
1966: Dave Robinson, LB
1966: Bob Skoronski, T
1966: Bart Starr, QB
1966: Willie Wood, S
1967: Herb Adderley, CB
1967: Don Chandler, K
1967: Willie Davis, DE
1967: Boyd Dowler, WR
1967: Forrest Gregg, T
1967: Bob Jeter, CB
1967: Jerry Kramer, G
1967: Dave Robinson, LB
1967: Willie Wood, S
1968: Donny Anderson, RB
1968: Carroll Dale, WR
1968: Forrest Gregg, T
1968: Willie Wood, S
1969: Carroll Dale, WR
1969: Gale Gillingham, G
1969: Bob Jeter, CB
1969: Dave Robinson, LB
1969: Willie Wood, S

1st-Round Draft Picks

1960: Tom Moore (5), RB, Vanderbilt
1961: Herb Adderley (12),
    CB, Michigan State
1962: Earl Gros (14), Back, LSU
1963: Dave Robinson (14), LB, Penn State
1964: Lloyd Voss (13), DE, Nebraska
1965: Donny Anderson (7),
    RB, Texas Tech;
    Larry Elkins (10), WR, Baylor
1966: Jim Grabowski (9), RB, Illinois;
    Gale Gillingham (13), G, Minnesota
1967: Bob Hyland (9), G, Boston College;
    Don Horn (25), QB, San Diego State
1968: Fred Carr (5), LB, UTEP;
    Bill Lueck (26), G, Arizona
1969: Rich Moore (12), DT, Villanova

HERB ADDERLY
GREEN BAY PACKERS — HALFBACK

MVP Books Collection

It was a difficult transition for Bart Starr as he went from championship quarterback in the 1960s to struggling head coach in the 1970s. And Lynn Dickey proved to be no Bart Starr under center. *Vernon Biever/Getty Images*

For Green Bay Packers fans, the decade of the 1970s was about learning to live without Vince Lombardi. Neither the city nor Lombardi coped very well without him prowling the sidelines.

Lombardi's final year coaching the Packers was 1967. He spent the 1968 season as general manager only, with Phil Bengston his anointed successor. A year later, Lombardi returned to coaching with the Washington Redskins, trying to replicate the kind of turnaround he had implemented in Green Bay.

The Redskins showed immediate signs of progress, but then stunningly Lombardi took ill and passed away in 1970. The quick demise of Lombardi from cancer was shocking for the people of Green Bay, who still appreciated what he had done for the team even if they couldn't understand why he would want to coach anywhere else.

Bengston was fired in Green Bay after the 1970 season. He was followed by Dan Devine and, by mid-decade, Packers hero Bart Starr.

Throughout all the changeovers, the Packers managed just two winning seasons in the decade. For the most part, Green Bay reverted to pre-Lombardi on the field. The fans still loved their team and supported it, but, spoiled by the fabulous '60s, they were disappointed time and again.

There were some holdover stars from the dynasty era. Starr was still pitching as the decade turned, and he was still throwing to Carroll Dale, but new talent was sorely needed. Even with the NFL-AFL merger completely accomplished and the teams no longer fighting over player acquisition, the Packers were not plugging holes in a timely way.

Once Starr retired after the 1971 season, the Packers went through starting quarterbacks even faster than they did head coaches. No Packers fan is likely to say that the '70s were his or her favorite decade.

While the Packers were winning their five NFL titles during the 1960s, it was not uncommon for seven, eight, or nine players (and sometimes even more) to be selected for Pro Bowl participation each year. If postseason honors were an indication of talent, the drop was swift and dramatic. In 1970, only lineman Gale Gillingham and defensive back Willie Wood were chosen All-Pro. In 1971, only Gillingham and fullback John Brockington received recognition.

In 1975 only linebacker Fred Carr was honored, and in 1976 and 1977 the Packers had no one selected for All-Pro recognition at all. Defensive back Willie Buchanon got the nod in 1978, but again in 1979 Green Bay was shut out. That was just supporting evidence that the Packers were a mediocre team.

The brightest new star in Green Bay was probably Brockington. He achieved 1,000-yard seasons even as the team lost games, at least for a little while. For a few years, Brockington paired with halfback MacArthur Lane, and the duo restored a bit of the image of the Packers as a three-yards-and-a-cloud-of-dust team in the tough NFL Central Division. The Central was starting to acquire its nickname as the "Black and Blue Division," and a heavy-duty running game fit right in.

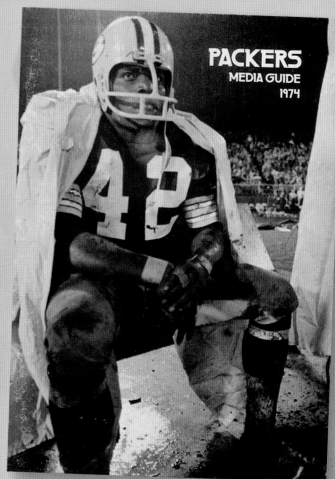

MVP Books Collection

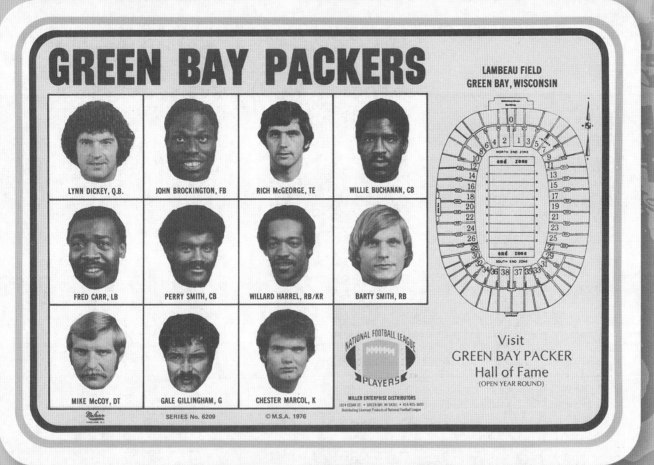

MVP Books Collection

1970

Game-by-Game

9/20	**L**, 0–40, vs. Detroit Lions
9/27	**W**, 27–24, vs. Atlanta Falcons
10/4	**W**, 13–10, vs. Minnesota Vikings
10/12	**W**, 22–20, at San Diego Chargers
10/18	**L**, 21–31, vs. Los Angeles Rams
10/25	**W**, 30–17, vs. Philadelphia Eagles
11/1	**L**, 10–26, at San Francisco 49crs
11/9	**L**, 10–13, vs. Baltimore Colts
11/15	**W**, 20–19, vs. Chicago Bears
11/22	**L**, 3–10, at Minnesota Vikings
11/26	**L**, 3–16, at Dallas Cowboys
12/6	**W**, 20–12, at Pittsburgh Steelers
12/13	**L**, 17–35, at Chicago Bears
12/20	**L**, 0–20, at Detroit Lions

Team Scoring

196 points scored (24th)

293 points allowed (19th)

Packers open and close the season with shutout losses to the Lions, play .500 otherwise in Phil Bengston's farewell season as coach.

After posting a feel-good season in 1969 with an 8–6 record, coach Phil Bengston had to feel good about 1970, his third year on the job after replacing legendary coach Vince Lombardi. Lombardi had paved the way for his defensive coordinator to get the big job, but Lombardi was gone.

In fact, by the time the season started, Lombardi was dead. He died on September 3, 17 days before Green Bay's season opener. The Packers got waxed 40–0 by the Detroit Lions that day, and although they won three straight after that, Green Bay was on its way to a 6–8 record, the second losing season under Bengston.

The season marked the beginning of a scheduling partnership between the old National Football League and the American Football League. After playing AFL teams in exhibition games, the old guard played some AFL teams in games that counted in the standings.

The Packers made their first official trip to San Diego to play the Chargers on October 12 and prevailed 22–20. Quarterback Bart Starr threw two touchdown passes but needed kicker Dale Livingston to boot three field goals, including the game-winner in the fourth quarter from 14 yards.

Green Bay played an unfriendly schedule, with its final five games on the road. The Packers lost four of those, ending the year much like they began it. The Lions posted a 20–0 shutout to bookend the opener. The day after the December 20 finale, Bengston resigned.

Donny Anderson leaps across the goal line for a touchdown in Green Bay's 30–17 win over Philadelphia on October 25. Anderson posted career bests with 853 yards rushing and 414 yards receiving in 1970. *AP Photo*

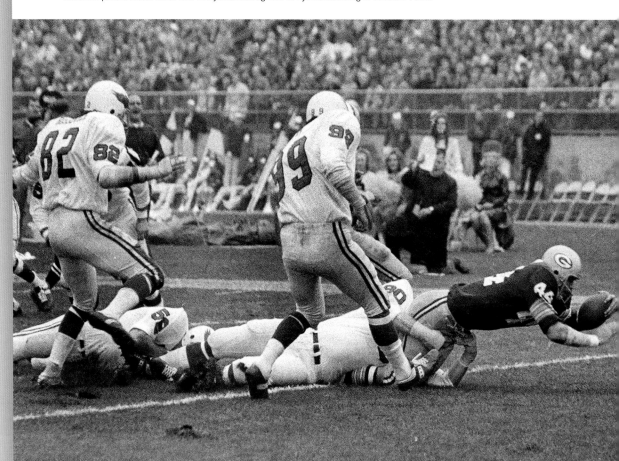

Gale Gillingham

A five-time Pro Bowl guard, Gale Gillingham spent his entire 10-year career with the Packers, splitting the decades of the 1960s and 1970s. In 1970, he was named First-Team All-Pro for the second year in a row.

The Wisconsin native, who played college ball at the University of Minnesota, was the Packers' No. 1 draft pick in 1966. He became a starter under coach Vince Lombardi and started in Super Bowl II, and he remained a starter under coach Bart Starr near the end of his career.

Gillingham also played under coach Dan Devine, who moved him to defensive tackle briefly in an experiment that ended with injury.

One thing the 6-foot-3, 255-pound Gillingham was noted for was lifting weights, which was somewhat frowned upon by coaches at the time. At first, Gillingham was a left guard who spelled Fuzzy Thurston. Then he took over for Thurston full-time. When Jerry Kramer retired, Gillingham moved to right guard.

"The hardest thing is that I don't know much about the people I'm playing against," Gillingham said of the new faces he ran into on the other side of the line. "I've never played against them before."

Switching to the right side after getting used to playing the left side also made for different assignments when Packers plays were called. "It's a little harder to pull," Gillingham said. "It's an unnatural pull, so it's a little bit harder on the trap plays because a right-handed guy, like I am, normally finds it easier to go to the right."

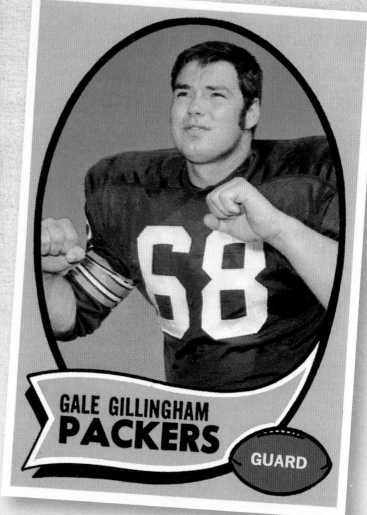

MVP Books Collection

1971

▶ 4–8–2   4th place ◀

Game-by-Game

9/19 **L**, 40–42,
vs. New York Giants

9/26 **W**, 34–13,
vs. Denver Broncos

10/3 **W**, 20–17,
vs. Cincinnati Bengals

10/10 **L**, 28–31, at Detroit Lions

10/17 **L**, 13–24,
vs. Minnesota Vikings

10/24 **L**, 13–30,
at Los Angeles Rams

11/1 **T**, 14–14, vs. Detroit Lions

11/7 **W**, 17–14,
at Chicago Bears

11/14 **L**, 0–3,
at Minnesota Vikings

11/22 **L**, 21–28,
at Atlanta Falcons

11/28 **L**, 21–29,
vs. New Orleans Saints

12/5 **T**, 16–16,
at St. Louis Cardinals

12/12 **W**, 31–10,
vs. Chicago Bears

12/19 **L**, 6–27, at Miami Dolphins

Team Scoring

274 points scored (13th)

298 points allowed (18th)

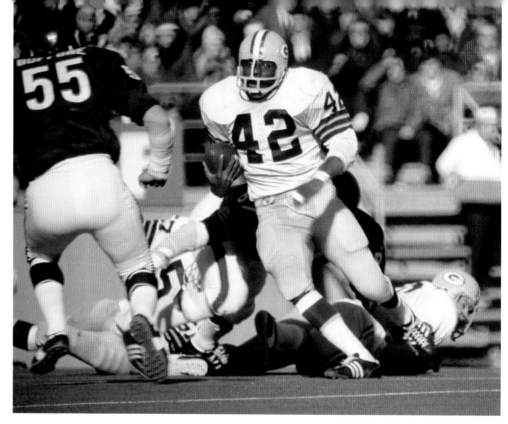

Fullback John Brockington tallied 142 yards against Chicago on November 7 during his remarkable rookie season of 1971. His 1,105 yards earned him a First-Team All-Pro selection, a place on the Pro Bowl team, and Rookie of the Year honors. *Vernon Biever/Getty Images*

To replace Phil Bengston, Packers management went outside the team. Starting fresh, Green Bay hired prominent college coach Dan Devine. After a few years as an assistant coach at Michigan State, Devine became first the Arizona State head coach and then the Missouri coach for years when the Packers tabbed him. He was allowed to take on the general manager's role in Green Bay as well.

Devine was born in Augusta, Wisconsin, and grew up in Minnesota near the state line, so this was a homecoming. "In no way could I have left Missouri for any other college job and for very few professional opportunities," Devine said.

Devine had been a consistent big winner in college, but he had no NFL background, and in his last year at Missouri he had a losing record. Devine may have divined that he would have a difficult tenure in Green Bay when, in his first regular-season game, he was run over along the sidelines and suffered a broken leg.

The play occurred in the fourth quarter, and Devine was taken to the hospital before the final gun. He had to listen to the end of the game on the radio.

Not only was Devine injured, but insult was added to injury when the Packers lost 42–40 to the New York Giants. Green Bay was on its way to a 4–8–2 record. Quarterback Bart Starr was still around, but not healthy. Backup Zeke Bratkowski started the opener, but then Devine turned the job over to Scott Hunter, a rookie sixth round pick out of Alabama. Starr got a couple of starts at the end of the year.

A different rookie made a bigger impact than Hunter. Fullback John Brockington, the team's No. 1 draft choice out of Ohio State, rushed for 1,105 yards. Holdover halfback Donny Anderson added 757 yards.

PACKERS HEADLINE

Top draft pick John Brockington tallies 1,105 rushing yards to set a franchise rookie record while tearing up NFL defenses.

John Brockington

It was unlikely, but in his first few years at fullback, powerful John Brockington was a worthy successor to Hall of Famer Jim Taylor. Brockington, a No. 1 draft choice out of Ohio State, was named NFL Offensive Rookie of the Year in 1971 after he rushed for 1,105 yards and scored eight touchdowns.

"He's my kind of people," said Packers coach Dan Devine, who was a big believer in a strong running game.

Entering his first training camp, Brockington focused on becoming a starter. "That was the only thing I wanted to do then," he said. "It kills me not to play."

One reason Brockington did not set loftier first-year goals than simply starting was his lack of familiarity with the caliber of NFL play and the knowledge that not all highly touted newcomers do well.

"Sure you have doubts," Brockington said. "There's no league on top of this. And you read about a lot of top prospects, No. 1s, who don't make the grade."

At the time, Brockington's 1,105 yards were the most by a rookie in NFL history. He didn't stop there, either. Brockington rushed for 1,027 yards in 1972 and 1,144 yards in 1973.

A three-time Pro Bowl player, Brockington rushed for 5,185 yards and 30 touchdowns in his pro career, which lasted from 1971 to 1977.

MVP Books Collection

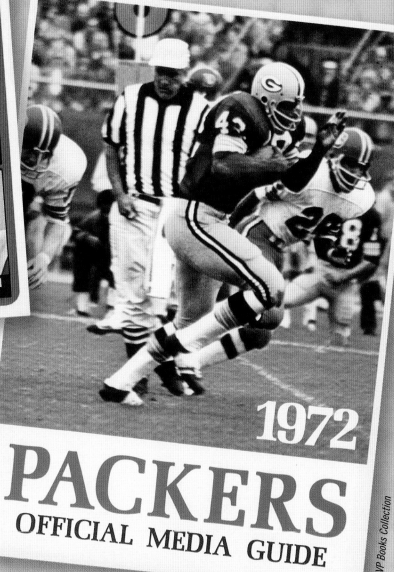

MVP Books Collection

1972

▶ 10–4　1st place ◀

Game-by-Game

9/17	W, 26–10, at Cleveland Browns
9/24	L, 14–20, vs. Oakland Raiders
10/1	W, 16–13, vs. Dallas Cowboys
10/8	W, 20–17, vs. Chicago Bears
10/16	W, 24–23, at Detroit Lions
10/22	L, 9–10, vs. Atlanta Falcons
10/29	L, 13–27, vs. Minnesota Vikings
11/5	W, 34–24, vs. San Francisco 49ers
11/12	W, 23–17, at Chicago Bears
11/19	W, 23–10, at Houston Oilers
11/26	L, 16–21, at Washington Redskins
12/3	W, 33–7, vs. Detroit Lions
12/10	W, 23–7, at Minnesota Vikings
12/17	W, 30–20, at New Orleans Saints

Playoffs

12/24	L, 3–16, at Washington Redskins

Team Scoring

304 points scored (11th)

226 points allowed (4th)

"The Pack Is Back" with their best post-Lombardi record and a trip to the postseason.

Employing the same catchy theme used a couple of years earlier, fans enjoyed chanting "The Pack Is Back" in 1972 because it seemed to be in Dan Devine's second season. The Packers finished 10–4, their most regular-season wins since 1966. There were even bumper stickers proclaiming "It's Fine With Devine."

After losing two games to the Detroit Lions by a combined 60–0 margin in 1971, the Packers retaliated by sweeping Detroit, 24–23 and 33–7. The venerable Bart Starr retired, leaving the quarterback job to second-year man Scott Hunter. Hunter started every game, but he completed just 43.2 percent of his passes while throwing six touchdown passes and nine interceptions.

It was the ground game that opponents feared. The 225-pound John Brockington was a battering ram, rushing for 1,027 yards and eight touchdowns. Donny Anderson was traded to the St. Louis Cardinals for MacArthur Lane, and the new halfback helped give the Packers a big one-two punch out of the backfield. Lane gained 821 yards from scrimmage.

The Packers also came up with a new kicker, Chester Marcol, who scored 128 points. The Pack won four of their first five games.

Although Hunter seemed to have a grip, however shaky, on the signal-caller's role, his new backup was a familiar face in Green Bay. Jerry Tagge, drafted out of Nebraska, had grown up in Green Bay, played high school football there, and, as a youngster, sold concessions at Lambeau Field.

On the field, Tagge attempted 29 passes as a rookie and completed 10 of them for 154 yards.

As coach Dan Devine is hoisted up by players in the background, Pete Lammons (86), Scott Hunter (16), and John Brockington (42) celebrate Green Bay securing its first postseason berth of the post-Lombardi era. The 23–7 victory over the Vikings on December 10 clinched the NFC Central Division crown. *Vernon Biever/Getty Images*

The Packers' first-round pick in 1972, cornerback Willie Buchanon (28) was a three-time Pro Bowler in seven seasons with Green Bay, but his 1973 season was cut short when he broke his leg during a game against the Rams on October 21, shown here earlier in that contest. *AP Photo/NFL Photos*

Game-by-Game

9/17	W, 23–7, vs. New York Jets	
9/23	T, 13–13, vs. Detroit Lions	
9/30	L, 3–11, at Minnesota Vikings	
10/7	W, 16–14, at New York Giants	
10/14	T, 10–10, vs. Kansas City Chiefs	
10/21	L, 7–24, at Los Angeles Rams	
10/28	L, 0–34, at Detroit Lions	
11/4	L, 17–31, vs. Chicago Bears	
11/11	W, 25–21, vs. St. Louis Cardinals	
11/18	L, 24–33, at New England Patriots	
11/26	L, 6–20, at San Francisco 49ers	
12/2	W, 30–10, vs. New Orleans Saints	
12/8	L, 7–31, vs. Minnesota Vikings	
12/16	W, 21–0, at Chicago Bears	

Team Scoring

202 points scored (22nd)

259 points allowed (14th)

PACKERS HEADLINE

Quarterback carousel produces erratic, disappointing season.

The Dan Devine bandwagon hit a speed bump and lost a wheel in 1973. The Packers finished 5–7–2, and the Pack was back in trouble. Nothing illustrated Devine's frustration more than a 34–0 loss to the Detroit Lions in October.

"It was a very, very, very horrible, nightmarish type of game," Devine said. "I'm personally humiliated."

This was an erratic season, with a win here, a loss there, and a tie there. The Packers never put together a long winning streak, but in October they went into a three-game tailspin in which Devine realized that Scott Hunter was not the permanent solution at quarterback.

Devine had patiently waited for Hunter to develop, but he hadn't improved even with experience. Devine didn't seem to think popular local boy Jerry Tagge was ready for action, either. So Green Bay sent draft picks to the Miami Dolphins for Jim Del Gaizo and started him.

That didn't work, either, and down the stretch Devine turned to Tagge. Quarterback controversies with two men in the mix are never considered to be healthy. With three players vying for one slot, things get messy. Tagge had the best stats—to a point—with 56 completions in 106 tries for a 52.8 percentage. However, he threw for just two touchdowns while heaving seven interceptions.

Brockington recorded his third straight 1,000-yard rushing season, and halfback MacArthur Lane added another 500-plus yards. The limited strike ability of the passing attack was obvious; Lane, out of the backfield, was the leading receiver with 27 catches.

Larry McCarren

The only time the center gets attention is when a hike is muffed between his hands and the quarterback's. But Larry McCarren stayed around Green Bay so long—first as a player, then as a broadcaster—he became one of the best-known figures surrounding the team.

McCarren, a twelfth-round draft pick out of the University of Illinois, was the 308th player taken in the 1973 NFL draft. He wasn't supposed to make the team, but he became a 12-year fixture for the Packers on the offensive line.

Actually, McCarren didn't truly make the team out of training camp his rookie year. He was signed to the then-called taxi squad and hung around, working hard. By the tenth game of the season, he was on the roster. He eventually made two Pro Bowls and was chosen for the Packers Hall of Fame.

One way McCarren advanced through the ranks, and a distinguishing characteristic of his career, was how hard he worked on the practice field. "Everybody here wants to be good," said his offensive line coach, Bill Curry, "but there are just some who want it more than others. Larry's willing to do the extra stuff you have to do to become a top-flight football player. Larry's intensity is unusual in that he's not so intense that he has the aura of gloom about him. He's got a sense of humor. He's able to laugh at himself."

If it sounded old-fashioned, McCarren didn't care when he provided answers to reporters who asked him why he pushed himself so hard.

"I guess it's important to me to be good at what you do, just as a matter of pride," McCarren said. "It's pretty simple."

Compared to later generations of linemen, McCarren was a shrimp. He stood 6-foot-3, but at his peak he weighed about 255 pounds. That was after gaining weight following college, when he was around 20 pounds lighter.

Bulking up by lifting weights made a big difference in McCarren's career. It made it harder to push him around, and the Packers coaches, including Curry, noticed what was happening.

"He was almost a different player because he added so much strength," Curry said of McCarren after his taxi

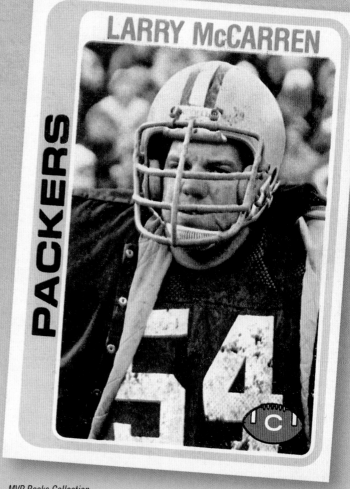

MVP Books Collection

squad ride and first two years on the team. "He could do things he couldn't think of doing before."

McCarren went through a series of Packers head coaches and assistants, and many offensive line partners, until one day he woke up and was an elder statesman.

"I have seen a lot of things change since I came up," McCarren said. "I've gone from one of the youngest to one of the older guys around. It happens gradually, though."

McCarren played through the 1984 season and then moved to the other side of the microphone for interviews, carving out a lengthy Wisconsin sportscasting career. He was sports director at a Green Bay TV station for more than 20 years, worked on sports talk radio, and did Packers analysis.

I f 1973 taught coach Dan Devine anything, it was that he was undermanned at quarterback and that none of the three at his disposal looked like a winner. Desperate for help, the Packers took a major gamble for 1974. They traded five draft choices, including two future first-round picks, to the Los Angeles Rams for John Hadl. And that was after trading a draft choice for Jack Concannon. The Hadl trade is regarded as possibly the worst in franchise history.

Jerry Tagge was still around, but Scott Hunter was out of the picture. It was Hadl's team to lead. Hadl was a big-league quarterback who had led the San Diego Chargers to great success. But he was 34.

Hadl was the starter, but his career was going downhill. With the Packers, Hadl completed only 48.4 percent of his passes for three touchdowns and eight interceptions. Tagge threw one touchdown pass and 10 interceptions. Concannon recorded one touchdown pass and three interceptions.

As Green Bay headed toward a 6–8 record, fullback John Brockington's production dropped to 883 yards on a puny 3.3 yards per carry. It also didn't help that training camp was disrupted by a labor dispute between the owners and the players union. The defense did yeoman work, five times holding opponents to a touchdown or less.

Devine sensed that he might be fired at season's end even with a year left on his contract, so he looked for a college job. He hit the jackpot with Notre Dame, and as soon as the campaign ended, he resigned. After posting a record of 25–27–4 in four seasons with Green Bay, Devine won 76 percent of his games in six seasons at Notre Dame and claimed the 1977 national championship with Joe Montana at quarterback.

Center Larry McCarren blocks as quarterback John Hadl hands off to running back John Brockington during a 34–0 win against the San Diego Chargers on November 24. It was the third straight victory with the veteran Hadl under center. *Vernon Biever/Getty Images*

▶ **6–8   3rd place** ◀

Game-by-Game

9/15	**L**, 17–32, vs. Minnesota Vikings
9/22	**W**, 20–13, at Baltimore Colts
9/29	**W**, 21–19, vs. Detroit Lions
10/6	**L**, 7–27, vs. Buffalo Bills
10/13	**W**, 17–6, vs. Los Angeles Rams
10/21	**L**, 9–10, at Chicago Bears
10/27	**L**, 17–19, at Detroit Lions
11/3	**L**, 6–17, vs. Washington Redskins
11/10	**W**, 20–3, vs. Chicago Bears
11/17	**W**, 19–7, at Minnesota Vikings
11/24	**W**, 34–0, vs. San Diego Chargers
12/1	**L**, 14–36, at Philadelphia Eagles
12/8	**L**, 6–7, at San Francisco 49ers
12/15	**L**, 3–10, at Atlanta Falcons

Team Scoring

210 points scored (21st)

206 points allowed (5th)

PACKERS HEADLINE

More quarterback woes as Packers complete a mere five touchdown passes, their lowest total since 1949.

143

▶ 4–10   4th place ◀

Game-by-Game

9/21	**L**, 16–30, vs. Detroit Lions	
9/29	**L**, 13–23, at Denver Broncos	
10/5	**L**, 7–31, vs. Miami Dolphins	
10/12	**L**, 19–20, at New Orleans Saints	
10/19	**W**, 19–17, at Dallas Cowboys	
10/26	**L**, 13–16, vs. Pittsburgh Steelers	
11/2	**L**, 17–28, vs. Minnesota Vikings	
11/9	**L**, 14–27, at Chicago Bears	
11/16	**L**, 10–13, at Detroit Lions	
11/23	**W**, 40–14, vs. New York Giants	
11/30	**W**, 28–7, vs. Chicago Bears	
12/7	**L**, 3–24, at Minnesota Vikings	
12/14	**L**, 5–22, at Los Angeles Rams	
12/21	**W**, 22–13, vs. Atlanta Falcons	

Team Scoring

226 points scored (20th)

285 points allowed (13th)

PACKERS HEADLINE

Bart Starr returns to Green Bay as head coach, produces first double-digit loss season since 1958.

At training camp before the 1975 season, former quarterback legend Bart Starr traded in shoulder pads for a whistle, taking over a club that had three losing seasons in the previous four years under Dan Devine. Starr didn't do much better during his nine-year tenure, securing only two winning seasons. *AP Photo*

Green Bay management was in exactly the situation it hadn't wanted to be in after Vince Lombardi left. The Packers had become a revolving door for coaches. Although he had no head coaching experience, quarterback Bart Starr was an icon in the community—a legendary player linked to the glory years—and everyone knew he was a smart leader.

Rather than bring in an unknown face, the Packers went to Starr and offered him the job. Starr had been out of football, working in the business world, but the opportunity appealed to him. He could bring his old team back to prominence. It would be a challenge, but going back to Green Bay felt right.

It was not right initially, as the Packers finished 4–10. At least Starr knew how to coach quarterbacks. This was John Hadl's second chance to lead the Packers, and he threw for 2,095 yards while recording a 54.1 completion rate. However, the big problem was his 21 interceptions stacked next to six TD passes.

John Brockington was no longer Brockington at fullback. He totaled 434 yards, with his average per carry dropping again to 3.0. Brockington did run for seven touchdowns.

The Packers opened with four straight losses, and after one win they ripped off four more losses. They got a little better over the season's last month, even thumping rival Chicago 28–7.

Coach Starr

When Bart Starr retired as a player for the Green Bay Packers in 1971 after 16 seasons, he was bound for the Hall of Fame for his exploits as a quarterback. A graduate of the University of Alabama, he was also bound for the South again, where he immersed himself in business.

Starr did not expect to receive a telephone call imploring him to come back and coach his old team, which had fallen on hard times and been through two coaches since Vince Lombardi. He was in demand for product endorsements, and he gave lectures at corporate meetings. He was removed from pro football and didn't thinking about coaching. He probably never would have done it if it hadn't been the Packers asking for help.

With five championships on his résumé, Starr had not trained to become a head coach. Many of his friends did not want him to take the job because they wondered if he would fail and tarnish his pristine image. But Starr said yes. "This is the organization that gave me a chance," he said.

His reasoning was as simple as that, and it typified his character. That type of outlook was one of the reasons Packers management wanted him back. When he began work as the boss, Starr realized there were many things he didn't know about running a team.

"There were a helluva lot of things they didn't tell me when I signed on with this outfit," Starr said early in his tenure.

Starr was no miracle worker, going 4–10 his first season. For a man weaned on Vince Lombardi's tight discipline and demanding learning curve, Starr was dismayed when his team didn't improve during the season.

"We never reached the stage I thought we should have reached," he said. "We were still making mistakes late in the season—in many cases, the same mistakes that we had made earlier. That wouldn't be so bad if this were a young team. But we're not a young team."

The talent was thin enough that an entire revamping of the roster was in order, and between 1975 when he started and 1983 when he finished, Starr made all of the changes. He got better at the coaching thing, yet the team never quite clicked long enough for a true breakthrough.

Starr led the Packers to two winning seasons and three 8–8 seasons. Something always happened in those .500 years to prevent Green Bay from scoring that one more win that would have made the record a much more palatable 9–7.

There were three losing seasons before the Packers at last recorded even an 8–7–1 winning season, but consistent winning never followed.

If Green Bay fans expected the second coming of Lombardi, they were mistaken. Starr was the extension of Lombardi on the field, but their personalities differed. "Vince was a hollerer, and I'm not," Starr said.

Starr probably had a lot to holler about, too. He finished his coaching stint with a record of 52–76–3.

MVP Books Collection

1976

▶ 5–9   4th place ◀

Game-by-Game

9/12	**L, 14–26,** vs. San Francisco 49ers
9/19	**L, 0–29,** at St. Louis Cardinals
9/26	**L, 7–28,** at Cincinnati Bengals
10/3	**W, 24–14,** vs. Detroit Lions
10/10	**W, 27–20,** vs. Seattle Seahawks
10/17	**W, 28–13,** vs. Philadelphia Eagles
10/24	**L, 14–18,** at Oakland Raiders
10/31	**L, 6–27,** at Detroit Lions
11/7	**W, 32–27,** vs. New Orleans Saints
11/14	**L, 13–24,** at Chicago Bears
11/21	**L, 10–17,** vs. Minnesota Vikings
11/28	**L, 10–16,** vs. Chicago Bears
12/5	**L, 9–20,** at Minnesota Vikings
12/12	**W, 24–20,** at Atlanta Falcons

Team Scoring

218 points scored (23rd)

299 points allowed (21st)

The Packers' meager offense tallies a total of 36 yards in a September loss to the Bengals, producing the lowest single-game total in team history.

Presumably, when fans announced that the Pack was back, they meant more than just Bart Starr. But the famous quarterback-turned-coach had little to work with—even at quarterback. After two chances to lead the Packers fizzled, John Hadl was gone.

The Packers did have a new face on the scene to handle the job. Lynn Dickey had played sparingly for the Houston Oilers after being drafted out of Kansas State, and he had some gifts that Starr felt he could work with. Dickey needed work, but the Packers threw him into the full-time QB role immediately.

At his introductory press conference the year before, Starr asked Green Bay fans for their patience. This season was one example of why patience was needed. The Packers were not within shouting distance of being a good team.

Dickey threw for 1,465 yards, but once again, as it had been for the preceding several years, the big problem was the horrible ratio of touchdown passes (seven) to interceptions (14). The Packers finished 5–9 with Dickey at the controls.

John Brockington rushed for 406 yards, but for the first time since 1970 he was not the team's leading rusher. Willard Harrell, out of the University of the Pacific, outgained him with 435 yards.

The Packers started the season 0–3, but they set off a flurry of excitement by beating the Detroit Lions, Seattle Seahawks, and Philadelphia Eagles to reach 3–3. Then the Packers won only two of their remaining contests.

In 1976, wide receiver Steve Odom (left) caught 23 passes for 456 yards while Willard Harrell was the team's top rusher with 435 yards and 435 carries. *Vera Anderson/Getty Images*

Lynn Dickey

Lynn Dickey was a late bloomer in the pros. He hardly played in his early years with the Houston Oilers, and he didn't look ready to play in his first years with the Green Bay Packers. At the time, it seemed the only thing he had in common with Joe Willie Namath was that they both got attention for wearing white shoes.

Dickey was held back by injury after injury to various parts of his body. But when he was at last healthy and had gained experience, he blossomed into a top-notch quarterback for the Packers.

The 6-foot-3, 215-pound Dickey had a strong arm, but he had the bad habit of throwing more passes to opponents than his own guys. The Packers obtained Dickey from Houston in a trade for quarterback John Hadl, cornerback Ken Ellis, and a draft choice in 1976. From 1976 to 1979, the combination of Dickey's erratic throwing and serious injuries kept him from being a reliable starter. Everything went wrong.

"It's very frustrating," Dickey said. "You get very impatient playing behind somebody."

Among Dickey's problems were missing the entire 1978 season while recovering from a badly broken leg that was slow to heal and required two surgeries. When he came back in 1979, he was a benchwarmer behind David Whitehurst. But things turned Dickey's way, really for the first time in a Packers uniform, near the end of the season. Dickey became the starter again, and he kept that job going into training camp in 1980.

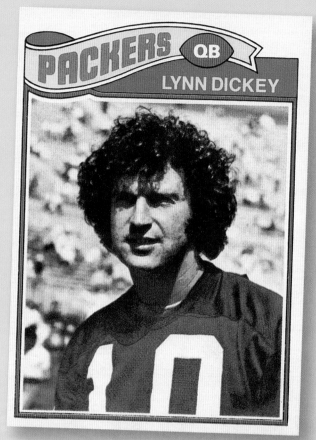

MVP Books Collection

That was the season he truly blossomed as a Packer. He threw for 3,528 yards while completing 258 out of 478 passing attempts for a 58.2 percentage rate. He threw 15 touchdown passes.

Dickey spent the next five years as Green Bay's starting quarterback, playing until he was 36, and in 1983 he put up staggering numbers. Dickey hurled 484 throws, 289 going for completions. His percentage was 59.7, and his 4,458 passing yards and 32 touchdown passes led the league. Dickey made All-Pro that season.

In a 1980 game, Dickey completed 35 of 51 attempts, including 15 straight, for 418 yards against Tampa Bay. In a 1983 game against Washington, Dickey steered Green Bay to a 48–47 win while throwing for 387 yards and three touchdowns.

Dickey performed well when healthy, but he took a terrible beating from football injuries. From hip surgery to Achilles problems, he faced them all and kept coming back. Given his personal history, it was no surprise that Dickey's career ended with an injury. He hurt his neck near the end of the 1985 season, and that was it.

Yet long into retirement, Dickey said he was glad he had kept on playing.

"I didn't want to wake up one day when I was older and regret not giving it all I had to play as long as I could," Dickey said. "I'm glad I didn't give up."

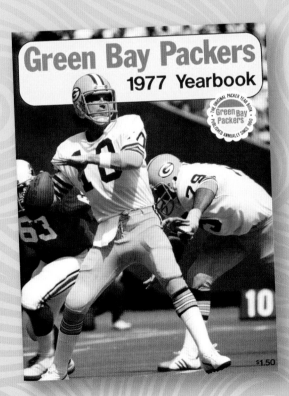

MVP Books Collection

▶ 4–10   4th place ◀

Game-by-Game

9/18	**W,** 24–20, at New Orleans Saints
9/25	**L,** 10–16, vs. Houston Oilers
10/2	**L,** 7–19, at Minnesota Vikings
10/9	**L,** 7–17, vs. Cincinnati Bengals
10/16	**L,** 6–10, at Detroit Lions
10/23	**W,** 13–0, at Tampa Bay Buccaneers
10/30	**L,** 0–26, vs. Chicago Bears
11/6	**L,** 10–20, at Kansas City Chiefs
11/13	**L,** 6–24, vs. Los Angeles Rams
11/21	**L,** 9–10, at Washington Redskins
11/27	**L,** 6–13, vs. Minnesota Vikings
12/4	**W,** 10–9, vs. Detroit Lions
12/11	**L,** 10–21, at Chicago Bears
12/18	**W,** 16–14, vs. San Francisco 49ers

Team Scoring

134 points scored (27th)

219 points allowed (10th)

PACKERS HEADLINE

Packers produce lowest point total since Curly Lambeau's final season as coach, in 1949.

The second Packers–Vikings meeting of 1977 was played in blizzard conditions at Lambeau Field, a stark contrast to the sunny climate at Metropolitan Stadium in Minnesota in early October. The results on the field, however, were similar, with two losses for the Packers. *Vernon Biever/Getty Images*

This was Bart Starr's third year as head coach, but the Packers showed no improvement, finishing 4–10. They were dull as well as bad, unable to score much or even gain many yards.

Lynn Dickey was still the quarterback, but when he went out for the season with a terribly broken leg with five games left, the numbers illustrating his basic problem were not any better than the year before: five touchdown passes, 14 interceptions.

David Whitehurst stepped in, and his stats were worse. He had a lower completion percentage, threw just one TD pass in five games, and tossed seven interceptions.

Barty Smith was both the new rushing leader with 554 yards as well as the leading receiver with 37 catches. No player on the team scored more than Steve Odom's three touchdowns.

The offense was so pitiful that the Packers scored 10 or fewer points 11 times in 14 games. The year's high mark was 24 points in the opener in a win over the New Orleans Saints. Willard Harrell's 75-yard punt return for a touchdown was one of the highlight plays of the season, and the Packers actually led that game 24–0 at halftime.

In all, Green Bay scored 134 points. The defense wasn't all that bad, surrendering just 219 points and never once giving up as many as 30 in a game.

Veteran fullback John Brockington carried 11 times for 25 yards in the early going and then was cut, ending his Packers career.

▶ 8–7–1   2nd place ◀

Game-by-Game

9/3	W, 13–7, at Detroit Lions	
9/10	W, 28–17, vs. New Orleans Saints	
9/17	L, 3–28, vs. Oakland Raiders	
9/24	W, 24–3, at San Diego Chargers	
10/1	W, 35–14, vs. Detroit Lions	
10/8	W, 24–14, vs. Chicago Bears	
10/15	W, 45–28, vs. Seattle Seahawks	
10/22	L, 7–21, at Minnesota Vikings	
10/29	W, 9–7, vs. Tampa Bay Buccaneers	
11/5	L, 3–10, at Philadelphia Eagles	
11/12	L, 14–42, vs. Dallas Cowboys	
11/19	L, 3–16, at Denver Broncos	
11/26	T, 10–10 (OT), vs. Minnesota Vikings	
12/3	W, 17–7, at Tampa Bay Buccaneers	
12/10	L, 0–14, at Chicago Bears	
12/17	L, 14–31, at Los Angeles Rams	

Team Scoring

249 points scored (22nd)

269 points allowed (8th)

After three dismal years, it's possible that if the head coach's name wasn't Bart Starr, he might have been dumped. But 1978 looked like nirvana compared to recent seasons, as the Packers surged to an 8–7–1 record. Good news at last.

This was a totally refurbished Packers team. Only four starters remained from four seasons earlier. Starr installed David Whitehurst, who came out of Furman University, as his first-string quarterback and left him there all year. Lynn Dickey did not play a down in 1978.

Whitehurst completed 51.2 percent of his passes, and while interceptions were still a worry (17 of them), he also threw 10 touchdown passes. That meant that for the first time in a while Green Bay moved the ball through the air.

A huge reason for that was the arrival of wide receiver James Lofton, a future Hall of Famer. Drafted in the first round out of Stanford in 1978, Lofton caught 46 passes for 818 yards, an average per catch of 17.8 yards. His talent was quite apparent.

Surprisingly, Terdell Middleton, who had 35 carries during the entire 1977 season, produced a 1,000-yard rushing year. With 1,116 yards rushing and 34 catches, Middleton, who had been a third-round draft pick by the St. Louis Cardinals out of Memphis, had the season of his life.

The Packers won six of their first seven games to give Green Bay fans some thrills, but they couldn't sustain the momentum and lost five of their last seven.

During their 24–3 win over the Chargers in San Diego, the Packers managed only 92 yards passing, including this grab by rookie James Lofton, but a blocked punt return and an interception return resulted in 14 points for Green Bay. *Richard Stagg/Getty Images*

Chester Marcol

Polish-born kicker Chester Marcol was one of the most unlikely success stories in NFL history. Born in Opole, Poland, in 1949, Marcol immigrated to the United States when he was 14 after the death of his father by suicide.

Marcol was an accomplished soccer player, but he had no knowledge of American football. He was attending high school in Michigan when a gym teacher taught him the rudiments of placekicking. Marcol went to Division II Hillsdale College (located in the town of the same name in Michigan), where he kept improving, and Green Bay made him a second-round pick in the 1972 draft.

Jerry Tagge, Marcol's Packers roommate, joked that Marcol would have been a first-rounder, "but by the time [teams] found Hillsdale, the first round was over."

Marcol was an immediate sensation, winning National Football Conference Rookie of the Year honors and being chosen All-Pro as well after scoring 128 points. In 10 seasons in the NFL, Marcol scored 525 points.

Packers teammates called him the "Polish Messiah." Marcol said he never let misses bother him. "I always forget the ones I miss," Marcol said. "Once it's over, there's nothing you can do about it."

Kicking, Marcol said, is mostly mental. "Heck, everybody has the mechanics down," he said. "I guess it's a lot like putting. You run in hot streaks."

Later, Marcol suffered with a cocaine addiction, attempted to commit suicide, and incurred permanent damage to his esophagus. Marcol survived and wrote an autobiography in 2011.

AP Photo/NFL Photos

GREEN BAY PACKERS
1973 YEAR BOOK
$1.50

MVP Books Collection

As Green Bay slid toward the bottom of the NFC Central in 1979, Tampa Bay catapulted to the top. In the teams' first meeting, on September 16, the Buccaneers held Terdell Middleton, seen here receiving the ball from quarterback David Whitehurst, to 22 rushing yards. *Vernon Biever/Getty Images*

After all of the euphoria of 1978, the Packers took two giant steps backward in 1979, finishing 5–11. For the first time, criticism of coach Bart Starr ratcheted up. The defense sprouted Swiss-cheese-like holes, and longtime coach Dave Hanner was fired after 28 years as defensive coordinator.

Quarterback David Whitehurst was the starter again, but Lynn Dickey came back healthy and took over the last four games.

It turned out that the Terdell Middleton miracle of 1978 had an expiration date. After his 1,100-yard year, Middleton rushed for 495 yards. Eric Torkelson (401 yards) nearly matched him.

There was to be no title in Titletown this year, although the Packers beat the Minnesota Vikings for the first time in five years. Green Bay opened with a stultifying 6–3 loss to the Chicago Bears, and two four-game losing streaks mixed in destroyed hope for a good season.

On October 1, when the Packers topped the New England Patriots 27–14, it was the first time *Monday Night Football* broadcast from Green Bay. Previous Monday night games hosted by the Packers were shown from Milwaukee.

One area that showed great promise was the receiving corps. In his second year, James Lofton grabbed 54 passes for 968 yards. But he had a new partner running downfield in tight end Paul Coffman, who caught 56 passes. Lofton had some issues. He gave a middle-finger salute to fans at one point after being booed for a fumble, and that became a lightning rod for criticism.

Game-by-Game

9/2	L, 3–6, at Chicago Bears	
9/9	W, 28–19, vs. New Orleans Saints	
9/16	L, 10–21, vs. Tampa Bay Buccaneers	
9/23	L, 21–27 (OT), at Minnesota Vikings	
10/1	W, 27–14, vs. New England Patriots	
10/7	L, 7–25, at Atlanta Falcons	
10/14	W, 24–16, vs. Detroit Lions	
10/21	L, 3–21, at Tampa Bay Buccaneers	
10/28	L, 7–27, at Miami Dolphins	
11/4	L, 22–27, vs. New York Jets	
11/11	W, 19–7, vs. Minnesota Vikings	
11/18	L, 12–19, at Buffalo Bills	
11/25	L, 10–21, vs. Philadelphia Eagles	
12/2	L, 21–38, at Washington Redskins	
12/9	L, 14–15, vs. Chicago Bears	
12/15	W, 18–13, at Detroit Lions	

Team Scoring

246 points scored (25th)

316 points allowed (13th)

PACKERS HEADLINE

Swiss-cheese defense gives up more than 150 yards rushing in 14 of 16 games.

THE 1970s RECORD BOOK

Team Leaders

(**Boldface** indicates league leader)

Scoring Leaders (Points)

1970: Dale Livingston, 64
1971: Lou Michaels, 43
1972: Chester Marcol, **128**
1973: Chester Marcol, 82
1974: Chester Marcol, **94**
1975: Joe Danelo, 53
1976: Chester Marcol, 54
1977: Chester Marcol, 50
1978: Terdell Middleton, 72
1979: Tom Birney & Chester Marcol, 28

Rushing Leaders (Carries / Yards / TDs)

1970: Donny Anderson, 170 / 761 / 5
1971: John Brockington, 216 / 1,105 / 4
1972: John Brockington, 274 / 1,027 / 8
1973: John Brockington, 265 / 1,144 / 3
1974: John Brockington, 266 / 883 / 5
1975: John Brockington, 144 / 434 / 7
1976: Willard Harrell, 130 / 435 / 3
1977: Barty Smith, 166 / 554 / 2
1978: Terdell Middleton, 284 / 1,116 / 11
1979: Terdell Middleton, 131 / 495 / 2

Passing Leaders (Completions / Attempts / Yards)

1970: Bart Starr, 140 / 255 / 1,645
1971: Scott Hunter, 75 / 163 / 1,210
1972: Scott Hunter, 86 / 199 / 1,252
1973: Jerry Tagge, 56 / 106 / 720
1974: John Hadl, 89 / 184 / 1,072
1975: John Hadl, 191 / 353 / 2,095
1976: Lynn Dickey, 115 / 243 / 1,465
1977: Lynn Dickey, 113 / 220 / 1,346
1978: David Whitehurst, 168 / 328 / 2,093
1979: David Whitehurst, 179 / 322 / 2,247

Receiving Leaders (Receptions / Yards / TDs)

1970: Carroll Dale, 49 / 814 / 2
1971: Carroll Dale, 31 / 598 / 4
1972: MacArthur Lane, 26 / 285 / 0
1973: MacArthur Lane, 27 / 255 / 1
1974: John Brockington, 43 / 314 / 0
1975: Ken Payne, 58 / 766 / 0
1976: Ken Payne, 33 / 467 / 4
1977: Barty Smith, 37 / 340 / 1
1978: James Lofton, 46 / 818 / 6
1979: Paul Coffman, 56 / 711 / 4

Interceptions (Number / Yards / TDs)

1970: Willie Wood, 7 / 110 / 0
1971: Ken Ellis, 6 / 10 / 0
1972: Willie Buchanon, 4 / 62 / 0;
Ken Ellis, 4 / 106 / 1; Jim Hill, 4 / 37 / 0
1973: Jim Carter, 3 / 44 / 1; Ken Ellis, 3 / 53 / 1;
Jim Hill, 3 / 53 / 0
1974: Ted Hendricks, 5 / 74 / 0
1975: Perry Smith, 6 / 97 / 0
1976: Johnnie Gray, 4 / 101 / 1
1977: Steve Luke, 4 / 9 / 0; Mike McCoy, 4 / 2 / 0
1978: Willie Buchanon, 9 / 93 / 1
1979: Johnnie Gray, 5 / 66 / 0

WILLIE BUCHANON

PACKERS

CB

MVP Books Collection

First-Team All-Pros

1970: Gale Gillingham, G
1971: John Brockington, RB
1972: Ken Ellis, CB
1972: Chester Marcol, K
1974: Ted Hendricks, LB
1974: Chester Marcol, K
1978: Willie Buchanon, CB

Pro Bowl Selections

1970: Fred Carr, LB
1970: Carroll Dale, WR
1970: Gale Gillingham, G
1970: Willie Wood, S
1971: John Brockington, RB
1971: Gale Gillingham, G
1972: John Brockington, RB
1972: Bob Brown, DT
1972: Fred Carr, LB
1972: Chester Marcol, K
1973: John Brockington, RB
1973: Willie Buchanon, CB
1973: Jim Carter, LB
1973: Ken Ellis, CB
1973: Gale Gillingham, G
1974: Willie Buchanon, CB
1974: Ken Ellis, CB
1974: Gale Gillingham, G
1974: Ted Hendricks, LB
1974: Chester Marcol, K
1975: Fred Carr, LB
1975: Steve Odom, WR
1978: Willie Buchanon, CB
1978: Ezra Johnson, DE
1978: James Lofton, WR
1978: Terdell Middleton, RB

1st-Round Draft Picks

1970: Mike McCoy (2), DT, Notre Dame;
Rich McGeorge (16), TE, Elon
1971: John Brockington (9), RB,
Ohio State
1972: Willie Buchanon (7), CB,
San Diego State;
Jerry Tagge (11), QB, Nebraska
1973: Barry Smith (21), WR, Florida State
1974: Barty Smith (12), RB, Richmond
1975: No pick
1976: Mark Koncar (23), OT, Colorado
1977: Mike Butler (9), DE, Kansas;
Ezra Johnson (28), DE,
Morris Brown
1978: James Lofton (6), WR, Stanford;
John Anderson (26), LB, Michigan
1979: Eddie Lee Ivery (15), RB,
Georgia Tech

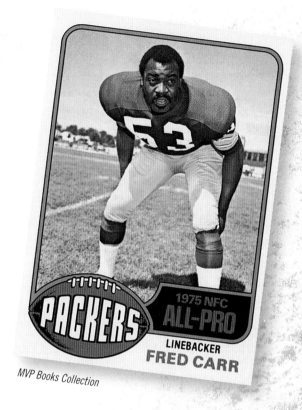

MVP Books Collection

MVP Books Collection

After three Pro Bowl selections in three seasons with San Diego, John Jefferson (83) joined James Lofton (80) in 1981 to form a dangerous wide-receiver tandem in Green Bay during the early 1980s. *Vernon Biever/Getty Images*

By 1980, it had probably sunk in for Packers fans that there was no going back to the 1960s. It was hard enough work to carve out a single winning season, never mind winning championships every other minute. Still at the helm, Bart Starr was trying to bring the Pack all the way back, but he stalled out about halfway there.

Starr presided over a string of .500 seasons, except for one not terribly satisfying winning campaign (5–3–1) in 1982 when the NFL lost games to labor unrest. Finally, the lack of progress caught up to Starr, and the team's leaders decided to dip into the history books once more for a successor.

All-Pro guard Forrest Gregg took over as coach in 1984. After a couple more 8–8 seasons were looked at as running in place, he supervised over two losing seasons. That was enough for the management team, and Gregg was ousted. This time, the club went outside the family in its search.

Lindy Infante, who had worked with the New York Giants, Cincinnati Bengals, and Cleveland Browns and was viewed as an offensive whiz, was hired to become the head man beginning with the 1988 season. Infante signed a five-year contract, and at his meet–Green Bay press conference, he predicted that winning would soon follow. Infante was the fifth Green Bay coach since Vince Lombardi, but he hurriedly distanced himself from Lombardi's accomplishments.

"I wouldn't begin to compare myself with those who have gone before me here," Infante said. "I don't consider myself any super-special human being. I'm just another guy who is going to try to get that job done. If hard work and dedication will get it done, we'll get it done."

The Packers promptly went out and didn't get it done in 1988 with a 4–12 record. It was another forgettable year, and to show how limited the fans' patience with Infante was, he was booed in an exhibition game. But in 1989, Infante produced a 10–6 team that offered the greatest degree of optimism for the future the Packers had experienced in years.

"He's not a screamer or a shouter," linebacker John Anderson said of Infante's coaching approach. "He pays a lot of attention to detail. If you screw up a play, you're going to run it again."

Starr and Gregg rode the arm of a healthy Lynn Dickey at quarterback to their 8–8 seasons, but that was the best they could all do. While frustration built among fans, who clamored for a new face behind center, the Packers got worse as soon as it happened.

Quarterback Randy Wright was a crowd pleaser, if only because he had played his college ball at Wisconsin. He replaced Dickey as the starting quarterback in 1986 and showed some style, throwing for 3,247 yards and 17 touchdowns, although he also tossed 23 interceptions. The Pack finished 4–12.

It was not until Don Majkowski, a.k.a. the "Majik Man," took over at quarterback and began airing it out that fans got some true excitement out of the position, though it didn't last long. Another exciting new player who came along near the end of the decade was wide receiver Sterling Sharpe.

Defense was an ongoing concern. Until linebacker Tim Harris was chosen in 1989, no Packers defensive player had been selected to the Pro Bowl since Willie Buchanon in 1978.

For the most part, the 1980s were another decade of minimal achievement for the Packers, with few playoff spots earned and no championships won.

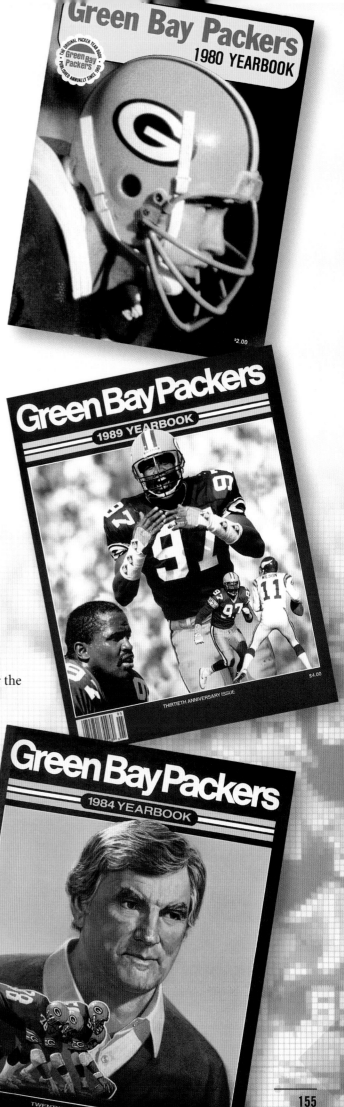

1980

Game-by-Game

09/07	**W**, 12–6 (OT), vs. Chicago Bears
09/14	**L**, 7–29, vs. Detroit Lions
09/21	**L**, 21–51, at Los Angeles Rams
09/28	**L**, 7–28, vs. Dallas Cowboys
10/05	**W**, 14–9, vs. Cincinnati Bengals
10/12	**T**, 14–14 (OT), at Tampa Bay Buccaneers
10/19	**L**, 21–26, at Cleveland Browns
10/26	**W**, 16–3, vs. Minnesota Vikings
11/02	**L**, 20–22, at Pittsburgh Steelers
11/09	**W**, 23–16, vs. San Francisco 49ers
11/16	**L**, 21–27, at New York Giants
11/23	**W**, 25–13, at Minnesota Vikings
11/30	**L**, 17–20, vs. Tampa Bay Buccaneers
12/07	**L**, 7–61, at Chicago Bears
12/14	**L**, 3–22, vs. Houston Oilers
12/21	**L**, 3–24, at Detroit Lions

Team Scoring

231 points scored (28th)

371 points allowed (22nd)

After making only three carries as a rookie in 1979, Eddie Lee Ivery emerged as a focal point of the Packers offense in 1980, attempting 202 rushes and gaining 831 yards while chipping in 50 pass receptions as well. *Ronald C. Modra/Sports Imagery/Getty Images*

Quarterback Lynn Dickey and receiver James Lofton help ratchet up passing game, but Packers still finish as lowest scoring team in the NFL.

With a month to go in the 1980 season, it appeared that the Packers had a winning record within reach. Then they lost their last four games in a row to finish 5–10–1. In the last three, the Packers couldn't score more than seven points.

The season began poorly when the Packers were snubbed by their first-round draft choice. Bruce Clark, a defensive end from Penn State picked fourth overall, signed with the Toronto Argonauts in the Canadian Football League.

Defense was a huge problem. The team allowed 371 points and suffered some losses by ego-devastating margins, such as 61–7 to the Chicago Bears and 51–21 to the Los Angeles Rams. This was possibly the weakest defense of the Bart Starr era, though there were a couple of solid efforts, too, such as a 12–6 win over the Bears early and a 16–3 victory over the Minnesota Vikings.

Quarterback Lynn Dickey was healthy enough to start every game, and he played well, completing 58.2 percent of his passes for 3,529 yards and 15 touchdowns. He was greatly aided by the talent of receiver James Lofton, who caught 71 balls.

Running back Eddie Lee Ivery, a No. 1 draft pick out of Georgia Tech in 1979, rushed for a team-high 831 yards. A college All-American, Ivery spent his entire eight-year NFL career with the Packers, but he would never again approach his single-season yardage total of 1980.

When the season ended, team management took away Starr's dual-role job as general manager.

Almost. That was the best that could be said of the 1981 season after the Packers started lousy, finished strong, and, at 8–8, missed reaching the playoffs by one game.

Eddie Lee Ivery, who had emerged as a top halfback the season before, was lost for the rest of the season following an injury in the opener. Quarterback Lynn Dickey did not stay completely healthy for two years in a row, and backup David Whitehurst started a couple of games.

Yet somehow, once they got rolling, the Packers produced a great second-half surge. It was as if someone flipped a switch to energize a moribund team, and that someone was kicker Jan Stenerud. After a long and successful career with the Kansas City Chiefs, Stenerud came to the Packers at age 38. In 1981, he scored 101 points while booting 22 out of 24 field goal attempts and 35 out of 36 extra points that season. On November 8, when Green Bay beat the New York Giants 26–24, Stenerud kicked four field goals and two extra points.

Going into the last game of the season in December, if the Packers could defeat the New York Jets in New York, they would finish 9–7 and make the playoffs. Only they got thumped, 28–3, by a Jets team that qualified for the playoffs as a result.

Veteran kicker Jan Stenerud brought added punch to a struggling team in 1981, making a career-best 92 percent of his field goal attempts and contributing 101 points. Although he spent only four seasons in Green Bay, he was inducted into the Packers Hall of Fame in 1991.
Focus on Sport/Getty Images

PACKERS HEADLINE

Hall of Fame kicker Jan Stenerud helps kick-start the Packers to six wins in final eight games.

1981

▸ **8–8   3rd place** ◂

Game-by-Game

9/6	W, 16–9, at Chicago Bears	
9/13	L, 17–31, vs. Atlanta Falcons	
9/20	L, 23–35, at Los Angeles Rams	
9/27	L, 13–30, vs. Minnesota Vikings	
10/4	W, 27–14, at New York Giants	
10/11	L, 10–21, vs. Tampa Bay Buccaneers	
10/18	L, 3–13, vs. San Francisco 49ers	
10/25	L, 27–31, at Detroit Lions	
11/1	W, 34–24, vs. Seattle Seahawks	
11/8	W, 26–24, vs. New York Giants	
11/15	W, 21–17, vs. Chicago Bears	
11/22	L, 3–37, at Tampa Bay Buccaneers	
11/29	W, 35–23, at Minnesota Vikings	
12/6	W, 31–17, vs. Detroit Lions	
12/13	W, 35–7, at New Orleans Saints	
12/20	L, 3–28, at New York Jets	

Team Scoring

324 points scored (14th)

361 points allowed (20th)

James Lofton

The Packers knew exactly what they were after and what they were getting when they made Stanford's James Lofton their No. 1 pick in the 1978 draft. He was a brilliantly gifted athlete who possessed super speed and had an NCAA long jump championship on his résumé for the Cardinal's track and field team.

Lofton stood 6-foot-3 and weighed 195 pounds. He could fly and he could jump, and as a rookie he caught 46 passes. That was just a warm-up act.

After being selected for the Pro Bowl in his debut season, he made six straight Pro Bowls from 1980 to 1985. He was named First-Team All-Pro in 1981, when he caught 71 passes for 1,294 yards—his second year in a row with 71 catches and more than 1,200 receiving yards. In 1983 and 1984, he averaged more than 22 yards per catch, both league highs.

Lofton was one of the best receivers in the NFL, and he added an entirely fresh dimension to the Packers' offense whenever they had a quarterback who could find him downfield. In the three and a half seasons in which Lofton teamed with John Jefferson, they made a deadly duo tearing up defensive backfields.

As popular as Lofton was with Packers fans, he occasionally tested their patience. He made the mistake of flipping the bird to fans when he was booed during a 1979 game, and he compounded that error with inflammatory comments afterward. The next season, he was more mature.

"It caused me to take a look at myself and who I am and what I'm trying to accomplish," Lofton said. "I realized that I had a bit of tunnel vision in that you get so locked up into yourself you don't look around and realize what's going on around you. The whole incident made me realize that I might be past the standpoint of having to accomplish things every week just to prove something. It helped me eliminate external frustrations, which has made me a better player."

Lofton said that even though he did well from the beginning of his career, it was a huge leap from college to the pros and a learning experience absorbing the speed of the game, even among linebackers who sometimes covered him. The better he played, the more he became a focus for opposing defenses.

"About 75 percent of the time, I see double coverage," Lofton said, "but that just makes me try harder. When you are doubled, you have to look for open areas and execute that much better."

Lofton played nine seasons in Green Bay and was selected to eight Pro Bowls in all. But his time in Wisconsin ended badly when he was accused of sexual assault. He denied the claim, was suspended for the last game of the 1986 season, was tried by a jury, and was found not guilty.

During his 16-season career, Lofton also played for the Buffalo Bills, Oakland Raiders, Philadelphia Eagles, and Los Angeles Rams. He retired in 1993 with 764 catches and 76 touchdowns, and he was elected to the Pro Football Hall of Fame.

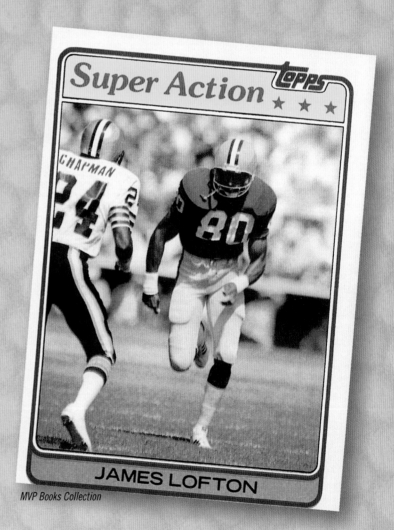

MVP Books Collection

This was a messy season in pro football, but it turned out to be the best it could have been for the Packers given the circumstances. Play began as scheduled, but with the Packers at 2–0 a strike was called, and it lasted 57 days. The Packers finished 5–3–1 in the abbreviated, nine-game season—and qualified for the playoffs for the first time since 1972.

Even better, Green Bay won its first-round playoff game, overwhelming the St. Louis Cardinals 41–16. Quarterback Lynn Dickey was superb, throwing for 260 yards and four touchdowns. Receiver John Jefferson caught two of them (six catches for 148 yards in all), and running back Eddie Lee Ivery scored two more touchdowns on the ground while gaining 67 yards.

"Our pass protection was excellent, and our passing attack was as good as we've had it," said coach Bart Starr.

That victory earned Green Bay a second playoff game, and while it did not turn out as well, the Packers put on a good show. After falling behind 20–7 at the half, they lost 37–26. Receiver James Lofton was the Packers' star in this one, catching five passes for 109 yards and one touchdown and also running 71 yards for another TD. Jan Stenerud kicked two field goals, and cornerback Mark Lee intercepted a pass and ran it back 22 yards for another score.

Off the field, longtime equipment manager Gerald "Dad" Braisher died at 81 before the season. Also, Dominic Olejniczak, team president since 1958, was replaced by Robert Parins.

1982

▶ 5-3-1   3rd place ◀

Game-by-Game

9/12	W, 35–23, vs. Los Angeles Rams
9/20	W, 27–19, at New York Giants
11/21	W, 26–7, vs. Minnesota Vikings
11/28	L, 13–15, at New York Jets
12/5	W, 33–21, vs. Buffalo Bills
12/12	L, 10–30, vs. Detroit Lions
12/19	T, 20–20 (OT), at Baltimore Colts
12/26	W, 38–7, at Atlanta Falcons
1/2/83	L, 24–27, at Detroit Lions

Playoffs

1/8/83	W, 41–16, vs. St. Louis Cardinals
1/16/83	L, 26–37, at Dallas Cowboys

Team Scoring

226 points scored (5th)

169 points allowed (11th)

PACKERS HEADLINE

Packers earn first playoff victory in 15 years during strike-shortened season.

In Green Bay's first postseason game in a decade, the Packers pounded the visiting St. Louis Cardinals, 41–16, in opening-round action. Lynn Dickey is seen here celebrating one of his four touchdown passes in the game. *AP Photo/Tom Lynn*

1983

▶ 8–8   2nd place ◀

Game-by-Game

9/4	**W**, 41–38 (OT), at Houston Oilers
9/11	**L**, 21–25, vs. Pittsburgh Steelers
9/18	**W**, 27–24, vs. Los Angeles Rams
9/26	**L**, 3–27, at New York Giants
10/2	**W**, 55–13, vs. Tampa Bay Buccaneers
10/9	**L**, 14–38, at Detroit Lions
10/17	**W**, 48–47, vs. Washington Redskins
10/23	**L**, 17–20 (OT), vs. Minnesota Vikings
10/30	**L**, 14–34, at Cincinnati Bengals
11/6	**W**, 35–21, vs. Cleveland Browns
11/13	**W**, 29–21, at Minnesota Vikings
11/20	**L**, 20–23 (OT), vs. Detroit Lions
11/27	**L**, 41–47 (OT), at Atlanta Falcons
12/4	**W**, 31–28, vs. Chicago Bears
12/12	**W**, 12–9 (OT), at Tampa Bay Buccaneers
12/18	**L**, 21–23, at Chicago Bears

Team Scoring

429 points scored (5th)

439 points allowed (26th)

During his breakout season in 1983, Lynn Dickey became the first Packers quarterback to throw for more than 4,000 yards in a season; his 4,458 total yards passing stood as a franchise record until Aaron Rodgers broke it in 2011. *Ronald C. Modra/Sports Imagery/Getty Images*

The half season of success in 1982 translated into only 8–8 in 1983. Offensively, the Packers could light it up with anyone, as quarterback Lynn Dickey had his finest year (4,458 yards). And veteran kicker Jan Stenerud had finest season for the Packers, scoring 115 points while making 52 of 52 extra-point attempts and 21 out of 26 field goal tries.

While Green Bay's offense scored 52 touchdowns and 429 points, the reason why the Packers were still a .500 team was that they also gave up 439 points.

At times, the Packers looked like the most exciting team in football, such as when they beat the Houston Oilers 41–38 in overtime in September on Stenerud's 42-yard field goal. In edging the Washington Redskins 48–47 in October, Dickey threw five touchdown passes and Stenerud nailed a field goal with 54 seconds remaining in a game that featured five lead changes in the last 15 minutes. There were other times the Packers looked like the most explosive team in football, such as in early October when they crushed the Tampa Bay Bucs 55–14.

The difference between finishing even and a winning season came down to the last game, appropriately enough against the Chicago Bears at Soldier Field. It was a freezing day on the shores of Lake Michigan, and the Bears prevailed 23–21 on a field goal by Bob Thomas with 10 seconds to go. The last-day defeat again cost the Packers a spot in the playoffs.

The nine-year coaching reign of Bart Starr ended the next day when he was fired, and five days later he was replaced by former Lombardi Era teammate Forrest Gregg.

PACKERS HEADLINE

Lynn Dickey goes deep with NFL-best 4,458 yards passing.

Paul Coffman

Paul Coffman became a three-time All-Pro at tight end, spending all but two of his NFL seasons with the Packers, but he was fortunate to even make it to the pros. Coffman, a 6-foot-3 225-pounder, went undrafted out of Kansas State in 1978.

Packers scouts had journeyed to Manhattan, Kansas, to work out the KSU quarterback and stumbled over Coffman. He did some running, but didn't impress enough to get drafted. However, later in training camp it became apparent that the Packers needed depth at tight end, and they ended up signing Coffman.

During his career, Coffman caught 339 passes for 4,340 yards and 42 touchdowns, and he regularly blocked bigger guys coming off the defensive line. He was neither exceptionally big nor fast, but he could play. Once placed in an environment in the middle of scrimmages and games, he showed his stuff.

"I think blue-collar workers can relate to me," Coffman said once. "I've had to work my way up the corporate ladder, so to speak."

Coffman was no rookie sensation, playing only on special teams, but during his second season, 1979, he solidified his reputation with 56 catches. Coffman realized that he landed with the right club. "Now I'm on a team that throws the ball a lot and uses the tight end in the passing game," he said.

Paul Coffman (82) with his partners-in-receiving, John Jefferson (83) and James Lofton (80), 1983. *Vernon Biever/Getty Images*

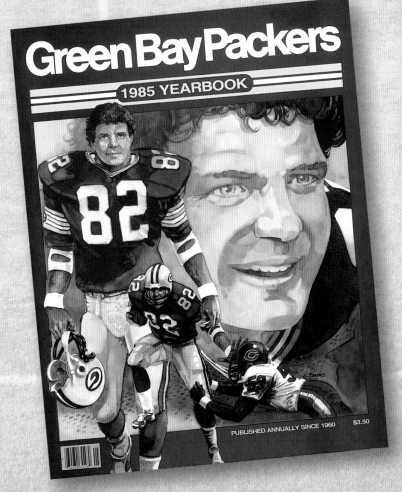

MVP Books Collection

1984

Game-by-Game

9/2	**W**, 24–23,	vs. St. Louis Cardinals
9/9	**L**, 7–28,	at Los Angeles Raiders
9/16	**L**, 7–9, vs. Chicago Bears	
9/23	**L**, 6–20, at Dallas Cowboys	
9/30	**L**, 27–30 (OT),	at Tampa Bay Buccaneers
10/7	**L**, 28–34,	vs. San Diego Chargers
10/15	**L**, 14–17,	at Denver Broncos
10/21	**L**, 24–30,	vs. Seattle Seahawks
10/28	**W**, 41–9, vs. Detroit Lions	
11/4	**W**, 23–13,	at New Orleans Saints
11/11	**W**, 45–17,	vs. Minnesota Vikings
11/18	**W**, 31–6,	vs. Los Angeles Rams
11/22	**L**, 28–31, at Detroit Lions	
12/2	**W**, 27–14,	vs. Tampa Bay Buccaneers
12/9	**W**, 20–14,	at Chicago Bears
12/16	**W**, 38–14,	at Minnesota Vikings

Team Scoring

390 points scored (7th)

309 points allowed (10th)

Green Bay's running attack (for lack of a better word) in 1984 featured Jessie Clark (33) and Gerry Ellis (31). Seen here blocking for Clark during a 28–7 loss to the Raiders, Ellis led the team with 123 rushes and 581 yards gained.
AP Photo/NFL Photos

Strong finish salvages .500 season in Forrest Gregg's coaching debut.

Those who felt Bart Starr should have been retained probably got very nervous when the Packers started the season 1–7 under new coach Forrest Gregg. Then they were happily stunned when the Packers went 7–1 down the stretch. At least it felt better going into the offseason.

Gregg won his first game 24–23 over the St. Louis Cardinals, and receiver James Lofton was the difference maker with seven catches for 134 yards. Quarterback Lynn Dickey said, "He has a way of coming up with the big plays."

Then the Packers spent the next seven weeks not coming up with the big plays, losing to the Chicago Bears 9–7, falling to Tampa Bay 30–27 in overtime, and losing three more games by six points or fewer.

Gregg became exasperated and started making personnel changes. The Packers, who started the year with Jan Stenerud as the kicker, replaced him with Eddie Garcia, and then dumped Garcia for Al Del Greco. Backup quarterback David Whitehurst was exiled in favor of rookie Randy Wright. Solid running back Eddie Lee Ivery was sidelined for six games due to injury.

At the end of October, the Packers pulverized the Detroit Lions 41–9 to begin the turnaround. The Packers ran up 439 yards, and Dickey threw four touchdown passes, two to Paul Coffman.

"Well, they just kicked our tails," said Detroit coach Monte Clark.

The only game Green Bay lost the rest of the season was a rematch to Detroit, 31–28, on national TV on Thanksgiving Day.

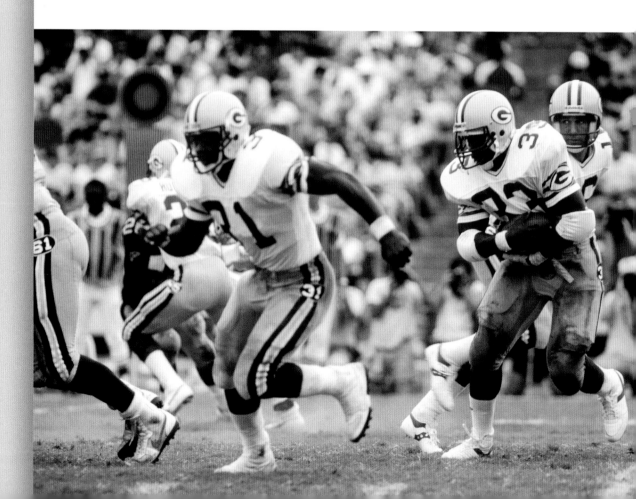

As with most of the NFL, the Packers were left in the dust by Walter Payton and the Chicago Bears in 1985, losing to the eventual Super Bowl champions twice in a three-week stretch. Payton ran for 192 yards in the 16–10 Bears victory at Lambeau Field on November 3. *Vernon Biever/Getty Images*

P roving that they could finish with exactly the same record by a completely different avenue, the Packers weren't as streaky in 1985 but ended up 8–8 again. Their longest winning streak was two in a row, but they finished .500 for the third campaign in a row.

While it seemed as though the Packers made it to 8–8 the hard way in 1984, there was nothing easier about 1985. Quarterback Lynn Dickey, on his way into retirement, was injured for part of the year. Longtime Seattle quarterback Jim Zorn was brought in to handle the reins and led the team to three wins in his five starts.

After trading away receiver John Jefferson, Green Bay relied more on the running game. Gerry Ellis averaged 5.5 yards per carry, though he was only the team's third-leading rusher in total yardage with 571. It was running back by committee. Eddie Lee Ivery rushed for 636 yards on 4.8 per carry, and Jessie Clark rushed for 633 yards on 4.3 per carry. The offensive line definitely opened holes.

In a season when 72 luxury boxes were added to Lambeau Field, there was one home game in which the fans could barely see the action, against Tampa Bay on December 1. A heavy snowfall pounded Green Bay the day before the game, and snow resumed, falling inch by inch steadily during the game. The weather was so bad that attendance was under 20,000 in the 57,000-seat building.

It wouldn't be Green Bay if there wasn't the occasional blizzard to contend with, and the Bucs had to cope with a blizzard of an offense, too, losing 21–0.

PACKERS HEADLINE

Running-backs-by-committee give Packers rejuvenated ground attack.

Game-by-Game

9/8	L, 20–26, at New England Patriots
9/15	W, 23–20, vs. New York Giants
9/22	L, 3–24, vs. New York Jets
9/29	L, 28–43, at St. Louis Cardinals
10/6	W, 43–10, vs. Detroit Lions
10/13	W, 20–17, vs. Minnesota Vikings
10/21	L, 7–23, at Chicago Bears
10/27	L, 10–37, at Indianapolis Colts
11/3	L, 10–16, vs. Chicago Bears
11/10	W, 17–27, at Minnesota Vikings
11/17	W, 38–14, vs. New Orleans Saints
11/24	L, 17–34, at Los Angeles Rams
12/1	W, 21–0, vs. Tampa Bay Buccaneers
12/8	L, 34–24, vs. Miami Dolphins
12/15	W, 26–23, at Detroit Lions
12/22	W, 20–17, at Tampa Bay Buccaneers

Team Scoring

337 points scored (16th)

355 points allowed (15th)

1986

▶ 4–12 4th place ◀

Game-by-Game

9/7 **L,** 3–31, vs. Houston Oilers

9/14 **L,** 10–24,
at New Orleans Saints

9/22 **L,** 12–25,
vs. Chicago Bears

9/28 **L,** 7–24,
at Minnesota Vikings

10/5 **L,** 28–34,
vs. Cincinnati Bengals

10/12 **L,** 14–21, vs. Detroit Lions

10/19 **W,** 17–14,
at Cleveland Browns

10/26 **L,** 17–31,
vs. San Francisco 49ers

11/2 **L,** 3–27,
at Pittsburgh Steelers

11/9 **L,** 7–16,
vs. Washington Redskins

11/16 **W,** 31–7,
vs. Tampa Bay Buccaneers

11/23 **L,** 10–12, at Chicago Bears

11/27 **W,** 44–40, at Detroit Lions

12/7 **L,** 6–32,
vs. Minnesota Vikings

12/14 **W,** 21–7,
at Tampa Bay Buccaneers

12/20 **L,** 24–55,
at New York Giants

Team Scoring

254 points scored (25th)

418 points allowed (27th)

Six-game losing streak to start the season— the longest in franchise history— leads to 12-loss campaign.

One thing became apparent in the years after Vince Lombardi walked away from the Green Bay Packers' sideline. No matter who the coach was that followed, nobody could build a defense that guarded the Packers' goal line the way he had.

Not Phil Bengston, who was a defensive specialist; not Hugh Devore or Ray McLean; not Gene Ronzani or Lisle Blackbourn; not Dan Devine, Bart Starr, or Forrest Gregg. Green Bay went 4–12 in 1986, and the defense allowed a horrendous 418 points. The 12 losses were the most to date in Packers history.

Seven times the D had 30 or more points hung on it, with the exclamation point being a last-game 55–24 loss to the New York Giants. Cornerback Mark Lee's nine interceptions was the defensive highlight of the year.

In an effort to bolster the defensive 11, Green Bay had selected Memphis linebacker Tim Harris in the fourth round of the 1986 draft. The 6-foot-6, 260-pounder contributed right away, leading the team with eight sacks. Harris would remain a standout on the Packers defense through 1990.

The season was a lost cause early. The Packers dropped their first six games, only once exceeding 14 points, and they eventually fell to 1–9. Gregg put his faith in Randy Wright at quarterback, hoping to make a local hero out of the former University of Wisconsin Badgers star. Given his inexperience, Wright did okay, throwing for 3,247 yards and 17 touchdowns, but he did toss 23 interceptions.

Gregg tried to turn over some aging talent, but the replacements he brought in didn't work out. Star receiver James Lofton was accused of sexual assault, and he was suspended by the team with one game remaining. Lofton was found not guilty, but he never played for the Packers again.

A fourth-round pick in 1986, linebacker Tim Harris was a standout on mediocre Green Bay defenses in the late 1980s. He led the squad with 8 sacks as a rookie and was the club sack leader in all four of his Packers seasons, including a franchise-record 19.5 in 1989.
Allen Steele/Allsport/Getty Images

Whether with regular players or replacement players, 1987 was a rough season for head coach Forrest Gregg (left). The 5–9–1 campaign was the final chapter in Gregg's coaching career, which concluded with a 25–37–1 overall record for the Packers. *Ronald C. Modra/Sports Imagery/Getty Images*

Game-by-Game

9/13	**L**, 0–20, vs. Los Angeles Raiders
9/20	**T**, 17–17 (OT), vs. Denver Broncos
10/4	**W**, 23–16, at Minnesota Vikings
10/11	**L**, 16–19 (OT), vs. Detroit Lions
10/18	**W**, 16–10 (OT), vs. Philadelphia Eagles
10/25	**W**, 34–33, at Detroit Lions
11/1	**L**, 17–23, vs. Tampa Bay Buccaneers
11/8	**L**, 24–26, vs. Chicago Bears
11/15	**L**, 13–24, at Seattle Seahawks
11/22	**W**, 23–3, at Kansas City Chiefs
11/29	**L**, 10–23, at Chicago Bears
12/6	**L**, 12–23, vs. San Francisco 49ers
12/13	**W**, 16–10, vs. Minnesota Vikings
12/19	**L**, 10–20, at New York Giants
12/27	**L**, 24–33, at New Orleans Saints

Team Scoring

255 points scored (26th)

300 points allowed (11th)

I n 1987, perhaps the most forgettable year in Packers history, Green Bay finished 5–9–1, but how that conclusion was reached was painful. Before the third week of the season, with the Packers' record at 0–1–1, the NFL went on strike. Only this time, unlike 1982, games were not canceled. Replacement players suited up for three weeks.

That year, because of the strike, the Packers had 21 different players make at least one rushing attempt and 19 different players catch at least one pass.

Alan Risher, out of Louisiana State, served as quarterback. Risher had played for the Arizona Wranglers in the short-lived United States Football League, and he had spent a year with the Tampa Bay Bucs. As Green Bay's QB, he went 2–1.

When the regular Packers were playing, Randy Wright, the starter the previous season, was on the job—until Don Majkowski began sneaking up on him and getting his share of snaps. Risher started three games and never played in the NFL again. Wright started seven games and Majkowski started five.

It was a lost year in many ways. Cornerback Mossy Cade was sent to prison for sexual assault. Defensive end Charles Martin got into a bar fight and was waived. The single-game highlight may have been the October 25, 34–33 victory over the Detroit Lions when Majkowski threw for 323 yards.

Forrest Gregg resigned in January, a few weeks after the season ended, to take the job as head coach at Southern Methodist University, his alma mater.

PACKERS HEADLINE

Replacement players go 2–1 during players' strike while regular Packers go 3–8–1.

1988

Game-by-Game

9/4	**L**, 7–34, vs. Los Angeles Rams
9/11	**L**, 10–13, vs. Tampa Bay Buccaneers
9/18	**L**, 17–24, at Miami Dolphins
9/25	**L**, 6–24, vs. Chicago Bears
10/2	**L**, 24–27, at Tampa Bay Buccaneers
10/9	**W**, 45–3, vs. New England Patriots
10/16	**W**, 34–14, at Minnesota Vikings
10/23	**L**, 17–20, vs. Washington Redskins
10/30	**L**, 0–28, at Buffalo Bills
11/6	**L**, 0–20, at Atlanta Falcons
11/13	**L**, 13–20, vs. Indianapolis Colts
11/20	**L**, 9–19, vs. Detroit Lions
11/27	**L**, 0–16, at Chicago Bears
12/4	**L**, 14–30, at Detroit Lions
12/11	**W**, 18–6, vs. Minnesota Vikings
12/18	**W**, 26–17, at Phoenix Cardinals

Team Scoring

240 points scored (26th)

315 points allowed (11th)

PACKERS HEADLINE

Lindy Infante becomes the 10th head coach in Packers history, leads them to 12 losses.

It was on to a new regime in 1988. Lindy Infante, a longtime college and NFL assistant known for his offensive creativity, was the new coach. But the record was the same old 4–12. The Packers lost Infante's first five games, won two, and then lost seven in a row. Nobody in Green Bay was singing, "Happy days are here again." They weren't even whispering it.

The end of the Randy Wright-at-quarterback experiment (as well as the end of Wright's NFL career) was punctuated by a four-touchdown, 13-interception half season, as well as injury. Don Majkowski emerged as the new No. 1 signal-caller. Majkowski did not set the town on fire, either, throwing for 2,119 yards. But his TD-to-interception performance (9 and 11, respectively) was a slight improvement.

When the Packers finally won a game in early October, they did it up right, crushing the New England Patriots 45–3. Fullback Brent Fullwood scored three touchdowns, and the defense had its best day of the year with five interceptions.

Fullwood was the leading rusher with 483 yards (the Packers did not gain very many). He was also the leading scorer with 48 points and the top kickoff return man, too. Fullwood had been the 1987 No. 1 pick out of Auburn, where he was overshadowed by Bo Jackson.

Somehow, the quarterbacking was mediocre enough to hold down Sterling Sharpe, the 1988 No. 1 pick out of South Carolina. As a rookie, Sharpe caught 55 passes, but only one for a touchdown.

When he signed on to replace Forrest Gregg as the Packers' head coach in 1988, Lindy Infante was given a five-year contract. He lasted only four seasons, leading the Pack to an uninspiring overall record of 24–40. *Jonathan Daniel/Getty Images*

Sterling Sharpe

From 1988 to 1994, Sterling Sharpe was the best Green Bay Packers receiver since Don Hutson invented many of the routes he ran in the 1930s, and he broke some of Hutson's records, too. A No. 1 draft pick out of South Carolina, Sharpe became a five-time Pro Bowl selection thanks to extraordinary moves and sure hands.

Even before Brett Favre arrived at quarterback, Sharpe excelled. But once they were paired, they were unstoppable. During a career abbreviated by injury when he was 29, Sharpe led the NFL three times in catches and twice in receiving yards.

He caught 595 passes for 8,134 yards and 65 touchdowns in seven seasons. In 1992, Sharpe, who stood 6-foot and weighed 205 pounds, led the league in passes caught, yards gained, and touchdown receptions. He was a star of the first magnitude.

Sharpe loved to play football so much that he was often seen smiling on the field, even if the Packers were losing or had a bad record.

"People see me smiling on television even though we're 0–6," Sharpe said, "and they don't understand it. The Packers coaches don't, either. They think my attitude is too nonchalant, that I'm not intense enough and don't take it seriously. I don't go out there with a game face. They try to get me to look on it as a business, to grit my teeth and be grim. That's going to be awfully hard for me to do because I'm having so much fun."

Sharpe started having fun very early in his NFL career. He caught 56 passes as a rookie and 90 as a second-year man. Going into the 1992 season, Sharpe was considered so valuable to the Packers that he signed a 10-year, $15.5 million contract with the club. Then, that year, Favre's first season in Green Bay, Sharpe set an NFL record with 108 receptions. The next year, he caught 112 passes.

"As long as we win, if I catch 40, I'm happy," Sharpe said, never making a big deal about his records.

In two games near the end of the 1994 season, Sharpe complained to team doctors after taking big hits that something felt wrong with his neck. Close and continual examination showed that Sharpe had a problem with damaged vertebrae. He was immediately grounded for the last game of the regular season, and then he was informed he had to retire or face the risk of paralysis.

The unfortunate injury drove Sharpe from the sport, although he made a smooth transition into broadcasting and still works for the NFL Network and sometimes ESPN after spending years with that organization. His younger brother, Shannon Sharpe, also became an excellent NFL receiver. Shannon played for 14 seasons and was part of three Super Bowl title teams.

He gave one of his Super Bowl rings to his brother because Sterling missed out when the Packers later won their crown in 1997.

STERLING SHARPE
WR • Packers

PRO SET • THE OFFICIAL NFL CARD

MVP Books Collection

Vernon Biever/Getty Images

Don Majkowski

His flame burned bright, but it didn't burn long. Don Majkowski became the Packers' first-string quarterback and stunned the team and the league with a fantastic 1989 season. He completed 58.9 percent of his passes for 4,318 yards and 27 touchdowns.

As the Packers repeatedly won close games on their way to 10 victories that year, it was natural for Majkowski, the purveyor of late-game heroics, to be tabbed the "Majik Man." Majkowski had been in the league in 1987 and 1988, but he hadn't gained much attention.

"I hadn't really done anything up until this year," Majkowski said. "You're going to get overlooked if there's nothing to look at."

Once the season started, fans couldn't take their eyes off of him.

"I'm a much better player this year," Majkowski said. "I'm proud of the fact that I'm doing a lot better because I worked so hard to get here."

For Green Bay, that was the understatement of the year.

Majkowski was born in Buffalo, attended the University of Virginia, and wasn't drafted until the tenth round by the Packers in 1987. He was the 255th player selected, so the odds against him surviving training camp weren't all that good. That was his first achievement. Then he got some playing time—also a surprise. By 1988 he was the part-time starter, and in 1989 he led the NFL in passes completed (355), passes attempted (599), and yards gained.

By that season, some people were comparing Majkowski to the Chicago Bears' Super Bowl–winning quarterback Jim McMahon, but McMahon never had such a prolific throwing year. The leadership qualities were singled out, but when presented with the argument, Majkowski said not so fast.

"It's strictly coincidence," he said. "I'm not trying to be like anybody else."

Majkowski's rise from barely known in Wisconsin to being touted all around the league was a swift one. He made All-Pro in 1989. And before the next season's training camp began, his exalted status was evident. He was already requested for visits by seriously ill children through the Make-A-Wish Foundation.

After one super season, following his limited playing time, Majkowski was barely known to his constituency as a person. He played the role of "Majik Man" on game day almost as if he was slipping into a superhero pair of tights instead of a No. 7 jersey, but the rest of the time he was a private man and somewhat quiet. He put on his shoulder pads and his game face at the same time.

"I look across the field and at our opponent and I feel the adrenaline pumping," Majkowski said.

Unfortunately for Majkowski and the Packers, his ride atop the wave of all-star success and popularity was short-lived. In the tenth game of the 1990 season, Majkowski was dumped by a defender and suffered a torn rotator cuff in his throwing shoulder. He underwent surgery, and although he returned to the Packers through 1992 and played a few years with other teams, he was never the same.

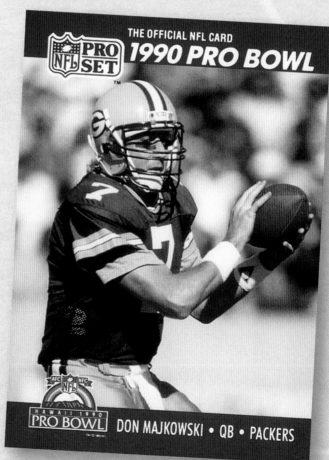

MVP Books Collection

Quarterback Dan Majkowski emerged as a leader in the Packers huddle and a Pro Bowl–caliber quarterback in the NFL in 1989. Unfortunately for Packers fans and the "Majik Man," the success didn't last. *George Rose/Getty Images*

All at once, coach Lindy Infante's alleged offensive credentials began to look quite real. Out of nowhere, the Packers went 10–6. Out of nowhere, quarterback Don Majkowski became the second coming of Johnny Unitas. Receiver Sterling Sharpe became a superstar.

This season, Majkowski became known as the "Majik Man." Starting every game, he threw for 4,315 yards and 27 touchdowns. It was the best Packers quarterback season since Lynn Dickey's in 1983 and one of the best ever in terms of big numbers.

The 6-foot, 205-pound Sharpe played huge, gathering in 90 passes for 1,423 yards and 12 touchdowns to make his first All-Pro team.

On the other side of the ball, the 18th-ranked defense had little to offer beyond All-Pro linebacker Tim Harris. Absolutely terrorizing opposing quarterbacks, Harris recorded 19.5 sacks—a franchise record that stands to this day.

For all the thrills the Packers generated on offense, they barely eked out victories. Known as the "Cardiac Pack," Green Bay won four games by one point, and they won seven games by fewer than five points. Nobody walked out on a Packers game that season, especially not the midseason home game against the Chicago Bears.

With a fourth down on the Bears' 14-yard line and 32 seconds left in the fourth quarter, Majkowski took the snap, rolled right, and completed a pass to Sharpe in the end zone. An official declared that Majkowski had his foot just over the line of scrimmage, nullifying the play. But officials' review of instant replay showed that the call was wrong. The touchdown stood, and the Packers won 14–13.

In subsequent years, the Bears' media guide referred to the loss as the "Instant Replay Game," as if they refused to acknowledge it.

For their surprising 10–6 final record— the Packers' best since 1972—Infante was chosen the NFL Coach of the Year. Three years later, he was fired as Green Bay's head coach.

PACKERS HEADLINE

The "Majik Man" emerges as a star at QB, while linebacker Tim Harris sets franchise record with 19.5 sacks.

Game-by-Game

9/10	L, 21–23, vs. Tampa Bay Buccaneers
9/17	W, 35–34, vs. New Orleans Saints
9/24	L, 38–41, at Los Angeles Rams
10/1	W, 23–21, vs. Atlanta Falcons
10/8	W, 31–13, vs. Dallas Cowboys
10/15	L, 14–26, at Minnesota Vikings
10/22	L, 20–23, at Miami Dolphins
10/29	W, 23–20 (OT), vs. Detroit Lions
11/5	W, 14–13, vs. Chicago Bears
11/12	L, 22–31, at Detroit Lions
11/19	W, 21–17, at San Francisco 49ers
11/26	W, 20–19, vs. Minnesota Vikings
12/3	W, 17–16, at Tampa Bay Buccaneers
12/10	L, 3–21, vs. Kansas City Chiefs
12/17	W, 40–28, at Chicago Bears
12/24	W, 20–10, at Dallas Cowboys

Team Scoring

362 points scored (8th)

356 points allowed (18th)

THE 1980s RECORD BOOK

Team Leaders

(**Boldface** indicates league leader)

Scoring Leaders (Points)
1980: Gerry Ellis, 48
1981: Jan Stenerud, 101
1982: Jan Stenerud, 64
1983: Jan Stenerud, 115
1984: Al Del Greco, 61
1985: Al Del Greco, 95
1986: Al Del Greco, 80
1987: Max Zendejas, 61
1988: Brent Fullwood, 48
1989: Chris Jacke, 108

Rushing Leaders (Carries / Yards / TDs)
1980: Eddie Lee Ivery, 202 / 831 / 3
1981: Gerry Ellis, 196 / 860 / 4
1982: Eddie Lee Ivery, 127 / 453 / 9
1983: Gerry Ellis, 141 / 696 / 4
1984: Gerry Ellis, 123 / 581 / 4
1985: Eddie Lee Ivery, 132 / 636 / 2
1986: Kenneth Davis, 114 / 519 / 0
1987: Kenneth Davis, 109 / 413 / 3
1988: Brent Fullwood, 101 / 483 / 7
1989: Brent Fullwood, 204 / 821 / 5

Passing Leaders (Completions / Attempts / Yards)
1980: Lynn Dickey, 278 / 478 / 3,529
1981: Lynn Dickey, 204 / 354 / 2,593
1982: Lynn Dickey, 124 / 218 / 1,790
1983: Lynn Dickey, 289 / 484 / **4,458**
1984: Lynn Dickey, 237 / 401 / 3,195
1985: Lynn Dickey, 172 / 314 / 2,206
1986: Randy Wright, 263 / 492 / 3,247
1987: Randy Wright, 132 / 247 / 1,507
1988: Don Majkowski, 178 / 336 / 2,119
1989: Don Majkowski, **353 / 599** / 4,318

Receiving Leaders (Receptions / Yards / TDs)
1980: James Lofton, 71 / 1,226 / 4
1981: James Lofton, 71 / 1,294 / 8
1982: James Lofton, 35 / 696 / 4
1983: James Lofton, 58 / 1,300 / 8
1984: James Lofton, 62 / 1,361 / 7
1985: James Lofton, 69 / 1,153 / 4
1986: James Lofton, 64 / 840 / 4
1987: Walter Stanley, 38 / 672 / 3
1988: Sterling Sharpe, 55 / 791 / 1
1989: Sterling Sharpe, **90** / 1,423 / 12

Interceptions (Number / Yards / TDs)
1980: Johnny Gray, 5 / 54 / 0
1981: Maurice Harvey, 6 / 217 / 0;
  Mark Lee, 6 / 50 / 0
1982: John Anderson, 3 / 22 / 0
1983: John Anderson, 5 / 54 / 1;
  Tim Lewis, 5 / 111 / 0
1984: Tom Flynn, 9 / 106 / 0
1985: Tim Lewis, 4 / 4 / 0
1986: Mark Lee, 9 / 33 / 0
1987: Dave Brown, 3 / 16 / 0
  Jim Bob Morris, 3 / 135 / 0
1988: Mark Murphy, 5 / 19 / 0
1989: Dave Brown, 6 / 12 / 0

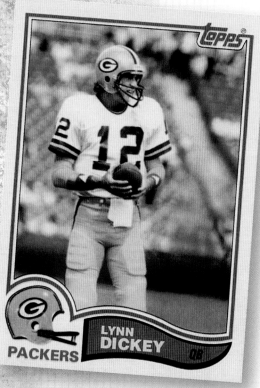

MVP Books Collection

First-Team All-Pros

1981: James Lofton, WR
1989: Tim Harris, LB
1989: Sterling Sharpe, WR

Pro Bowl Selections

1980: James Lofton, WR
1981: James Lofton, WR
1982: Paul Coffman, TE
1982: John Jefferson, WR
1982: James Lofton, WR
1982: Larry McCarren, C
1983: Paul Coffman, TE
1983: James Lofton, WR
1983: Larry McCarren, C
1984: Paul Coffman, TE
1984: James Lofton, WR
1985: James Lofton, WR
1989: Brent Fullwood, RB
1989: Tim Harris, LB
1989: Don Majkowski, QB
1989: Sterling Sharpe, WR

1st-Round Draft Picks

1980: Bruce Clark (4), DT, Penn State;
George Cumby (26), LB, Oklahoma
1981: Rich Campbell (6), QB, California
1982: Ron Hallstrom (22), G, Iowa
1983: Tim Lewis (11), CB, Pittsburgh
1984: Alphonso Carreker (12), DE,
Florida State
1985: Ken Ruettgers (7), OT,
Southern California
1986: No pick
1987: Brent Fullwood (4), RB, Auburn
1988: Sterling Sharpe (7), WR,
South Carolina
1989: Tony Mandarich (2), OT,
Michigan State

Green Bay Packer Hall of Fame

MVP Books Collection

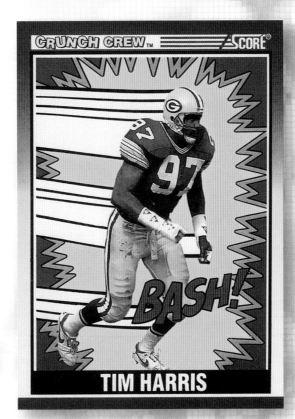

MVP Books Collection

THE 1990s

The decade began with Lindy Infante as head coach and ended with Ray Rhodes as head coach, and 1990 and 1999 were two of the three losing seasons of the decade. In between, it was the best Packers decade since the 1960s, and that was due to coach Mike Holmgren.

From 1992 to 1998, Holmgren led the Packers to winning records every season except one, and that was a .500 campaign. At the end of the 13–3 campaign of 1996, the Packers won the Super Bowl. It was the first franchise championship in 30 years. Another 13–3 season followed, and the Packers earned their way back to the Super Bowl, though they lost that one.

By then, a guy named Brett Favre was entrenched at quarterback. A daredevil gunslinger of a leader, Favre routinely set team passing records and chased the NFL passing marks. He was brash and colorful and could throw the ball most of the 100 yards of the field.

Holmgren made his mark as offensive coordinator with the San Francisco 49ers before being hired to run the operation in Green Bay. He was somewhat round-faced and sported a thick mustache, a combination that led to his nickname of "The Walrus."

The Super Bowl success did not come overnight, although some measurement of success did. Holmgren's tenure began with three straight 9–7 seasons, the latter two of them involving trips to the playoffs. Under Holmgren, the Pack went to the playoffs six straight years.

Favre, who came out of Southern Mississippi, was acquired in a trade with the Atlanta Falcons after sitting on the bench as a rookie. Favre's success spelled the end of Don Majkowski at quarterback even after the previous incumbent was healthy again. Favre and receiver Sterling Sharpe clicked to make beautiful music together. And then Green Bay added some additional worthy receivers in Robert Brooks and Antonio Freeman.

For the first several years under Holmgren, the Packers basically outscored people. The defense was still a bit rocky. But everything came together smoothly in 1996, when the point differential between the offense (456) and defense (210) was jaw-dropping.

Green Bay fans witnessed a new generation of stars, from high-scoring kicker Ryan Longwell to fullback Edgar Bennett to running back Dorsey Levens to defensive back LeRoy Butler and defensive end Reggie White.

General manager Ron Wolf began to turn the franchise around as soon as he got to Green Bay prior to the 1992 season, including hiring Holmgren as coach. *MVP Books Collection*

With a new head coach in Mike Holmgren and a new quarterback in Brett Favre, the Packers entered a new era in the 1990s. The decade saw six straight postseason appearances, two trips to the Super Bowl, and one NFL title. *Jonathan Daniel/Allsport/Getty Images*

As a career pro football man, Wolf found it easy to talk up the Packers' history and tradition.

"I think it's the best place in the National Football League to play football," Wolf said. "You have first-rate facilities. Anything a player needs is given to him within limits."

Wolf remained at the helm for a decade, departing after the 2000 season, during which time he pushed the team into an era of prosperity it hadn't experienced since the glory days of Vince Lombardi. Wolf presided over six playoff teams and one world champion.

The Packers continued to add to their trophy case during the 1990s. *MVP Books Collection*

While Holmgren presided over the on-field happenings, new general manager Ron Wolf, who was handed the job in late 1991, was the man who assembled the talent. "I was brought here to win," Wolf said early in his tenure, and he provided the tools to do so.

Almost immediately, Wolf made major decisions. He was responsible for firing Infante and hiring Holmgren. He traded for Favre. The Packers recorded back-to-back winning seasons for the first time in more than 25 years. Wolf had previously worked in personnel for the Oakland Raiders, Tampa Bay Bucs, and New York Jets, but he called the Packers GM position "the ultimate job."

Wolf quickly became known for his dedication to the job around the Packers' offices. "Ron Wolf spends every minute of every waking hour thinking about what he can do to make this football team better," said team president Bob Harlan.

1990

▸ 6–10   4th place ◂

Game-by-Game

9/9	**W, 36–24,** vs. Los Angeles Rams
9/16	**L, 13–31,** vs. Chicago Bears
9/23	**L, 3–17,** vs. Kansas City Chiefs
9/30	**W, 24–21,** at Detroit Lions
10/7	**L, 13–27,** at Chicago Bears
10/14	**L, 14–26,** at Tampa Bay Buccaneers
10/28	**W, 24–10,** vs. Minnesota Vikings
11/4	**L, 20–24,** vs. San Francisco 49ers
11/11	**W, 29–16,** at Los Angeles Raiders
11/18	**W, 24–21,** at Phoenix Cardinals
11/25	**W, 20–10,** vs. Tampa Bay Buccaneers
12/2	**L, 7–23,** at Minnesota Vikings
12/9	**L, 14–20,** vs. Seattle Seahawks
12/16	**L, 0–31,** at Philadelphia Eagles
12/22	**L, 17–24,** vs. Detroit Lions
12/30	**L, 13–22,** at Denver Broncos

Team Scoring

271 points scored (23rd)

347 points allowed (18th)

PACKERS HEADLINE

Injuries and a porous offensive line set back Packers offense.

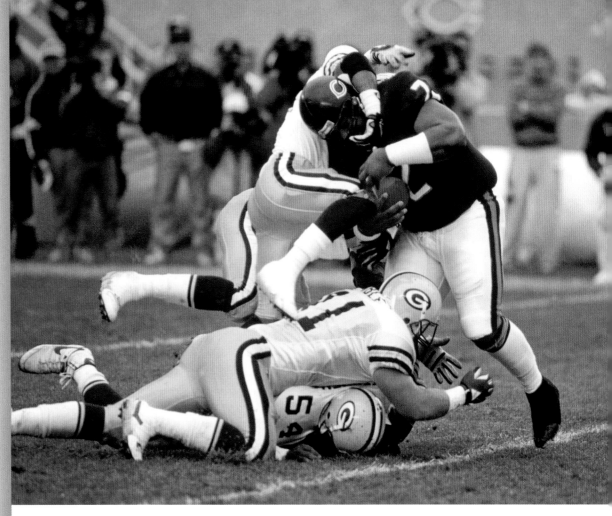

It took four Packers defenders to bring down Chicago's William "The Refrigerator" Perry during a 27–13 loss to the Bears. The defense didn't have much better luck stopping smaller-sized opponents in 1990. *Jonathan Daniel/Getty Images*

The happy face that Lindy Infante drew on the town in 1989 with a 10–6 record vanished quickly in 1990, along with his job of head coach soon after. Infante used up his year of goodwill earned, as the Packers finished 6–10.

So brilliant the year before, quarterback Don Majkowski was doing fine in 1990 until he got hurt in the tenth game, ending his season. Fill-in Anthony Dilweg took control in one of the more unexpected story lines of the season. Dilweg, from Duke, was the grandson of Packers great Lavvie Dilweg, who had played for the team in the 1920s and 1930s.

Anthony Dilweg completed 101 of 192 passes for 1,267 yards and eight touchdowns after moving up on the depth chart. It was the only season in which Dilweg saw substantial action in an NFL career that lasted less than three years. Anthony was born in 1965 and his grandfather died in 1968, so Lavvie never saw him play.

Green Bay didn't have much of an offense. The team's leading rusher was Michael Haddix with just 311 yards. The Packers were hoping that No. 1 draft pick Darrell Thompson out of Minnesota would be their marquee runner, but he rushed for just 264 yards and one touchdown and never made it big in Green Bay. The offensive line, which surrendered a league-leading 62 sacks in 1990, surely didn't help the ground attack.

Among the bright spots were receiver Sterling Sharpe, who made 67 catches for 1,105 yards, and kicker Chris Jacke, who scored 97 points.

A season-ending five-game losing streak left the Packers reeling.

The second losing season in a row under Lindy Infante after the miracle season of 1989 meant the end of the line for the coach. After starting 1–6, Infante was probably lucky he lasted the whole season. The Packers finished 4–12, and soon they had a new coach in Mike Holmgren.

It didn't help that quarterback Don Majkowski was in the repair shop for part of the season with a hamstring injury. Mike Tomczak started much of the year in his only season in Green Bay. It was a little like rent-a-QB. Tomczak played okay, completing 53.8 percent of his passes while recording 11 touchdowns and nine interceptions.

The best thing the Packers had going for them, no matter who was throwing, was receiver Sterling Sharpe, who caught 69 passes. The second-leading receiver was Vince Workman with 42 catches. Up until then, the 5-foot-10, 215-pounder was a backfield benchwarmer. Overall, Green Bay's offense was anemic, ranking No. 22 in the league, and the ground game was extremely weak.

Forget about a single back rushing for 100 yards in a single game; the *team* couldn't break the 100-yard mark on the ground for the first 11 games. Only Darrell Thompson, with 93 yards, rushed for more than 76 in a game.

The Packers had to be glad they had the 3–13 Tampa Bay Bucs in the Central Division with them, because they accounted for two of the Packers' wins.

PACKERS HEADLINE

Third season of double-digit losses in four years spells end for Lindy Infante.

1991

▸ 4–12   4th place ◂

Game-by-Game

9/1	L, 3–20, vs. Philadelphia Eagles	
9/8	L, 14–23, at Detroit Lions	
9/15	W, 15–13, vs. Tampa Bay Buccaneers	
9/22	L, 13–16, at Miami Dolphins	
9/29	L, 21–23, at Los Angeles Rams	
10/6	L, 17–20, vs. Dallas Cowboys	
10/17	L, 0–10, vs. Chicago Bears	
10/27	W, 27–0, at Tampa Bay Buccaneers	
11/3	L, 16–19 (OT), at New York Jets	
11/10	L, 24–34, vs. Buffalo Bills	
11/17	L, 21–35, vs. Minnesota Vikings	
11/24	W, 14–10, vs. Indianapolis Colts	
12/1	L, 31–35, at Atlanta Falcons	
12/8	L, 13–27, at Chicago Bears	
12/15	L, 17–21, vs. Detroit Lions	
12/21	W, 27–7, at Minnesota Vikings	

Team Scoring

273 points scored (22nd)

313 points allowed (18th)

Green Bay fans at both Lambeau Field and Milwaukee County Stadium (shown here) had little reason to cheer in 1991, as the Packers won only two home games all season. On October 6, they fell just short in a 20–17 loss to the Cowboys. *Rick Stewart/ Getty Images*

Mike Holmgren

The Packers had been running through coaches the way a speed dater disposes of possible matches when they finally hired Mike Holmgren as head coach in 1992. Holmgren promptly led Green Bay to six consecutive playoff berths, one Super Bowl championship, and another Super Bowl appearance.

Holmgren had been the promising head coach in waiting after putting in distinguished service as an assistant coach. If he hadn't hungered for more power and a concurrent general manager slot when he left for the Seattle Seahawks in 1998, he might still be the Packers' coach.

After leading Green Bay to its first back-to-back winning seasons since Vince Lombardi, Holmgren was given a three-year contract extension by general manager Ron Wolf. "That is what the game is all about," Wolf said of winning. "His record more or less speaks for itself."

Going 75–37, Holmgren won 67 percent of his regular-season games and was a good match with the Packers, who had seasons in which they twice won 13 games on his watch and won 11 in another year.

The Packers won their first Super Bowl in 29 years in January 1997, a victory that represented the twelfth NFL championship in franchise history. The glow from that win spread far and lingered long, and even at the start of the next season Holmgren was conscious of working to put it aside.

"I worked them very hard to keep the hammer on them because I know there is a natural tendency, it's human nature, to relax a little bit after something like that," Holmgren said.

Holmgren's veterans, who seemed to understand the pitfalls of complacency, also dug in. They wanted a repeat.

"Fortunately, my team leaders want it as bad as I want it again," Holmgren said. "They convey that to the younger players, and that makes the coaches' job a lot easier. I equate it to a college having a great group of seniors that bring a team along."

The Packers put themselves in position to win the Super Bowl again, but they lost at game's end to the Denver Broncos.

In interviews by then, Holmgren was telegraphing his desire to someday become a coach-general manager somewhere. And that was even after Green Bay named a street for him. He asked team higher-ups for permission to explore such jobs if they opened.

"I've learned a tremendous amount about personnel and the mechanics of it," Holmgren said. "I think I've always been a fair evaluator of talent, but I have really learned from Ron [Wolf] a lot of things about just the structure of doing it correctly. But my first love is still coaching."

Eventually, after the 1998 season, Holmgren did get an offer to fulfill his dream. He left for Seattle to coach and manage the Seahawks, but he never approached the success he had in Green Bay. Later, he moved on to the Cleveland Browns as team president, and that franchise did not respond to his touch, either. Holmgren left Cleveland after the 2012 season.

Peter Brouillet/Getty Images

The Packers' turnaround was fast under Mike Holmgren. The team won five more games than it had in 1991, going 9–7, and won six of the last seven contests. The passing-attack turnaround was just as stunning, as the controls were turned over to a strong-armed newcomer named Brett Favre.

Favre had spent his rookie year on the bench with the Atlanta Falcons, for whom he threw just four passes and completed none. The first pass of his pro career was an interception run back for a touchdown. One of the other passes was an interception, and Favre was also sacked. Although Atlanta gave Favre a $1.4 million, multiyear contract after making him a second-round pick, coach Jerry Glanville didn't like him. In an infamous statement, he said it would "take a plane crash" for Favre to start.

The Packers liked Favre better, and they traded a first-round pick for him. Poor Don Majkowski got hurt again, and Favre stepped in as quarterback. It was somewhat like the New York Yankees' Wally Pipp sitting out in favor of Lou Gehrig. Favre became the NFL iron man, starting every game for the Packers through 2007.

In 15 games, Favre completed 64.1 percent of his passes for 18 touchdowns. His infectious personality and never-give-up attitude helped transform the team. Even though Favre and Sterling Sharpe spent less than a full season working together, Sharpe caught 108 passes for 1,461 yards and 13 touchdowns. It was apparent that the passing game was now going to be a Green Bay strength.

Taking over as a sub during a 31–3 defeat to Tampa Bay, Brett Favre made his Packers regular-season debut on September 13, 1992. A week later, he came in for an injured Don Majkowski—and didn't relinquish his place under center in Green Bay for 15 years. *Allen Kee/Getty Images*

PACKERS HEADLINE

Brett Favre and Mike Holmgren usher in new era in Green Bay.

Game-by-Game

9/6	L, 20 –23 (OT), vs. Minnesota Vikings
9/13	L, 3–31, at Tampa Bay Buccaneers
9/20	W, 24–23, vs. Cincinnati Bengals
9/27	W, 17–3, vs. Pittsburgh Steelers
10/4	L, 10–24, at Atlanta Falcons
10/18	L, 6–17, at Cleveland Browns
10/25	L, 10–30, vs. Chicago Bears
11/1	W, 27–13, at Detroit Lions
11/8	L, 7–27, at New York Giants
11/15	W, 27–24, vs. Philadelphia Eagles
11/22	W, 17–3, at Chicago Bears
11/29	W, 19–14, vs. Tampa Bay Buccaneers
12/6	W, 38–10, vs. Detroit Lions
12/13	W, 16–14, at Houston Oilers
12/20	W, 28–13, vs. Los Angeles Rams
12/27	L, 7–27, at Minnesota Vikings

Team Scoring

276 points scored (17th)

296 points allowed (15th)

Brett Favre

The quarterback who showed up in 1992 after wasting a year on the Atlanta Falcons' bench soon became a virtual god in Green Bay. Brett Favre was good right away and exceeded expectations almost immediately on his way to setting a slew of Packers and NFL records and being acclaimed as one of the greatest quarterbacks of all time.

A native of Mississippi and a permanent resident of that state, Favre starred at Southern Mississippi. He had a powerful arm and the guts of a gambler, and he could lead a football team with his athleticism and attitude. Except for his uncomfortable parting from Green Bay when it was deemed that his age was interfering with the progress of the team, Favre could do little wrong in the city for 16 years.

Even after his first season, Favre's personality was obvious to the masses. Steve Mariucci, then a Green Bay assistant coach, said, "I don't think for him there will be any of that Hollywood stuff, the glamour, the lights and the glitter. He's a country kid for life, and he likes to be that way." Mariucci was right.

Favre helped make the Packers a winner, and he kept them winning throughout his stay in Wisconsin. At 6-foot-2 and 225 pounds, he was tough for defenders to bring down. He hardly ever got injured, and he always played when he was hurt, setting an NFL record with 297 consecutive starts at quarterback. He even played days after his father died, performing brilliantly.

"I knew my dad would have wanted me to play," Favre said of the victory, in which he threw for 399 yards and four touchdown passes.

Favre's talent was apparent to coach Mike Holmgren, but he knew the young Favre liked to party as well. Holmgren rode Favre hard enough to squeeze out his potential.

"He jumps on me harder than anyone else," Favre said. "He wants me to be as good as them [Joe Montana and Steve Young, whom Holmgren worked with in San Francisco]. It all starts with the quarterback. I just happen to be the one who catches the most abuse."

Jonathan Daniel/Getty Images

Favre was a smiling presence on the Packers bench for 16 seasons.
Jonathan Daniel/Getty Images

With Favre at the helm, the Packers won eight division titles, captured one Super Bowl, and played in another. In a career that wrapped up with the Minnesota Vikings after a stopover with the New York Jets, Favre's on-again, off-again angst about retirement became a national soap opera.

When he finally did pack up his cleats for good, Favre was an 11-time Pro Bowl selection who had set NFL records with 6,300 completions, 508 touchdown passes, 71,838 yards, and 186 wins. He won the league's MVP Award three times in a row. And although he made more money as he went along, Favre became the first NFL player to be paid $6 million for a season.

Right after he earned his second Most Valuable Player Award, Favre made it clear that football was his first love.

"The one place I feel at home is on the football field," he said. "I can kind of escape everything."

He always enjoyed the heck out of Green Bay's deeply committed football fans. They filled Lambeau Field on the coldest of game days.

"I saw a couple of big, fat guys sitting there with no shirts on," Favre said of one chilly contest, "and I'm like, 'Wow, I'm bundled up and I'm thinking those guys are going to be dead when the game's over.'"

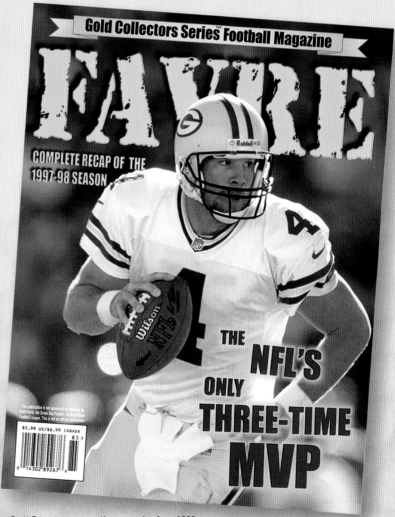

Brett Favre commemorative magazine from 1998.
MVP Books Collection

LeRoy Butler

The odds were against LeRoy Butler becoming much of an athlete after childhood illness kept him in a wheelchair for some time. But he outgrew his physical problems, became a high school star so good that he was named to the Florida All-Century Team, and then shined at Florida State University.

Picked in the second round of the 1990 draft, Butler was a hard-hitting, 6-foot, 200-pound defensive back who became a four-time Pro Bowl choice. He intercepted 38 passes in his 12-season NFL career, all spent with the Packers.

In a way, Butler personified the 1990s for the Pack, spending the entire decade with the team. He went through the tough times before coach Mike Holmgren made the club a winner, and he was still in the lineup after Holmgren departed following two Super Bowl appearances.

One of Butler's enduring contributions to Packers lore was his creation of the "Lambeau Leap."

The famous celebration, in which Packers players who score touchdowns jump into the end zone stands to celebrate briefly with fans, got its start on December 26, 1993, against the Los Angeles Rams. Butler tackled a player hard, causing a fumble. The ball bounced to defensive end Reggie White, who lumbered along and then tossed a lateral to Butler, who took the ball in for a touchdown. He was so excited that he leapt up to the fans. Fans loved the bonding move, but since it was ironically started by a defensive player, it took Butler teammate Robert Brooks, a receiver who scored more often, to really popularize the move. The Lambeau Leap has remained a Packers staple after touchdowns for 20 years.

Butler retired before the start of the 2002 season, though that was not his plan. A lingering problem from a broken shoulder blade suffered against the Atlanta Falcons forced him to quit. Besides the interceptions, Butler was in on nearly 1,000 tackles in his career, made 12 fumble recoveries, and scored three touchdowns on the defensive side. Butler also managed to collect 20.5 sacks from either his cornerback or safety positions on blitzes.

In retirement, Butler has remained visible by raising money for his LeRoy Butler Foundation, a charitable organization. One of the fundraising items is a cookbook that he wrote. He is so into cooking now that he will go to a private home and cook a meal for a party. Also, during the 2012 season, Butler did a weekly analysis breaking down Packers games with a *Milwaukee Journal* sports reporter. The theme was "X's and O's with LeRoy Butler."

AP Photo/Todd Ponath

New reception record for Sterling Sharpe, and playoff success for the Packers

The 1993 Packers repeated their 9–7 record from the season before, marking the first time since 1966–1967 that the team had two straight winning seasons. That season, defensive back LeRoy Butler introduced the "Lambeau Leap," spontaneously jumping into the stands after scoring a touchdown.

In a major coup, the Packers signed star defensive end Reggie White as a free agent after he left the Philadelphia Eagles. White was on his way to being a 13-time All-Pro, and he became the cornerstone of the defense.

Sterling Sharpe caught 112 passes, breaking his own franchise record, set the previous year (108). He caught 10 passes in three different games while tallying 1,274 receiving yards.

There was another special aspect to the season—the Pack qualified for the playoffs. At one point, Green Bay was sitting at 1–3, but after the wobbly start the Packers tore off a 6–1 stretch and didn't even need a last-day victory to make the playoffs. The loss in the finale was to the Detroit Lions, the first-round foe. But a week later, Green Bay prevailed 28–24 in a postseason thriller.

In a stupendous game, Lions star Barry Sanders returned from an injury to rush for 169 yards, Green Bay defender George Teague ran an interception back 101 yards for a touchdown, and the Packers pulled the game out with 55 seconds left. Favre rolled to his right and made a heave across his body for a 40-yard touchdown pass to Sharpe, his third score of the day.

The season ended a week later in the next round of the playoffs when the Dallas Cowboys put up a 17-point second quarter to win 27–17. Sharpe again starred with six catches for 129 yards.

Sterling Sharpe set a franchise record with 112 catches during the regular season, and then in the opening game of the playoffs against Detroit, he caught five passes for 101 yards and three touchdowns in the 28–24 victory.
Betsy Peabody Rowe/Getty Images

Game-by-Game

9/5	W, 36–6,	vs. Los Angeles Rams
9/12	L, 17–20,	vs. Philadelphia Eagles
9/26	L, 13–15,	at Minnesota Vikings
10/3	L, 14–36,	at Dallas Cowboys
10/10	W, 30–27,	vs. Denver Broncos
10/24	W, 37–14,	at Tampa Bay Buccaneers
10/31	W, 17–3,	vs. Chicago Bears
11/8	L, 16–23,	at Kansas City Chiefs
11/14	W, 19–17,	at New Orleans Saints
11/21	W, 26–17, vs. Detroit Lions	
11/28	W, 13–10,	vs. Tampa Bay Buccaneers
12/5	L, 17–30, at Chicago Bears	
12/12	W, 20–13,	at San Diego Chargers
12/19	L, 17–21,	vs. Minnesota Vikings
12/26	W, 28–0,	vs. Los Angeles Raiders
1/2/94	L, 20–30, at Detroit Lions	

Playoffs

1/8/94	W, 28–24, at Detroit Lions
1/16/94	L, 17–27, at Dallas Cowboys

Team Scoring

340 points scored (6th)

282 points allowed (9th)

Reggie White

Sundays were holy days for a couple of reasons for Reggie White, perhaps the best defensive lineman of his time. He was a very religious man for one, and his profession put him on the field trying to sack quarterbacks for another. White's addition to the Packers in 1993 helped mature the defense into a Super Bowl–caliber unit. White being public about his religion and his skills at football gained him the nickname "Minister of Defense."

During a professional career that began with the Memphis Showboats of the United States Football League in 1984 after college play at Tennessee, White had a Hall of Fame career mostly with the Philadelphia Eagles and the Packers. He was chosen for the Pro Bowl 13 times, was a two-time NFL Defensive Player of the Year, and retired with 198 sacks and more than 1,100 tackles.

At 6-foot-5 and 290 pounds, White was a feared pass rusher who altered other teams' offensive strategy. While the Packers bid for White after he left the Eagles, it did not seem likely they would sign him. Free agents were showing a preference for warm-weather climates. But White joined the Pack, and fans went gaga right from training camp, mobbing him for autographs.

"When I walked out there and saw all those people, that was an experience like no other," White said of the preseason Packers enthusiasm. "Just to see that many people out for a professional scrimmage was incredible."

What attracted White to Green Bay was the tradition of winning championships, the image of Vince Lombardi, and the long history of the team in the NFL. White said he was awed strolling around team buildings and soaking in the past.

"I walk through the [Packers] Hall of Fame and see all of Lombardi's words and all the players who made this a great team, and it's a special feeling," he said. "The atmosphere and the history, it's just unbelievable. You truly get an appreciation for what football means here."

There was so much excitement when White signed with Green Bay that he felt a need to tamp down some of it.

"This is not the Green Bay Reggies," White said. "It's the Green Bay Packers."

A few years later, the Packers did win a Super Bowl with White in the lineup and played in a second one.

White almost retired before the 1998 season because of a degenerative disc in his back, but the retirement lasted two days. He returned saying that God told him he should keep playing and it should be in Green Bay.

White wrapped up his career with one season with the Carolina Panthers in 2000. In 2004, when he was only 43, White suffered a heart attack and died at his home in North Carolina.

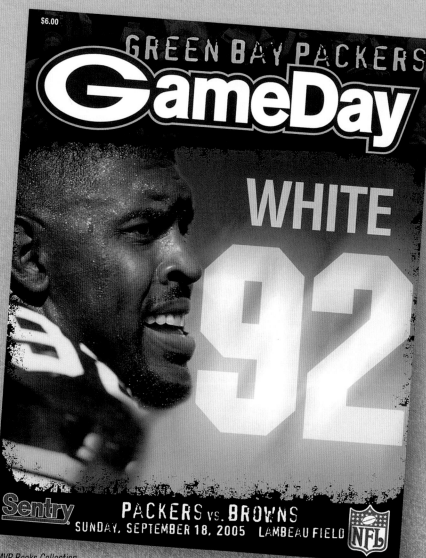

MVP Books Collection

The Green Bay defensive front—Sean Jones, Steve McMichael, Matt Brock, John Jurkovic, Don Davey, Bryce Paup, and Reggie White—held Detroit's Hall of Fame running back Barry Sanders to -1 yard rushing during the Packers' 16–12 victory in the NFC Wildcard Playoff on December 31, 1994. *Vernon Biever/Getty Images*

Although fans expected more, it took all the Packers could muster to produce a third straight 9–7 season in 1994 after a three-game, midseason losing streak. The team rallied to win three in a row to make the playoffs again.

Young quarterback Brett Favre was working toward true stardom, throwing for 3,882 yards and 33 touchdowns. Receiving partner Sterling Sharpe just kept rolling along with 94 catches, 18 of them for touchdowns. As often as Favre threw (582 times), there were plenty of balls to go around. Running back Edgar Bennett caught 78 passes, and receiver Robert Brooks caught 58.

The Packers beat the Chicago Bears (40–3!), Atlanta Falcons, and the Tampa Bay Bucs to sneak into the playoffs on the last day of the regular season. However, Sharpe complained of stinging sensations in his neck in both games, and he wound up missing the playoffs. The first game was a rematch with the Detroit Lions. This time, the game was in Green Bay and the Packers hustled to a 16–12 win at Lambeau Field.

Defense was paramount, a rarity for the Packers in recent years. But the D held Lions star Barry Sanders down. In the worst game of his career, he rushed for minus-one yard in 13 attempts. Dorsey Levens scored the only TD for the Packers, and Chris Jacke kicked field goals of 51, 32, and 28 yards.

The next week provided a rematch against the Dallas Cowboys, but it wasn't even close. Green Bay lost 35–9.

PACKERS HEADLINE

Green Bay enjoys back-to-back playoff seasons for the first time since the Lombardi era.

1994

▶ 9–7   2nd place ◀

Game-by-Game

9/4	W, 16–10, vs. Minnesota Vikings
9/11	L, 14–24, vs. Miami Dolphins
9/18	L, 7–13, at Philadelphia Eagles
9/25	W, 30–3, vs. Tampa Bay Buccaneers
10/2	L, 16–17, at New England Patriots
10/9	W, 24–17, vs. Los Angeles Rams
10/20	L, 10–13 (OT), at Minnesota Vikings
10/31	W, 33–6, at Chicago Bears
11/6	W, 38–30, vs. Detroit Lions
11/13	W, 17–10, vs. New York Jets
11/20	L, 20–29, at Buffalo Bills
11/24	L, 31–42, at Dallas Cowboys
12/4	L, 31–34, at Detroit Lions
12/11	W, 40–3, vs. Chicago Bears
12/18	W, 21–17, vs. Atlanta Falcons
12/24	W, 34–19, at Tampa Bay Buccaneers

Playoffs

12/31	W, 16–12, at Detroit Lions
1/8/95	L, 9–35, at Dallas Cowboys

Team Scoring

382 points scored (4th)

287 points allowed (5th)

Dorsey Levens

At his best, Dorsey Levens was very good for the Green Bay Packers, twice rushing for more than 1,000 yards in a season and being the lead back on a Super Bowl champion.

Levens came out of Georgia Tech as a fifth-round pick in 1994, and he used his solid, 6-foot-1, 230-pound size to good advantage. He frequently shared the Packers backfield with Edgar Bennett, giving the team two extra-large backs at once—when they were both healthy at the same time. Levens was chosen for the Pro Bowl in 1997.

During his eight-year Packers career, Levens rushed for 3,937 yards, averaged 3.9 yards per carry, and scored 28 rushing touchdowns and 16 receiving touchdowns. He ranks sixth on the all-time franchise list in rushing yardage and attempts. Sometimes he was the Packers' lead back—such as in 1997 when he set a franchise mark with 329 rushing attempts (surpassed by Ahman Green in 2003)—and sometimes he was in the lineup as Green Bay rushed by committee.

"These guys are the best," Levens said. "We all lean on each other."

After a one-year stop with the Giants sandwiched between two years in Philadelphia, Levens retired in 2004 with 4,955 rushing yards for his career.

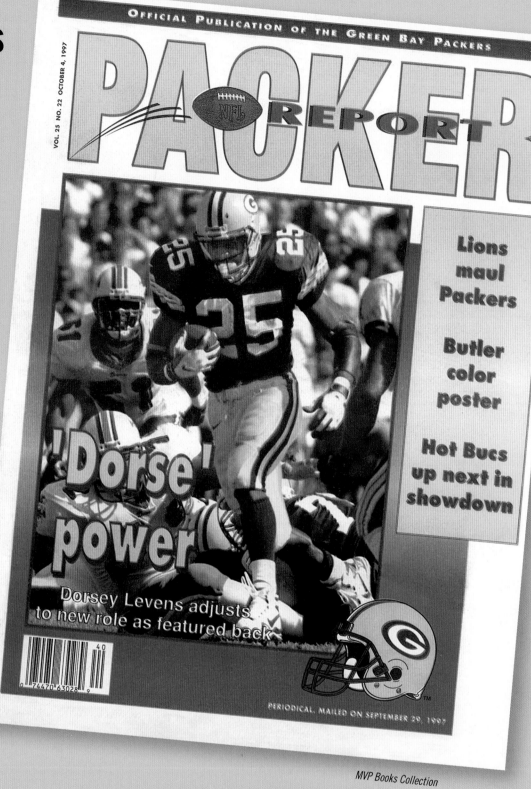

OFFICIAL PUBLICATION OF THE GREEN BAY PACKERS

$2.0

VOL 25 NO. 22 OCTOBER 4, 1997

PACKER REPORT

NFL

'Dorse' power

Dorsey Levens adjusts to new role as featured back

Lions maul Packers

Butler color poster

Hot Bucs up next in showdown

0 74470 63028 9   40

PERIODICAL, MAILED ON SEPTEMBER 29, 1997

MVP Books Collection

Edgar Bennett

Edgar Bennett pretty much lives and breathes Packers football. He had his best years in the NFL in Green Bay from 1992 and 1997, and he has returned repeatedly for different off-field roles later in life, including working in the front office in player personnel and as an assistant coach.

Bennett was a fourth-round draft choice of the Pack out of Florida State, where he was surrounded by so much backfield talent that it was a like a sneak preview of being in the pros. Bennett overlapped with five other backs who went on to play in the NFL, including Zach Crockett, William Floyd, and Amp Lee. He showed the type of versatility with Green Bay that he displayed with FSU, both as a runner and a pass catcher.

A 6-foot, 220-pound fullback, Bennett was a member of the Packers' championship team of 1996. In the Super Bowl, he rushed for 40 yards and caught one pass in the victory over the New England Patriots.

Bennett rushed for nearly 4,000 yards in his career while scoring 21 touchdowns. His best year was 1995, when he rushed for 1,067 yards and caught 61 passes. The biggest problem Bennett faced in his career was a torn Achilles tendon, but he came back from that.

Bennett led the Packers in rushing in three different seasons, despite working with Dorsey Levens and others. "We just complement each other," Bennett said of making the rotation work. "We find ways to win."

Jonathan Daniel/Allsport/Getty Images

1995

▶ 11–5   1st place ◀

Game-by-Game

9/3	**L**, 14–17, vs. St. Louis Rams
9/11	**W**, 27–24, at Chicago Bears
9/17	**W**, 14–6, vs. New York Giants
9/24	**W**, 24–14, at Jacksonville Jaguars
10/8	**L**, 24–34, at Dallas Cowboys
10/15	**W**, 30–21, vs. Detroit Lions
10/22	**W**, 38–21, vs. Minnesota Vikings
10/29	**L**, 16–24, at Detroit Lions
11/5	**L**, 24–27, at Minnesota Vikings
11/12	**W**, 35–28, vs. Chicago Bears
11/19	**W**, 31–20, at Cleveland Browns
11/26	**W**, 35–13, vs. Tampa Bay Buccaneers
12/3	**W**, 24–10, vs. Cincinnati Bengals
12/10	**L**, 10–13 (OT), at Tampa Bay Buccaneers
12/16	**W**, 34–23, at New Orleans Saints
12/24	**W**, 24–19, vs. Pittsburgh Steelers

Playoffs

12/31	**W**, 37–20, vs. Atlanta Falcons
1/6/96	**W**, 27–17, at San Francisco 49ers
1/14/96	**L**, 27–38, at Dallas Cowboys

Team Scoring

404 points scored (6th)

314 points allowed (4th)

Packers record most wins since 1966 but are thwarted by the Cowboys yet again in the postseason.

The 11–5 record that the Packers compiled in 1995 was the best for the team in about 30 years—and it was a sturdy 11–5. All five losses were close (three by a field goal), and there was no doubt that this was a playoff team. Green Bay won the Central Division by a game over the Detroit Lions.

But there was a big void. Sterling Sharpe was forced to retire following his end-of-season neck injury in 1994. The five-time Pro Bowl selection was only 29.

Also, the Packers stopped playing home games in Milwaukee for the first time since the 1930s. When the lease at County Stadium expired in 1994, the Packers committed to playing all future home games at Lambeau Field.

Quarterback Brett Favre continued to electrify crowds, throwing for 4,413 yards and 38 touchdowns, and Robert Brooks assumed the role of No. 1 receiver with 102 catches. Running back Edgar Bennett had an outstanding season with 61 catches and a team-high 1,067 yards rushing.

Green Bay opened the playoffs with a 37–20 triumph over the Atlanta Falcons. Antonio Freeman ran a punt back 76 yards for a TD. A week later, the Pack held off the 49ers in San Francisco, 27–17. The defense was sterling, causing four turnovers and sacking Steve Young three times.

For the third year in a row, the Packers met the Dallas Cowboys in the playoffs and lost, this time 38–27. Emmitt Smith rushed for 150 yards and three touchdowns.

Receiver Robert Brooks was often leaving defenders in his wake while accumulating a franchise-record 1,497 receiving yards in 1995. In the losing effort against Dallas in the NFC title game, Brooks caught six passes for 105 yards and two touchdowns. *Al Bello/Getty Images*

1996

In their finest season in three decades, the Green Bay Packers added another title to the Titletown résumé by capturing Super Bowl XXXI. They ran through a 13–3 regular season and entered the playoffs on fire. Their last three margins of victory were 35, 28, and 28, and overall they outscored foes 456–210.

Quarterback Brett Favre recorded the same type of season he had in 1995 with 3,899 yards and 39 touchdowns, though he had a new favorite target in Antonio Freeman, who logged 56 catches and nine touchdowns. Tight end Keith Jackson caught 10 touchdown passes. Eight players had at least 23 receptions for the year.

The Packers handled the San Francisco 49ers easily in the first round of the playoffs, 35–14, as Desmond Howard made two big punt returns. The Packers had to fight to top the Carolina Panthers, 30–13, in the next round. They did it on touchdowns by Freeman and running backs Dorsey Levens and Edgar Bennett as well as three field goals from Chris Jacke.

Green Bay advanced to its first Super Bowl in 29 years to face the New England Patriots in New Orleans. At 10–0, the game seemed as if it could be a possible Packers runaway. After New England took a 14–10 lead, the Patriots retaliated with monster plays—an 81-yard TD pass from Favre to Freeman and a Howard 99-yard kickoff return, the latter coming after the Patriots had climbed to within six points.

The final was 35–21 Packers, and Green Bay had its twelfth NFL championship.

PACKERS HEADLINE

Green Bay claims its 12th NFL championship with victory in Super Bowl XXXI.

The Packers clinched their second consecutive NFC Central Division title on December 8 when they trounced the Broncos 41–6 at Lambeau Field. They went on to win the final two games of the season to finish at 13–3—their highest win total since 1962. *Brian Bahr/Allsport/Getty Images*

▶ **13–3   1st place** ◀

Game-by-Game

9/1	W, 34–3, at Tampa Bay Buccaneers
9/9	W, 39–13, vs. Philadelphia Eagles
9/15	W, 42–10, vs. San Diego Chargers
9/22	L, 21–30, at Minnesota Vikings
9/29	W, 31–10, at Seattle Seahawks
10/6	W, 37–6, at Chicago Bears
10/14	W, 23–20 (OT), vs. San Francisco 49ers
10/27	W, 13–7, vs. Tampa Bay Buccaneers
11/3	W, 28–18, vs. Detroit Lions
11/10	L, 20–27, at Kansas City Chiefs
11/18	L, 6–21, at Dallas Cowboys
11/24	W, 24–9, at St. Louis Rams
12/1	W, 28–17, vs. Chicago Bears
12/8	W, 41–6, vs. Denver Broncos
12/15	W, 31–3, at Detroit Lions
12/22	W, 38–10, vs. Minnesota Vikings

Playoffs

1/4/97	W, 35–14, vs. San Francisco 49ers
1/12/97	W, 30–13, vs. Carolina Panthers
1/26/97	W, 35–21, vs. New England Patriots

Team Scoring

456 points scored (1st)

210 points allowed (1st)

Desmond Howard (81) returning a kick for a touchdown during Super Bowl XXXI against the New England Patriots. *Peter Brouillet/Getty Images*

Super Bowl XXXI

Defeating the New England Patriots, 35–21, in the Super Bowl on January 26, 1997, culminated 30 years of dreaming in Green Bay. At last, the Packers, winners of 11 previous NFL titles, added another championship trophy to their collection.

After taking the early lead, and then falling behind 14–10 after the first quarter, the Packers led the rest of the game. While Brett Favre threw for 246 yards and two touchdowns and Antonio Freeman topped 100 yards in receiving, the real spark was provided by return man Desmond Howard.

Howard, who had won the Heisman Trophy at Michigan, became the first and only special teams player to win the Super Bowl MVP Award. Howard ran a kickoff back 99 yards for a touchdown, and including his punt returns he totaled 244 all-purpose yards.

"We went into the locker room at halftime and said we can break a return," Howard said. "We saw things we thought we could exploit coming out in the second half. As I ran through the middle, I just basically followed Don Beebe's block. I was just another strong link in this very, very strong chain."

Beebe had played in four losing Super Bowls with the Buffalo Bills and finally won a championship ring. "I've been wanting to hold this thing for a long time," Beebe said of the Vince Lombardi Trophy. "And yes, I'm taking this thing home. These guys don't know that yet, but it's gonna sit on my mantle."

Another player very glad to become a Super Bowl champ deep into his career, and who deserved to touch the trophy, was defensive end Reggie White, who collected three sacks.

"Now I can sit back with my son for years and watch highlights of this Super Bowl, and he can see his daddy getting three sacks," White said.

It was a championship first for a lot of players, as well as coach Mike Holmgren as a head man after his winning experience as an assistant with San Francisco.

"I look at the faces of my players and my coaches and ownership in the locker room, I'm humbled by that," Holmgren said. "I'm overwhelmed by it. I'm so happy for those guys."

The people of Green Bay were pretty happy, too, and word had already come to Holmgren in the locker room how people in Wisconsin were reacting.

"The welcoming party sold out in four hours—60,000 tickets," Holmgren said. "And they had phone calls from a million and a half. So they've been with us through tough times and the bumps in the road as well."

Back in Green Bay when the team flew in, schools closed early and workers were let off the job early. Crowds flocked to the airport and stood on snow banks as the Packers departed from the plane, with White waving the trophy high. The Packers were whisked to Lambeau Field along a tickertape motorcade route that was lined six deep with fans.

"That's what it's about right here," White said, pointing to the trophy.

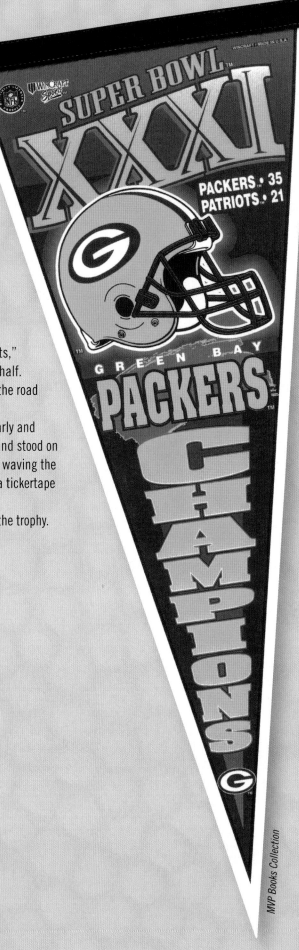

MVP Books Collection

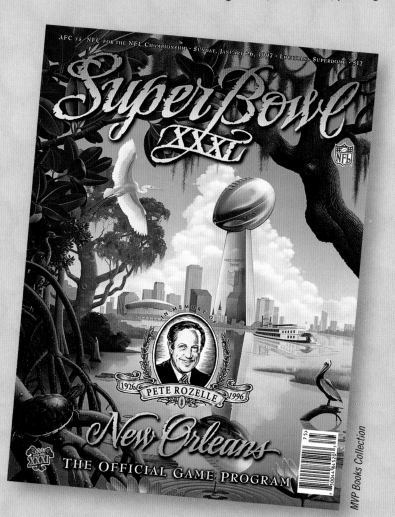

MVP Books Collection

1997

► **13–3   1st place** ◄

Game-by-Game

9/1	W, 38–24, vs. Chicago Bears
9/7	L, 9–10, at Philadelphia Eagles
9/14	W, 23–18, vs. Miami Dolphins
9/21	W, 38–32, vs. Minnesota Vikings
9/28	L, 15–26, at Detroit Lions
10/5	W, 21–16, vs. Tampa Bay Buccaneers
10/12	W, 24–23, at Chicago Bears
10/27	W, 28–10, at New England Patriots
11/2	W, 20–10, vs. Detroit Lions
11/9	W, 17–7, vs. St. Louis Rams
11/16	L, 38–41, at Indianapolis Colts
11/23	W, 45–17, vs. Dallas Cowboys
12/1	W, 27–11, at Minnesota Vikings
12/7	W, 17–6, at Tampa Bay Buccaneers
12/14	W, 31–10, at Carolina Panthers
12/20	W, 31–21, vs. Buffalo Bills

Playoffs

1/4/98	W, 21–7, vs. Tampa Bay Buccaneers
1/11/98	W, 23–10, at San Francisco 49ers
1/25/98	L, 24–31, vs. Denver Broncos

Team Scoring

422 points scored (2nd)

282 points allowed (5th)

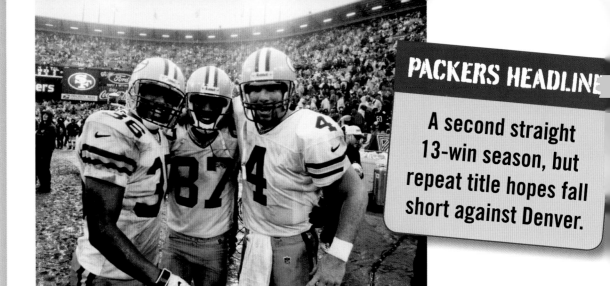

PACKERS HEADLINE

A second straight 13-win season, but repeat title hopes fall short against Denver.

Safety LeRoy Butler, receiver Robert Brooks, and quarterback Brett Favre get ready to celebrate their victory over the San Francisco 49ers in the NFC Championship Game, sending the Packers back to the Super Bowl. *James V. Biever/Getty Images*

Green Bay's 1997 season was almost as great as 1996, except for an unhappy ending. The Packers finished 13–3 again in the regular season and battled through the playoffs to reach the Super Bowl, except this time they lost to the Denver Broncos.

For the most part, Green Bay was dominant during the regular season. Quarterback Brett Favre had clearly become the face of the team, and his bombs-away attack was the symbol of the offense. He threw for 35 touchdowns. Target Mr. A-1 was Antonio Freeman, who made 81 catches and scored 12 TDs.

Also, seemingly for the first time since the heyday of Jim Taylor, the Packers had a back to pile up the yards. Dorsey Levens ran for 1,435 yards and seven touchdowns. Rookie kicker Ryan Longwell provided 120 points with his foot, including a perfect 48-for-48 in extra point attempts.

The defense did its part all season, especially in the first two rounds of the playoffs. Green Bay topped Tampa Bay 21–7 and then, in the NFC Championship Game, defeated the San Francisco 49ers 23–10.

The Super Bowl in San Diego was a showdown between Favre and Denver's John Elway, and the Broncos won 31–24. Green Bay got two touchdowns from Freeman and mounted a 95-yard drive, but Denver scored last on a Terrell Davis one-yard run to break a 24–24 deadlock.

Off the field, the Packers went public late in the year with their first stock offering since 1950, allowing for the sale of up to 400,000 shares in the team at $200 apiece in order to raise $80 million in capital. The primary goal was to raise money for a renovation of Lambeau Field.

The Packers were the only major professional sports franchise in the United States owned by the community. It was the fourth time the franchise had made an offering like this since its inception in 1919.

Packers stock comes with specific rules. It cannot be sold for more than face value, it won't appreciate in value, and no one is allowed to own more than 200 shares.

The stock sale began in November 1997 and concluded in March 1998. During that time period, 120,000 shares of Packers stock were sold, raising $24 million. The total accumulated was less than the stated goal, but Packers President Bob Harlan said the team was not disappointed.

"The goal was very difficult to determine," Harlan said. "We had not tried a stock sale in 47 years. We really did not know where this would take us. We are delighted."

By selling 120,000 shares, Harland said, "We've made the statement that we are America's team, and I think this goes to prove it one more time."

Super Bowl XXXII

Determined to repeat as NFL champions, the Packers fought their way back to the Super Bowl on January 25, 1998, to face the Denver Broncos. In a classic matchup of quarterbacks, it was Brett Favre against John Elway.

The evenly played game was determined at the end of the fourth quarter when Broncos star Terrell Davis scored the winning touchdown. On the day, Davis ran for 157 yards and three touchdowns. Denver won 31–24.

"They got 10 points off of our turnovers, and I think that was the difference in the game," said Favre, who threw for 256 yards and three touchdowns. "They blitzed and we picked it up for the most part, and we made two mistakes."

It was 7–7 after the first quarter, 17–14 Denver at halftime, and 24–17 after three quarters. The Packers tied the game at 24–24 in the fourth quarter, but they couldn't hold Denver out of the end zone one more time.

"We knew that we could come back if we had to," said Green Bay tackle Adam Timmerman, "but we just kind of ran out of time."

All season, the Packers had been motivated to win a second straight title. They got to the big game and played the big game even until the end, but still went home with the L.

"I'm hurt, don't get me wrong," said defensive end Reggie White. "I know I'm still going to have to deal with this one."

Leroy Butler, who had been a key player in the Super Bowl victory over the New England Patriots the previous year, echoed that frustration from the Green Bay locker room.

"It is very disappointing," Butler said after the loss. "We played in it last year and won. We felt confident. We had a lot riding on this game. They had a great game plan. They wanted it more than we did."

MVP Books Collection

Brett Favre looks to pass during Super Bowl XXXII against the Denver Broncos. *Kevin Reece/Getty Images*

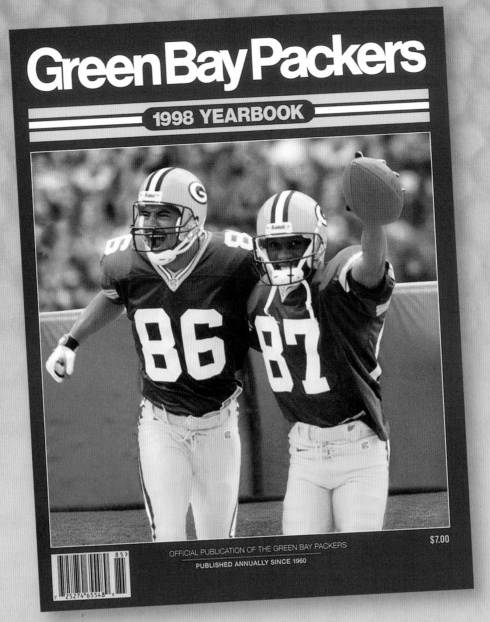

Robert Books (87) with Antonio Freeman on the 1998 Packers yearbook. *MVP Books Collection*

Robert Brooks

Like his good friend and receiving partner Antonio Freeman, Robert Brooks was a third-round draft choice. He felt he should have been taken sooner than the sixty-second slot the Packers used to grab him out of South Carolina in 1992.

Although injuries hampered the 6-foot, 180-pound receiver's career, Brooks had some terrific moments and seasons for the Packers from 1992 to 1998. In 1993, Brooks was the NFL kickoff return leader with a 26.6-yards-per-return average.

When Sterling Sharpe's career ended due to injury in 1995, Brooks faced pressure. But he came through with 102 catches for 13 touchdowns. The most spectacular play was a 99-yard touchdown pass from Brett Favre on *Monday Night Football* to help beat the Chicago Bears.

"After that draft," Brooks said, "I was like, 'In the end, it will take care of itself.' All the guys who got drafted before me, you can go down the list, see where they're at, and what their situations are. I feel like I'm in the better position out of all of them."

Brooks was a member of two Packers Super Bowl teams. He could not play in Green Bay's victory because of a knee injury, but the next year Brooks won the NFL's Comeback Player of the Year Award. He caught 60 passes and topped 1,000 yards receiving.

"I know that I really liked Robert Brooks," said Packers general manager Ron Wolf. "We had Robert Brooks rated as a first-round player."

Antonio Freeman

Coming out of Virginia Tech, Antonio Freeman joined the Packers in 1995 and shined through the 2001 season. Freeman shifted teams a few times after that, but he returned to Green Bay for a year at the tail end of his career. In all, Freeman, who formed a terrific pitch-and-catch partnership with Brett Favre, caught 477 passes for 7,251 yards and 61 touchdowns.

The 6-foot-1, 200-pound receiver felt snubbed when he dropped to the third round on draft day. He turned that frustration into motivation.

"When you're in the third round now," Freeman said, "you say to yourself, 'I've got to prove these guys wrong. I've got to show everybody I can play.'"

In his second year, Freeman caught 56 passes. Then he had 81- and 84-catch seasons. In 1998, he led the NFL with 1,424 yards gained on receptions.

In one 1998 game, Freeman grabbed eight passes against the Chicago Bears after rushing back to action from a broken jaw that was wired shut. Freeman gained 103 yards and earned admiration for his stout-hearted play.

"I think most people wouldn't have played," said quarterback Brett Favre. "He took some hits and he had some big catches."

Freeman helped the Packers win Super Bowl XXXI with an 81-yard touchdown pass play, and he was All-Pro in 1998. "When I saw that safety come up, I knew that all I had to do was make him stumble or move the wrong way," Freeman said of his Super Bowl TD.

Antonio Freeman (86) lifted up by teammate Robert Books (87). *Al Bello/Getty Images*

1998

▶ 11–5   2nd place ◀

Game-by-Game

9/6	W, 38–19, vs. Detroit Lions
9/13	W, 23–15, vs. Tampa Bay Buccaneers
9/20	W, 13–6, at Cincinnati Bengals
9/27	W, 37–30, at Carolina Panthers
10/5	L, 24–37, vs. Minnesota Vikings
10/15	L, 20–27, at Detroit Lions
10/25	W, 28–10, vs. Baltimore Ravens
11/1	W, 36–22, vs. San Francisco 49ers
11/9	L, 20–27, at Pittsburgh Steelers
11/15	W, 37–3, at New York Giants
11/22	L, 14–28, at Minnesota Vikings
11/29	W, 24–16, vs. Philadelphia Eagles
12/7	L, 22–24, at Tampa Bay Buccaneers
12/13	W, 26–20, vs. Chicago Bears
12/20	W, 30–22, vs. Tennessee Oilers
12/27	W, 16–13, at Chicago Bears

Playoffs

1/3/99	L, 20–27, at San Francisco 49ers

Team Scoring

408 points scored (6th)

319 points allowed (11th)

Roell Preston returns kicks for a team-record 1,497 yards, but the Pack misses return to the Super Bowl.

As an NFL gimmick in 1998, the Packers played a summer exhibition game in Tokyo against the Kansas City Chiefs and were given a couple of Japanese players to suit up. The real 1998 season began with the Packers looking perfectly capable of another run to the Super Bowl. They won their first four games, stumbled a few times in midseason, and charged to the regular-season finish line with three straight victories. However, 11–5 Green Bay did not capture the Central Division. The Minnesota Vikings went 15–1.

Although the Brett Favre–to–Antonio Freeman tandem was deadly, with Freeman amassing 84 catches and 14 touchdowns and Favre throwing for 31 scores, the offensive support system was weaker. No rusher hit 400 yards. Second-year kicker Ryan Longwell followed up his stellar rookie season by scoring 128 in 1998.

The Packers entered the playoffs feeling good. They drew the San Francisco 49ers, a team they had beaten three straight years in the playoffs. Only now it was San Francisco's turn, as the 49ers knocked out the Packers 30–27 in a stunning, demoralizing finish.

Green Bay led 27–23 when 49ers quarterback Steve Young completed a Hail Mary pass to Terrell Owens, who outfought four defenders for the ball in the end zone, with three seconds left.

This marked a team-record six consecutive years in the playoffs for the Packers, and when the season ended, defensive end Reggie White retired.

In the third Pro Bowl season of his career, tight end Mark Chmura collected 47 receptions and 4 touchdown catches in 1998. Here he leaps over a Bengals defender during Green Bay's 13–6 win in Cincinnati. *Harry How/Getty Images*

Reunited—and it doesn't feel so good for Brett Favre, whose Packers lost to Mike Holmgren's Seahawks on November 1, 1999, in the former coach's first trip back to Green Bay after leaving the club. *James Biever/Getty Images*

Game-by-Game

9/12	W, 28–24, vs. Oakland Raiders
9/19	L, 15–23, at Detroit Lions
9/26	W, 23–20, vs. Minnesota Vikings
10/10	W, 26–23, vs. Tampa Bay Buccaneers
10/17	L, 10–31, at Denver Broncos
10/24	W, 31–3, at San Diego Chargers
11/1	L, 7–27, vs. Seattle Seahawks
11/7	L, 13–14, vs. Chicago Bears
11/14	L, 13–27, at Dallas Cowboys
11/21	W, 26–17, vs. Detroit Lions
11/29	W, 20–3, at San Francisco 49ers
12/5	W, 35–19, at Chicago Bears
12/12	L, 31–33, vs. Carolina Panthers
12/20	L, 20–24, at Minnesota Vikings
12/26	L, 10–29, at Tampa Bay Buccaneers
1/2/00	W, 49–24, vs. Arizona Cardinals

Team Scoring

357 points scored (10th)

341 points allowed (20th)

While the finish to the 1998 playoffs was shocking, coach Mike Holmgren's decision to forsake the Packers for the Seattle Seahawks pretty much matched it. Holmgren walked because he could be both coach and general manager in Seattle, and he wanted the increased control and responsibility.

Holmgren departed after leading Green Bay to six straight playoff seasons, the best run of any coach by far since Vince Lombardi in the 1960s. His replacement was Ray Rhodes, who abruptly became available because of a 3–13 season at the end of a three-year tenure with the Philadelphia Eagles, for whom he had also been NFL Coach of the Year. Rhodes previously had been an assistant with the Packers and had won five Super Bowl rings as a key assistant with the San Francisco 49ers.

Under Rhodes, the Packers slipped to 8–8 in 1999. Brett Favre threw for 4,091 yards, but his touchdown passes were down. Antonio Freeman shone with 74 catches, and Dorsey Levens bounced back to his old form with 1,034 yards rushing.

Green Bay got off to a 3–1 start, but it didn't win the close ones, losing games by two, four, and one point from midseason on. Green Bay was 7–5 when a controversial call versus the Carolina Panthers led to a 33–31 loss. Even though the Packers were only 8–8, they missed the playoffs due to a tiebreaker. In what many people believed was a hasty move, Rhodes was fired after just one season on the job.

PACKERS HEADLINE

Mike Holmgren's departure means departure from the postseason for first time in seven years.

THE 1990s RECORD BOOK

Team Leaders

(**Boldface** indicates league leader)

Scoring Leaders (Points)
1990: Chris Jacke, 97
1991: Chris Jacke, 85
1992: Chris Jacke, 96
1993: Chris Jacke, 128
1994: Sterling Sharpe, 108
1995: Chris Jacke, 94
1996: Chris Jacke, 114
1997: Ryan Longwell, 120
1998: Ryan Longwell, 128
1999: Ryan Longwell, 113

Rushing Leaders (Carries / Yards / TDs)
1990: Michael Haddix, 98 / 311 / 0
1991: Darrell Thompson, 141 / 471 / 1
1992: Vince Workman, 159 / 631 / 2
1993: Darrell Thompson, 169 / 654 / 3
1994: Edgar Bennett, 178 / 623 / 5
1995: Edgar Bennett, 316 / 1,067 / 3
1996: Edgar Bennett, 222 / 899 / 2
1997: Dorsey Levens, 329 / 1,435 / 7
1998: Darick Holmes, 93 / 386 / 1
1999: Dorsey Levens, 279 / 1,034 / 9

Passing Leaders (Completions / Attempts / Yards)
1990: Don Majkowski, 150 / 264 / 1,925
1991: Mike Tomczak, 128 / 238 / 1,490
1992: Brett Favre, 302 / 471 / 3,227
1993: Brett Favre, 318 / 522 / 3,303
1994: Brett Favre, 363 / 582 / 3,882
1995: Brett Favre, 359 / 570 / **4,413**
1996: Brett Favre, 325 / 543 / 3,899
1997: Brett Favre, 304 / 513 / 3,867
1998: Brett Favre, **347** / 551 / **4,212**
1999: Brett Favre, 341 / **595** / 4,091

Receiving Leaders (Receptions / Yards / TDs)
1990: Sterling Sharpe, 67 / 1,105 / 6
1991: Sterling Sharpe, 69 / 961 / 4
1992: Sterling Sharpe, **108** / **1,461** / **13**
1993: Sterling Sharpe, **112** / 1,274 / 11
1994: Sterling Sharpe, 94 / 1,119 / **18**
1995: Robert Brooks, 102 / 1,497 / 13
1996: Antonio Freeman, 56 / 933 / 9
1997: Antonio Freeman, 81 / 1,243 / 12
1998: Antonio Freeman, 84 / **1,424** / 14
1999: Antonio Freeman, 74 / 1,074 / 6
        Bill Schroeder, 74 / 1,051 / 5

Interceptions (Number / Yards / TDs)
1990: LeRoy Butler, 3 / 42 / 0
        Jerry Holmes, 3 / 39 / 0
        Mark Murphy, 3 / 6 / 0
1991: LeRoy Butler, 3 / 76 / 0
        Chuck Cecil, 3 / 27 / 0
        Mark Murphy, 3 / 6 / 0
1992: Chuck Cecil, 4 / 52 / 0
1993: LeRoy Butler, 6 / 131 / 0
1994: Terrell Buckley, 5 / 38 / 0
1995: LeRoy Butler, 5 / 105 / 0
1996: Eugene Robinson, 6 / 107 / 0
1997: LeRoy Butler, 5 / 4 / 0
1998: Tyrone Williams, 5 / 40 / 0
1999: Mike McKenzie, 6 / 4 / 0

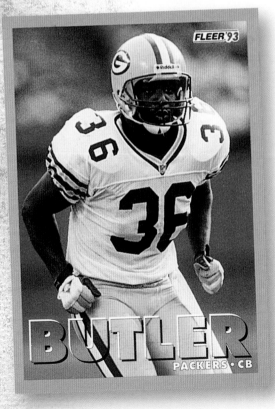

MVP Books Collection

First-Team All-Pros

1992: Sterling Sharpe, WR
1993: LeRoy Butler, S
1993: Chris Jacke, K
1993: Sterling Sharpe, WR
1995: Brett Favre, QB
1995: Reggie White, DE
1996: LeRoy Butler, S
1996: Brett Favre, QB
1997: LeRoy Butler, S
1997: Brett Favre, QB
1998: LeRoy Butler, S
1998: Antonio Freeman, WR
1998: Reggie White, DE

Pro Bowl Selections

1990: Sterling Sharpe, WR
1992: Chuck Cecil, S
1992: Brett Favre, QB
1992: Sterling Sharpe, WR
1993: LeRoy Butler, S
1993: Brett Favre, QB
1993: Sterling Sharpe, WR
1993: Reggie White, DE
1994: Bryce Paup, LB
1994: Sterling Sharpe, WR
1994: Reggie White, DE
1995: Mark Chmura, TE
1995: Brett Favre, QB
1995: Reggie White, DE
1996: LeRoy Butler, S
1996: Brett Favre, QB
1995: Keith Jackson, TE
1996: Reggie White, DE
1996: Frank Winters, C
1997: LeRoy Butler, S
1997: Mark Chmura, TE
1997: Brett Favre, QB
1997: Travis Jervey, RB
1997: Dorsey Levens, RB
1997: Reggie White, DE
1998: LeRoy Butler, S
1998: Mark Chmura, TE
1998: Antonio Freeman, WR
1998: Roell Preston, WR
1998: Reggie White, DE

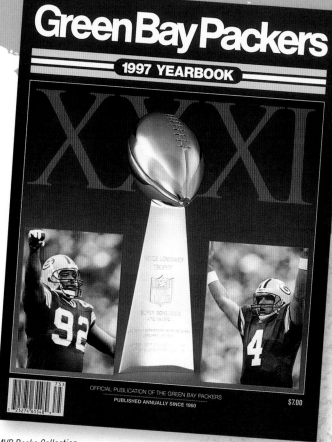

MVP Books Collection

1st-Round Draft Picks

1990: Tony Bennett (18), LB, Mississippi;
Darrell Thompson (19), RB,
Minnesota
1991: Vinnie Clark (19), CB, Ohio State
1992: Terrell Buckley (5), CB,
Florida State
1993: Wayne Simmons (15), LB, Clemson;
George Teague (29), S, Alabama
1994: Aaron Taylor (16), G, Notre Dame
1995: Craig Newsome (32), CB,
Arizona State
1996: John Michels (27), OT,
Southern California
1997: Ross Verba (30), G, Iowa
1998: Vonnie Holliday (19), DE,
North Carolina
1999: Antuan Edwards (25), S, Clemson

MVP Books Collection

Passing of the torch. Brett Favre led the Packers back to championship contention during the 1990s before handing the reins over to Aaron Rodgers, who quickly brought Green Bay back to the Super Bowl as the starting quarterback.
Joe Robbins/Getty Images

THE 2000s

The new millennium has been good to the Green Bay Packers. From 2000 to 2012, the Packers had nine seasons of at least 10 victories. One iconic quarterback departed and another arrived. And the storied franchise added a thirteenth NFL title to its lengthy list of achievements.

After an 11–5 regular season in 2009 under coach Mike McCarthy, the Packers ran the table in the playoffs to win Super Bowl XLV, 31–25, over the Pittsburgh Steelers.

Brett Favre ended his lengthy and record-breaking run as Packers quarterback. He was replaced by king-in-waiting Aaron Rodgers, who had spent almost three complete seasons of inaction on the bench before getting his chance. Rodgers immediately emerged as one of the best quarterbacks in the league, and he led the Packers to their Super Bowl triumph.

With the turn of the decade, the Packers hired Mike Sherman as coach to replace Ray Rhodes after his single season at the helm had resulted in an 8–8 record. Sherman had a lengthy apprenticeship as a college assistant and had spent two years as a Packers assistant before taking over as the head man in 2000.

After a 9–7 start in 2000, Sherman led the Packers to four straight double-digit-victory campaigns, including three consecutive division titles from 2002 to 2004. But after he stumbled with a losing record in 2005, he was ousted. McCarthy, who had worked with a variety of college and pro teams, including the Packers as an assistant, took over the top spot.

After an 8–8 season, the Packers exploded with a 13–3 mark in 2007, which helped McCarthy weather a losing season before he bounced back with the Super Bowl title. In 2011, the Packers compiled the best single-season record in team history, going 15–1, but they lost in the second round of the playoffs.

Overlapping with Favre and Rodgers was running back Ahman Green, who set team records for rushing, and receiver Donald Driver. Both were key cogs in the offense for years. In four of his first five seasons as the starting quarterback, Rodgers exceeded 4,000 yards in passing, and in 2011 he threw for 45 touchdowns—more than Favre ever had in a season.

In September 2005, the Packers retired jersey No. 92 in honor of Reggie White, who had shockingly passed away the previous year. It was only the fifth number retired in team history. White joined Tony Canadeo (3), Don Hutson (14), Bart Starr (15), and Ray Nitschke (66) as the only Packers with retired jerseys.

Unlike the Chicago Bears, who chose to shut down their home stadium of Soldier Field for renovation for more than a year and play home games 150 miles away at the University of Illinois, the Packers chose to make more drawn-out, piecemeal renovations to Lambeau Field. By choosing that route, the Packers played every home game in Green Bay.

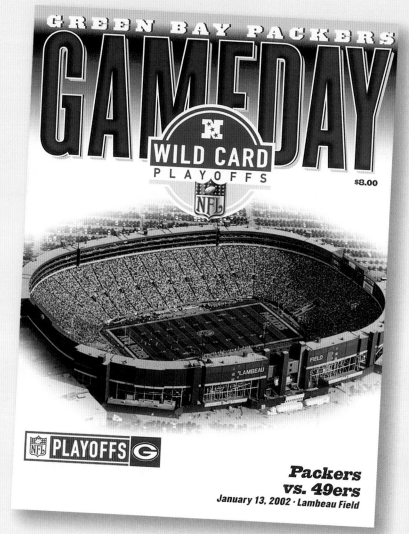

Between 2000 and 2012, the Packers reached the postseason nine times, including six NFC North Division titles. *MVP Books Collection*

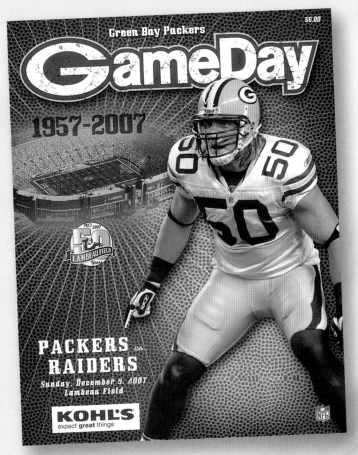

For a fifth time, the team offered stock for sale to community members and football fans. The sale, which ran from December 2011 to February 2012, was supposed to include 250,000 shares of stock at $250 each. That was the initial plan. However, 268,000 shares were sold. That brought to approximately 5 million the number of shares of stock in the Packers. There was also a brief window for international sales this time, and 2,000 shares were sold in Canada.

The stock offering raised $143 million in order to add 6,700 seats to Lambeau and upgrade the scoreboard (including video boards) and the sound system. That updating work was scheduled to be complete in time for the 2013 season.

Linebacker A. J. Hawk graces the cover of a game program from 2007. *MVP Books Collection*

2000

▶ **9–7   3rd place** ◀

Game-by-Game

9/3   L, 16–20, vs. New York Jets

9/10   L, 18–27, at Buffalo Bills

9/17   W, 6–3,
       vs. Philadelphia Eagles

9/24   W, 29–3,
       at Arizona Cardinals

10/1   L, 24–27,
       vs. Chicago Bears

10/8   L, 24–31, at Detroit Lions

10/15 W, 31–28,
       vs. San Francisco 49ers

10/29 L, 20–28,
       at Miami Dolphins

11/6   W, 26–20 (OT),
       vs. Minnesota Vikings

11/12 L, 15–20,
       at Tampa Bay Buccaneers

11/19 W, 26–24,
       vs. Indianapolis Colts

11/27 L, 14–31,
       at Carolina Panthers

12/3   W, 28–6,
       at Chicago Bears

12/10 W, 26–13,
       vs. Detroit Lions

12/17 W, 33–28,
       at Minnesota Vikings

12/24 W, 17–14 (OT),
       vs. Tampa Bay Buccaneers

Team Scoring

353 points scored (11th)

323 points allowed (14th)

During a 33–28 victory over the division-champion Vikings, unheralded receiver Bill Schroeder tied a career-best with eight catches, including a 3-yard touchdown run in the fourth quarter. *Elsa/Allsport/Getty Images*

200

PACKERS HEADLINE

New arrivals and unlikely heroes help drive winning season under new coach Mike Sherman.

The Mike Sherman coaching era began with two straight losses and a 2–4 start a year after Ray Rhodes was dismissed for going 8–8. But the season ended on an upswing, as the Packers won four straight games to salvage the situation.

A 9–7 record was not good enough for a playoff spot in a season in which the NFC Central Division was exceptionally tough. Four of the five teams had winning records, and Minnesota won the division crown with an 11–5 mark. The good news for the Packers was that in their closing stretch, they beat all three of those other teams.

The big addition to the offense was running back Ahman Green. Green, who came over from Seattle, was a sensation in Green Bay. He rushed for 1,175 yards, caught 73 passes, and scored 13 touchdowns.

An unlikely but popular success story was receiver Bill Schroeder. Schroeder had attended high school in Sheboygan, had played for tiny University of Wisconsin-LaCrosse, and had been drafted in the sixth round in 1994. He bounced around, playing for the Rhein Fire overseas, but in 1999 he stunned Green Bay fans by catching 74 passes for more than 1,000 yards. In 2000, he caught another 65. By the time his career ended a few years later, Schroeder had caught 304 passes.

The season also marked the real emergence of defensive back Darren Sharper. Sharper, who had been drafted out of William & Mary in 1997, began truly thriving in 2000 when he intercepted nine passes and earned his first Pro Bowl selection.

Kicker Ryan Longwell continued his string of 100 points or more points—which would eventually extend for eight consecutive seasons—by delivering a Packers-career-best 131 in 2000.

Darren Sharper

Getting noticed was a challenging aspect of Darren Sharper's pro football career. He played college ball at small William & Mary at the NCAA Division I-AA level. But this 6-foot-2, 210-pound defensive back was good enough to convince the Packers to take him in the second round of the 1997 draft.

Sharper played 14 years, most significantly with Green Bay for eight but also with the Minnesota Vikings and the New Orleans Saints. Sharper was a six-time All-Pro and a Super Bowl champion who intercepted 63 passes, which ranks sixth on the all-time list. In 2000, Sharper led the NFL in interceptions with nine. In all, he ran 11 interceptions back for touchdowns, one shy of the league record.

Sharper showed a knack for notching defensive touchdowns as a rookie even though he wasn't even sure he was going to be in the lineup regularly. That year, he scored on an interception return and a fumble return.

"I'm surprised," Sharper said, "because I didn't know from the beginning of the season how much I would be able to contribute."

That was a mere building block. The more Sharper played, the more effective he was.

"I think I've become a lot more aggressive," he said in his fourth season. "I feel it's as though me understanding what it is—at safety understanding the game better, and really getting a sense of what is going on out there . . . allowed me to . . . use my instincts."

Experience and talent combined to make Sharper one of the NFL's great ball-hawk defenders.

Jonathan Daniel/Allsport/Getty Images

2001

▸ 12–4   2nd place ◂

Game-by-Game

9/9	**W,** 28–6, vs. Detroit Lions
9/24	**W,** 37–0, vs. Washington Redskins
9/30	**W,** 28–7, at Carolina Panthers
10/7	**L,** 10–14, at Tampa Bay Buccaneers
10/14	**W,** 31–23, vs. Baltimore Ravens
10/21	**L,** 13–35, at Minnesota Vikings
11/4	**W,** 21–20, vs. Tampa Bay Buccaneers
11/11	**W,** 20–12, at Chicago Bears
11/18	**L,** 20–23, vs. Atlanta Falcons
11/22	**W,** 29–27, at Detroit Lions
12/3	**W,** 28–21, at Jacksonville Jaguars
12/9	**W,** 17–7, vs. Chicago Bears
12/16	**L,** 20–26, at Tennessee Titans
12/23	**W,** 30–7, vs. Cleveland Browns
12/30	**W,** 24–13, vs. Minnesota Vikings
1/6/02	**W,** 34–25, at New York Giants

Playoffs

| 1/13/02 | **W,** 25–15, vs. San Francisco 49ers |
| 1/20/02 | **L,** 17–45, at St. Louis Rams |

Team Scoring

390 points scored (5th)

266 points allowed (5th)

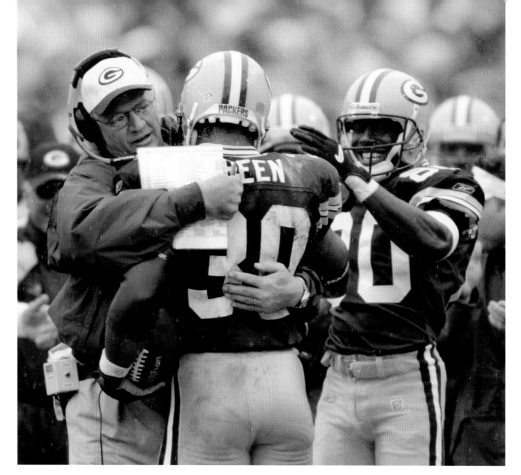

Coach Mike Sherman congratulates Ahman Green after the running back's 83-yard touchdown run helped Green Bay to its opening-game triumph over Detroit, kicking off what would be a 12-win season for the Packers. *Jonathan Daniel/Getty Images*

Everyone in Green Bay felt a lot better and a lot more secure with coach Mike Sherman in 2001, when the Packers finished 12–4 and qualified for the playoffs for the first time since 1998. Of the four losses, three came by six points or fewer. Although the Chicago Bears won the Central Division at 13–3, the Packers beat them twice.

Running back Ahman Green rushed for 1,387 yards, scored 11 touchdowns, and caught 62 passes. Quarterback Brett Favre found Green open more often than any of his wide receivers for the second year in a row. Ryan Longwell had certainly shown he was a cold-weather kicker for Green Bay, and his 104 points marked his fifth straight season with that many or more.

Closing with three straight wins, the Packers had momentum going into the playoffs and a home game against the San Francisco 49ers. The Packers pulled away from the visiting 49ers at Lambeau in the second half.

The Packers trailed 7–6 at halftime, and they were not throwing much. During the intermission, Favre convinced his coaches to let him air it out. He threw for 269 yards, 226 of them in the second half, and passed for touchdowns to Antonio Freeman and tight end Bubba Franks in a 25–17 victory.

However, the season ended the next week when the St. Louis Rams crushed the Pack 45–17, assisted by eight Green Bay turnovers.

PACKERS HEADLINE

Coach Mike Sherman takes over general manager duties and leads Green Bay to 12-win season.

Three come-from-behind wins in December lead the way for second straight 12-win campaign.

Green Bay was thinking big coming off the 2001 season, and it replicated a 12–4 finish to keep optimism high going into the playoffs. The league realigned divisions so that the Packers now played in something called the NFC North. Tampa Bay was moved out, so there were just four teams. Compared to the preceding season, the Chicago Bears and Minnesota Vikings both collapsed, and this time 12–4 was good enough to capture the division.

A seven-game winning streak, which ran from September to November, had the Packers feeling pretty good about themselves. They also won all eight home games during the regular season.

Kicker Ryan Longwell kept pumping out the points (128), Ahman Green kept cranking out the yards (1,240 on the ground), and Brett Favre kept firing the touchdown passes (27). He also gained a new favorite receiver. A steal in the 1999 draft, Donald Driver was a seventh-round pick (No. 213 overall) out of Alcorn State. He went from a previous high of 21 catches two seasons earlier to 70 in 2002, including nine TD receptions.

The season opened with a 37–34 Lambeau Field victory over the Atlanta Falcons, and Atlanta was the team Green Bay drew in the opening round of the playoffs. Entering the game, the Packers were 13–0 all time as a playoff host. But that streak ended. The Falcons, led by quarterback Michael Vick, controlled the tempo and the score, winning 27–7 over the favored Packers.

Tight end Bubba Franks had his second of three straight Pro Bowl seasons in 2002. He had a career-high 54 receptions that year, including a touchdown catch during the Packers' 30–20 win over the Bears in December. *Jonathan Daniel/Getty Images*

Game-by-Game

9/8	**W**, 37–34 (OT), vs. Atlanta Falcons
9/15	**L**, 20–35, at New Orleans Saints
9/22	**W**, 37–31, at Detroit Lions
9/29	**W**, 17–14, vs. Carolina Panthers
10/7	**W**, 34–21, at Chicago Bears
10/13	**W**, 28–10, at New England Patriots
10/20	**W**, 30–9, vs. Washington Redskins
11/4	**W**, 24–10, vs. Miami Dolphins
11/10	**W**, 40–14, vs. Detroit Lions
11/17	**L**, 21–31, at Minnesota Vikings
11/24	**L**, 7–21, at Tampa Bay Buccaneers
12/1	**W**, 30–20, vs. Chicago Bears
12/8	**W**, 26–22, vs. Minnesota Vikings
12/15	**W**, 20–14, at San Francisco 49ers
12/22	**W**, 10–0, vs. Buffalo Bills
12/29	**L**, 17–42, at New York Jets

Playoffs

1/4/03	**L**, 7–27, vs. Atlanta Falcons

Team Scoring

398 points scored (6th)

328 points allowed (12th)

Ahman Green

Perhaps the greatest running back in Packers history, Ahman Green starred for the University of Nebraska before being drafted by the Seattle Seahawks in 1998. Two years into his career, he joined Green Bay. The best years of his career were spent in Wisconsin running up yardage. When he retired in 2009, he was the franchise's all-time leading ground gainer.

The Packers were lucky the Seahawks didn't recognize Green's potential, and Green admitted he was overwhelmed when he first entered the NFL. The playbook seemed too much to digest.

"It was like trying to learn trigonometry overnight," Green said. "Sometimes I'd line up and be thinking, 'Where am I supposed to go?'"

Dwelling too much on the play calls, Green fumbled too much. But once he adapted in Green Bay, he became one of the league's brightest stars.

At 6-foot and 220 pounds, Green was both fast and strong. He also had good hands and a knack for getting open for passes coming out of the backfield.

Green recorded six 1,000-yard rushing seasons. In his 12-year career, he totaled 9,205 yards rushing with a lifetime average of 4.5 yards per carry. He also caught 378 passes for another 2,883 yards. Between ground travel and receptions, Green scored 74 touchdowns.

Green was invited to the Pro Bowl following the 2001 to 2004 seasons. Near the end of the 2003 season, he broke one of the Packers' most hallowed records. He surpassed Hall of Famer Jim Taylor's single-season best of 1,474 yards set in 1962 and ended the year with 1,883 yards.

Many, many times, Green prepared for games by watching tape of his hero and role model, Walter Payton, rushing for the Chicago Bears.

"Walter was the greatest," Green said. "If I don't watch the tape, I'm not focused. He's always been my idol, and I try to carry him on the field with me."

Despite pairing with pass-first Brett Favre in the backfield, Green became the team's offensive engine for several years. At one point, Favre joked to reporters that they should ask him, "Does Favre feel like he's the highest paid handoff guy in the league? The answer is yes."

Green remained in Green Bay after he retired. He is a part-owner of the Green Bay Blizzard, an indoor football team. In 2012, he also worked as an assistant high school coach in another community, where his stepson played football. Green works as a sports broadcaster in Green Bay and became a spokesman for the local symphony.

"It's the fans and the people in it," he said when explaining why he enjoyed living in Green Bay. "The support of the fans was huge through my playing days. It was an easy and simple decision to live here."

Matt Stroshane/Getty Images

A former Eagles defensive back, Al Harris joined the Packers in 2003 and provided some postseason heroics when his interception return for a touchdown in overtime won the Wild Card playoff game against the Seahawks. He went on to be a two-time Pro Bowler with Green Bay. *Elsa/Getty Images*

▸ **10–6   1st place** ◂

Game-by-Game

9/7	**L**, 25–30, vs. Minnesota Vikings
9/14	**W**, 31–6, vs. Detroit Lions
9/21	**L**, 13–20, at Arizona Cardinals
9/29	**W**, 38–23, at Chicago Bears
10/5	**W**, 35–13, vs. Seattle Seahawks
10/12	**L**, 34–40 (OT), vs. Kansas City Chiefs
10/19	**L**, 24–34, at St. Louis Rams
11/2	**W**, 30–27, at Minnesota Vikings
11/10	**L**, 14–17, vs. Philadelphia Eagles
11/16	**W**, 20–13, at Tampa Bay Buccaneers
11/23	**W**, 20–10, vs. San Francisco 49ers
11/27	**L**, 14–22, at Detroit Lions
12/7	**W**, 34–21, vs. Chicago Bears
12/14	**W**, 38–21, at San Diego Chargers
12/22	**W**, 41–7, at Oakland Raiders
12/28	**W**, 31–3, vs. Denver Broncos

Playoffs

1/4/04	**W**, 33–27 (OT), vs. Seattle Seahawks
1/11/04	**L**, 17–20 (OT), vs. Philadelphia Eagles

Team Scoring

442 points scored (4th)

307 points allowed (11th)

It was the year of Ahman Green. The Packers finished 10–6, and Green put together a spectacular season. He rushed for 1,883 yards, caught 50 passes, and scored 120 points on 20 touchdowns.

The 6-foot, 215-pound back was voted the NFC Offensive Player of the Year and selected for the second of his four Pro Bowls with the Packers.

On the way to establishing the new team rushing record, Green passed Jim Taylor, who had rushed for 1,474 yards in 1962. Green was humble when he cracked the mark.

"It lasted for a long time," Green said of the 41-year-old record. "I take my hat off to my O linemen and all the guys blocking for me. They know who they are. I couldn't have gotten here by myself."

In the same game against the San Diego Chargers, kicker Ryan Longwell scored eight points to break Don Hutson's team mark of 823 points, a record that had stood since 1945. Longwell collected a field goal and five extra points in the 38–21 victory.

"With the storied history of this franchise, any time you break a record it's unbelievable," Longwell said. "You're breaking a record of one of the legends of the game."

The Packers held off the Seattle Seahawks 33–27 in the first round of the playoffs. Green Bay broke a 27–27 tie in overtime on an Al Harris 52-yard interception return for a TD. But a week later, the Pack fell to the Philadelphia Eagles 20–17.

PACKERS HEADLINE

Ahman Green breaks franchise single-season rushing record, while kicker Ryan Longwell sets new all-time Packer scoring mark.

2004

▶ 10–6   1st place ◀

Game-by-Game

9/13   **W, 24–14,**
       at Carolina Panthers

9/19   **L, 10–21,**
       vs. Chicago Bears

9/26   **L, 31–45,**
       at Indianapolis Colts

10/3   **L, 7–14,**
       vs. New York Giants

10/11 **L, 27–48,**
       vs. Tennessee Titans

10/17 **W, 38–10, at Detroit Lions**

10/24 **W, 41–20,**
       vs. Dallas Cowboys

10/31 **W, 28–14,**
       at Washington Redskins

11/14 **W, 34–31,**
       vs. Minnesota Vikings

11/21 **W, 16–13,**
       at Houston Texans

11/29 **W, 45–17,**
       vs. St. Louis Rams

12/5   **L, 17–47,**
       at Philadelphia Eagles

12/12 **W, 16–13, vs. Detroit Lions**

12/19 **L, 25–28,**
       vs. Jacksonville Jaguars

12/24 **W, 34–31,**
       at Minnesota Vikings

1/2/05 **W, 31–14,**
       at Chicago Bears

Playoffs

1/9/05 **L, 17–31,**
       vs. Minnesota Vikings

Team Scoring

424 points scored (5th)

380 points allowed (23rd)

PACKERS HEADLINE

Packers win third straight division title but again fall in playoffs, upset by the division rival Vikings.

Slowed by an inexplicable four-game losing streak early in the season, the Packers recovered to finish 10–6 again. And again, they captured the NFC North title to advance to the playoffs.

After a season-opening victory, there was a lot of hand-wringing when the Packers lost to the Chicago Bears, Indianapolis Colts, New York Giants, and Tennessee Titans in consecutive games. But after that stretch, Green Bay played terrifically, winning six out of the last eight games on the schedule.

Brett Favre remained in top form at quarterback, completing 64.1 percent of his passes for 4,088 yards and 30 touchdowns. Javon Walker led all receivers with 89 catches, 1,382 yards, and 12 touchdowns. Ahman Green was not as overpowering as he had been in 2003, but he still rushed for 1,163 yards and caught 40 passes.

The Packers amassed a notable 424 points and scored more than 30 points seven times. They ranked fifth offensively in the league, but only twenty-third defensively. Darren Sharper led the team with four interceptions.

Twice during the regular season, the Packers edged NFC North rival Minnesota. The teams met for a third time in the first round of the playoffs at Lambeau Field. But Wild Card Sunday was too wild for Green Bay. The Packers trailed 17–3 after one quarter and lost 31–17.

Vikings quarterback Daunte Culpepper threw four touchdown passes and Favre threw four interceptions, and that was a huge difference in the game. With no fumbles, either, Minnesota did not make a turnover all day.

Ryan Longwell celebrates his game-winning field goal in the 34–31 victory over the Vikings on November 14. The kicker, who posted his eighth consecutive 100-point season in 2004, defeated Minnesota with another game-winning kick six weeks later, in another 34–31 final on December 24. *Jonathan Daniel/Getty Images*

Kabeer Gbaja-Biamila

It was obvious why Kabeer Gbaja-Biamila was nicknamed "KGB." And it was not because he had any association with the former Soviet Union's old secret police. It simplified pronunciation, and the initials made for easy headline writing in newspapers.

KGB was born in Los Angeles, the son of Nigerian parents, and played at San Diego State. The Packers chose the 6-foot-4, 250-pound linebacker in the 2000 NFL draft.

During his nine seasons with the Packers, KGB became a huge defensive force, disrupting other teams with his sterling ability to rush the passer. His 74.5 sacks set a Packers record.

KGB faced a tremendous mental challenge before a 2002 game, when his mother was killed in a car crash and his wife gave birth on the same day. Yet he played against the Vikings a few days later without practicing and after flying back and forth to California.

"I really didn't even feel like playing," KGB said. "But God gave me this strength. Oh, there was no question I was going to play."

In 2003, KGB signed a seven-year, $37.3 million contract.

"Kabeer has the rare ability to pressure and sack quarterbacks as well as create turnovers," said Packers coach Mike Sherman.

KGB's last name translates to "Big Man Come Save Me," and he played that role for the Packers while he put his original career idea on hold. He had planned on going into his father's plumbing business.

Joe Robbins/Getty Images

2005

▶ 4–12   4th place ◀

Game-by-Game

9/11	**L,** 3–17, at Detroit Lions
9/18	**L,** 24–26, vs. Cleveland Browns
9/25	**L,** 16–17, vs. Tampa Bay Buccaneers
10/3	**L,** 29–32, at Carolina Panthers
10/9	**W,** 52–3, vs. New Orleans Saints
10/23	**L,** 20–23, at Minnesota Vikings
10/30	**L,** 14–21, at Cincinnati Bengals
11/6	**L,** 10–20, vs. Pittsburgh Steelers
11/13	**W,** 33–25, at Atlanta Falcons
11/21	**L,** 17–20, vs. Minnesota Vikings
11/27	**L,** 14–19, at Philadelphia Eagles
12/4	**L,** 7–19, at Chicago Bears
12/11	**W,** 16–13 (OT), vs. Detroit Lions
12/19	**L,** 3–48, at Baltimore Ravens
12/25	**L,** 17–24, vs. Chicago Bears
1/1/06	**W,** 23–17, vs. Seattle Seahawks

Team Scoring

298 points scored (22nd)

344 points allowed (19th)

The disappointing ending to the 2004 season, with the upset loss to Minnesota in the playoffs, did not particularly presage the complete collapse of the Packers in 2005, when they finished a shocking 4–12. But that record got coach Mike Sherman fired.

Green Bay lost its first four games and seven of the first eight. At one point, the team record was 2–10 and nothing was going right. Their total points dropped from 424 in 2004 to 298, which ranked twenty-second in the league.

The biggest problem was the loss of star running back Ahman Green to injury. Green, a steady 1,000-yard-plus rusher, appeared in only five games and gained 255 yards. Green had also been an essential part of the offense as a reliable short-yardage receiver for quarterback Brett Favre.

Sherman tried several potential solutions. Samkon Gado, a native of Nigeria who had attended Liberty University—the religious school in Virginia founded by Jerry Falwell that competes at the NCAA Division I-AA level—went undrafted, but he signed as a free agent with the Kansas City Chiefs in 2005. A raw talent, Gado was waived, but he hooked on with the Packers.

Gado played parts of seven seasons in the NFL, but this year was the only time he was relied on to any extent, and he rushed for a team-leading 582 yards. He also caught 10 passes. Tony Fisher added 173 yards on the ground and caught 48 passes, as a committee was sought to make up for the absence of Green.

After leaving the Packers, Sherman landed as an assistant coach with the Houston Texans before serving as head coach at Texas A&M from 2008 to 2011. He returned to the NFL in 2012 as the Miami Dolphins' offensive coordinator.

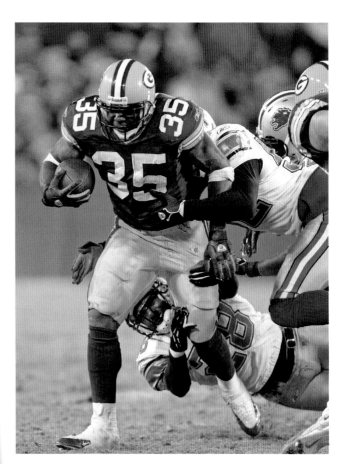

PACKERS HEADLINE

Green Bay plummets to the bottom of the division and posts first losing season of the millennium.

In a season that brought little cause for celebration in Green Bay, undrafted rookie running back Samkon Gado provided some unexpected sparks. In the Packers' 16–13 overtime win over the Lions, Gado plowed his way to 171 yards rushing and one touchdown. *Jonathan Daniel/Getty Images*

Domenic Centofanti/Getty Images

Charles Woodson

Before he completed his college football education at the University of Michigan (he decided he knew enough by the end of his junior year), Charles Woodson had won such honors at the Bronko Nagurski Trophy, the Jim Thorpe Award, the Chuck Bednarik Award, and the Heisman Trophy. Although he returned kicks for Michigan and was a part-time receiver, his main position was cornerback. He thus became the first primarily defensive player to win the Heisman.

Then he turned pro in 1998, toiling first with the Oakland Raiders before joining the Packers in 2006. As an eight-time Pro Bowl selection and three-time All-Pro (through 2012), Woodson had amassed 55 interceptions and more than 700 tackles as a cornerback and safety. He also forced 24 fumbles and collected 17 sacks. In 2006 and 2007, he served as Green Bay's main punt returner. In 2009, he was named the AP NFL Defensive Player of the Year.

The 6-foot-1, 202-pound defender is known for his hard hitting and extraordinary coverage. Although the Packers released the 37-year-old after the 2012 season, he had no plans to retire.

Woodson has been generous with the millions of dollars he has made from football. He donated $2 million to the children's hospital at Michigan, and he gave $100,000 to Hurricane Sandy relief efforts.

▶ 8–8   2nd place ◀

Game-by-Game

9/10	L, 0–26, vs. Chicago Bears
9/17	L, 27–34, vs. New Orleans Saints
9/24	W, 31–24, at Detroit Lions
10/2	L, 9–31, at Philadelphia Eagles
10/8	L, 20–23, vs. St. Louis Rams
10/22	W, 34–24, at Miami Dolphins
10/29	W, 31–14, vs. Arizona Cardinals
11/5	L, 10–24, at Buffalo Bills
11/12	W, 23–17, at Minnesota Vikings
11/19	L, 0–35, vs. New England Patriots
11/27	L, 24–34, at Seattle Seahawks
12/3	L, 10–38, vs. New York Jets
12/10	W, 30–19, at San Francisco 49ers
12/17	W, 17–9, vs. Detroit Lions
12/21	W, 9–7, vs. Minnesota Vikings
12/31	W, 26–7, at Chicago Bears

Team Scoring

301 points scored (22nd)

366 points allowed (25th)

PACKERS HEADLINE

Young coach Mike McCarthy sets Packers back on path to success.

New coach Mike McCarthy was not able to fix everything at once, but the Packers did finish 8–8 in his first season, a four-game improvement. Green Bay made news by winning its last four games in a row.

McCarthy was pretty much an unknown in Green Bay when hired, though he had spent one year with the team as quarterbacks coach. McCarthy didn't turn 43 until the 2006 season was underway. A native of Pittsburgh, he had played college ball at Baker University, an NAIA school in Kansas, and had begun his coaching career at the bottom as a graduate assistant at another small school in Kansas, Fort Hays State. He then worked his way up the coaching ladder one rung at a time.

McCarthy had the benefit of a healthy Ahman Green in the backfield. After missing two-thirds of the previous season, Green again had a 1,000-yard rushing season. He also resumed his role as a key outlet receiver, catching 46 passes.

At 37, quarterback Brett Favre did not have one of his best seasons, completing 56 percent of his passes and throwing an equal number of TD passes and interceptions—18 apiece. Favre was still good enough to keep rookie Aaron Rodgers on the bench for the second straight season. General manager Ted Thompson, who had hired McCarthy after replacing exiled coach-GM Mike Sherman, had made former Cal star Rodgers the team's No. 1 draft pick in 2005.

Another big draft pick came before the 2006 season, when the Packers selected linebacker A. J. Hawk out of Ohio State with the fifth overall pick. At 6-foot-1 and 248 pounds, Hawk is speedy for a midfield defender, and he immediately helped strengthen the Green Bay defense, starting all 16 games in his rookie season.

Defensive end Aaron Kampman terrorized opposing quarterbacks to the tune of 15.5 sacks in 2006. The Iowa native had been a fifth-round pick in 2002. *Tom Dahlin/Getty Images*

Mike McCarthy

The coach who few knew outside of the Packers organization when he was hired in 2006 won two-thirds of his games with Green Bay through the 2012 season, and Mike McCarthy also had a Super Bowl victory on his résumé.

McCarthy was a small-college player and started coaching as a small-college assistant, but by the time he became the Packers' head man, he had been an NFL assistant with four teams, including a brief stop in Green Bay. McCarthy's best credentials were his work as offensive coordinator for New Orleans and San Francisco.

When he was first announced as the Packers' new leader, McCarthy was not one of the best known assistants in the NFL, and his last 49ers team had ranked No. 32 in offensive production. Some Packers players didn't even know who McCarthy was.

"I'm aware of the criticism," McCarthy said. "But let's face it. I didn't get the job because our offense in San Francisco finished last in the league last season. I know people can take stats and twist them to say what they want. But getting a head job and being successful is more than just about stats. It's about fit."

One thing McCarthy, who was grateful for the chance, was about to prove quickly was that he was a good fit in Green Bay.

"It's a once-in-a-lifetime opportunity," he said.

Inescapable to McCarthy once he was granted the job was that he held the same title as the great Vince Lombardi once did.

"You can't help it," McCarthy said.

Right from the beginning with the Packers, McCarthy put more emphasis on weight lifting and building sturdier bodies. He said he wanted to have stronger men on the field. With McCarthy at the helm, Packers attendance at voluntary off-season workouts increased significantly.

Quarterback Brett Favre had begun his annual waffling about whether or not to retire, but McCarthy worked hard to convince Favre to stay in the game, talking to him frequently in Mississippi.

"He can still zip it," the coach said.

McCarthy's first season in Green Bay was nothing special at 8–8, but his program began to take hold in 2007 with a 13–3 record. A 6–10 mark was a bump in the road. But the 2010 season ended with the Packers as Super Bowl champions. They also have become big winners in the regular season each year, and in 2012 they made the playoffs for the fourth consecutive season.

As a motivational ploy, McCarthy had the players measured for championship rings during the night before the Super Bowl game against the Pittsburgh Steelers. It was as if to say, "If you play well, these will be yours."

When McCarthy's Packers won the Super Bowl, he saw his name go on a list that included Lombardi's.

"It feels awesome," McCarthy said of becoming champs. "It's great to bring the Vince Lombardi Trophy back to Green Bay."

MVP Books Collection

Greg Jennings

Greg Jennings did not come to Green Bay with a big reputation. He played his college ball at Western Michigan, and although he was a second-round draft pick, he arrived in Wisconsin with minimal fanfare in 2006.

But as soon as the 5-foot-11, 198-pound receiver got his chance, he seized it. Jennings was a member of the NFL's All-Rookie Team in 2006, and he was a big pass catcher for the Packers for seven seasons, a favorite target of Brett Favre and Aaron Rodgers.

Jennings caught Favre's 400th career touchdown pass on a 75-yard play in 2006, and he has twice been invited to the Pro Bowl. In seven seasons with Green Bay, Jennings had 425 catches, 6,537 yards receiving, and 53 touchdowns.

A member of the Super Bowl champion team after the 2006 season, Jennings was sidelined by injury during much of 2012. The timing was bad because it was the end of his three-year contract, so his future with the team was up in the air headed into the offseason as a free agent.

Jennings said he wanted to stay with the Packers, but with concerns about his injury and the fact that the team had a deep core of receivers on the roster, it quickly became clear that Jennings would be leaving Green Bay. In mid-March 2013, he signed a five-year, $47.5 million contract with the division-rival Minnesota Vikings.

The player has a charitable organization called the Greg Jennings Foundation, which makes contributions to benefit underprivileged children and other youth-oriented organizations. And Jennings has dabbled in television work, appearing on some regular shows and in commercials.

Dilip Vishwanat/Getty Images

Favre's final season in Green Bay falls short after tough playoff loss to New York.

From average to great in one year, Mike McCarthy had the Packers clicking in 2007 with a 13–3 regular-season record, thanks largely to another outstanding season from quarterback Brett Favre.

By the third week in November, the Packers were 10–1 and looking like a Super Bowl contender. They scored points in bunches and registered nine games with more than 30 points.

Favre looked 10 years younger, completing 66.5 percent of his passes for 4,155 yards and 28 touchdowns at age 38, which was not supposed to happen according to NFL aging measures.

Ahman Green was gone, but the new main running back, Ryan Grant, pumped his legs for 956 yards. Donald Driver caught 82 passes for more than 1,000 yards.

The Packers polished off the Seattle Seahawks 42–20 in a first-round playoff game. Recovering from the surprise of two quick Seattle touchdowns, the Green Bay defense clamped down in the second half, allowing only three points. Grant scored three touchdowns, all on short runs, and second-year man Greg Jennings, an emerging star at wide receiver, caught two touchdown passes from Favre.

That set up the NFC Championship Game at Lambeau Field against the New York Giants. The Giants had mustered a late-season run to sneak into the playoffs, and they upset the Packers 23–20. After the Packers sent the game into overtime on a fourth-quarter Mason Crosby field goal, the Giants won on a field goal. Then the Giants upset the undefeated New England Patriots in the Super Bowl.

Game-by-Game

9/9	W, 16–13, vs. Philadelphia
9/16	W, 35–13, at New York Giants
9/23	W, 31–24, vs. San Diego
9/30	W, 23–16, at Minnesota
10/7	L, 20–27, vs. Chicago
10/14	W, 17–14, vs. Washington
10/29	W, 19–13 (OT), at Denver
11/4	W, 33–22, at Kansas City
11/11	W, 34–0, vs. Minnesota
11/18	W, 31–17, vs. Carolina
11/22	W, 37–26, at Detroit
11/29	L, 27–37, at Dallas
12/9	W, 38–7, vs. Oakland
12/16	W, 33–14, at St. Louis
12/23	L, 7–35, at Chicago
12/30	W, 34–13, vs. Detroit

Playoffs

1/12/08	W, 42–20, vs. Seattle Seahawks
1/20/08	L, 20–23 (OT), vs. New York Giants

Team Scoring

435 points scored (4th)

291 points allowed (6th)

After charging through a 13–3 regular season, the Packers fell short in overtime in the NFC Championship Game against the Giants. Mason Crosby's 37-yard field goal tied the game at 20 to force the extra session. *Jamie Squire/Getty Images*

Aaron Rodgers

Packers fans heard about Aaron Rodgers' potential for so long while he sat on the bench behind play-every-down Brett Favre that they began to wonder if coaches and management were fibbing. Rodgers was a highly touted No. 1 draft pick out of California, but all the former Golden Bears star did was perform in practice and hardly ever see action.

However, after three years of showing his stuff in practice, teammates knew what to expect when Rodgers started.

"We weren't worried," said defensive back Al Harris. "We already knew how good he was."

Yet while his wait was agonizingly long, Rodgers emerged as a star as soon as he stepped in as quarterback. In his first few seasons as signal-caller, Rodgers not only delivered a Super Bowl title, but he ran up statistics that exceeded those of Favre at his best—an impressive feat considering that Favre retired holding many major NFL passing records.

The way the NFL has evolved in just the few years since Rodgers became a starter, it is inconceivable that he would wait long on the bench if drafted now. For years, the NFL philosophy was never to start rookies at quarterback because they would be in over their heads, and the crash courses some took usually produced a rash of interceptions as they learned on the job. But recently, at least a half dozen teams have thrown rookies into the job full-time at quarterback. Most have performed acceptably, and some have performed tremendously.

"I know I'm capable of greatness," Rodgers said. "And I'm expecting to reach that level. I've always seemed to have my best performances when I'm under the most pressure."

As soon as he stepped into the lineup, Rodgers showed that if he had experienced a learning curve in practice, he had absorbed all necessary knowledge. He swiftly piled up the touchdowns and the yards, quickly became a three-time Pro Bowl selection, and won the MVP Award in the Super Bowl. In his first five full-time seasons, Rodgers topped the 4,000-yard mark four times and barely missed it a fifth. He did not throw fewer than 28 touchdown passes in one of those seasons, and in 2011 he threw for 45 touchdowns—one of the best single-season marks ever.

Although Rodgers throws frequently, he is rarely picked off. After five years, Rodgers had thrown 171 touchdown passes and 46 interceptions. Only 1.7 percent of his passes were intercepted.

When the Packers offense was flowing, it was almost unstoppable. In a late December 2012 game against the Tennessee Titans, Green Bay won 55–7. It was an eye-opening final score, but not as important a win as the Super Bowl by any means.

"This is a great group of men we've put together here," Rodgers said of the Packers under coach Mike McCarthy. "They have a lot of character and we do a lot together. It's just great to share it with them."

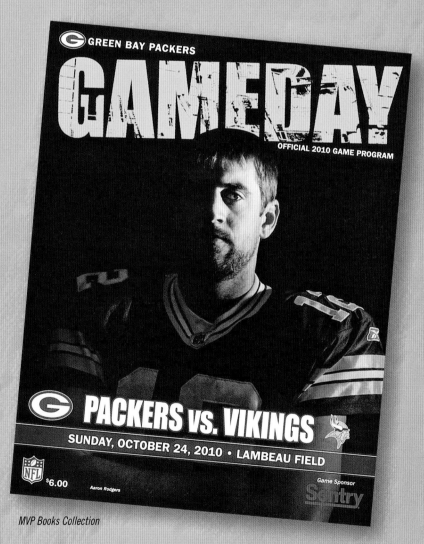

MVP Books Collection

Opposite: Al Bello/Getty Images

2008

Game-by-Game

9/8	W, 24–19, vs. Minnesota	
9/14	W, 48–25, at Detroit	
9/21	L, 16–27, vs. Dallas	
9/28	L, 21–30, at Tampa Bay	
10/5	L, 24–27, vs. Atlanta	
10/12	W, 27–17, at Seattle	
10/19	W, 34–14, vs. Indianapolis	
11/2	L, 16–19 (OT), at Tennessee	
11/9	L, 27–28, at Minnesota	
11/16	W, 37–3, vs. Chicago	
11/24	L, 29–51, at New Orleans	
11/30	L, 31–35, vs. Carolina	
12/7	L, 21–24, vs. Houston	
12/14	L, 16–20, at Jacksonville	
12/22	L, 17–20 (OT), at Chicago	
12/28	W, 31–21, vs. Detroit	

Team Scoring

419 points scored (5th)

380 points allowed (22nd)

PACKERS HEADLINE

Seven losses by less than a touchdown difference spells bad luck in Aaron Rodgers' debut turn as starter.

The Brett Favre will-he or won't-he saga about retirement took on gigantically odd proportions in 2008. Favre decided he did not want to retire, but the Packers decided they did not want him back and were turning over the first-string quarterback job to Aaron Rodgers.

Rodgers had been sitting around waiting to play more than about a dozen downs a season for three years. He was going to be under pressure replacing a legend regardless of circumstances, but the bad feelings that percolated between Favre and his team of the last 16 seasons divided the fan base, too.

Favre ended up spending an awkward season with the New York Jets. The Packers ended up having a lousy 6–10 season, but it wasn't Rodgers' fault. He had a very Favre-like year. Rodgers threw for 4,038 yards and 28 touchdowns compared to 13 interceptions.

In his second season as the feature back, Ryan Grant improved, too, rushing for 1,203 yards. As a team, the Packers scored 419 points.

But after a 4–3 start, the team took a dive, going 1–7 over the next eight weeks. The worst outing in the bunch was a 51–29 loss to the New Orleans Saints. That was a defensive fiasco, but the next four losses, all in a row, were more emblematic of not being able to make the big play to hold the opposition. On consecutive weeks, the Packers lost by four, three, four, and three points. It translated into a lost season.

Ryan Grant (25) celebrates after scoring a touchdown during Green Bay's 37–3 trouncing of the Bears on November 16. The second-year back exploded for 1,203 yards on the season, including a tremendous 145 against Chicago. *Doug Pensinger/Getty Images*

Offense clicks under Aaron Rodgers, who is named to his first Pro Bowl after a second-straight 4,000-yard season.

> ▸ 11–5   2nd place ◂

Game-by-Game

9/13	W, 21–15, vs. Chicago Bears	
9/20	L, 24–31, vs. Cincinnati Bengals	
9/27	W, 36–17, at St. Louis Rams	
10/5	L, 23–30, at Minnesota Vikings	
10/18	W, 26–0, vs. Detroit Lions	
10/25	W, 31–3, at Cleveland Browns	
11/1	L, 26–38, vs. Minnesota Vikings	
11/8	L, 28–38, at Tampa Bay Buccaneers	
11/15	W, 17–7, vs. Dallas Cowboys	
11/22	W, 30–24, vs. San Francisco 49ers	
11/26	W, 34–12, at Detroit Lions	
12/7	W, 27–14, vs. Baltimore Ravens	
12/13	W, 21–14, at Chicago Bears	
12/20	L, 37–36, at Pittsburgh Steelers	
12/27	W, 48–10, vs. Seattle Seahawks	
1/3/10	W, 33–7, at Arizona Cardinals	

Playoffs

1/10/10   L, 45–51 (OT), at Arizona Cardinals

Team Scoring

461 points scored (3rd)

297 points allowed (7th)

It was not exactly a tearful reunion when Aaron Rodgers and the Packers met Brett Favre and the Vikings for a nationally televised *Monday Night Football* game on October 5. Although Rodgers passed for 384 yards, the veteran Favre led his club to victory. *Jamie Squire/Getty Images*

Coming off a weird season, it was difficult to project the Packers' 2009 campaign. But they basically reversed their regular-season record, going 11–5. The Brett Favre drama played on throughout the land, but it was no longer an issue in Green Bay—except that he didn't retire again and signed with the rival Minnesota Vikings.

Green Bay became an offensive juggernaut behind Aaron Rodgers, who played like Favre at his best. Rodgers threw for 4,434 yards and 30 touchdowns while tossing only seven interceptions, a phenomenal ratio. The Pack averaged 28.2 points per game. Ryan Grant continued to excel in the backfield, rushing for 1,253 yards.

By signing with the Vikings, Favre added spice to the annual twice-a-year meetings with Minnesota. The first encounter came on October 5 in Minnesota, and the Vikings won 30–23. Minnesota built a 28–14 lead at halftime and held on. In their first meeting head-to-head, Rodgers went 26-for-37 for 384 yards, two touchdowns, and one interception. Favre went 24-for-31 for 271 yards, three touchdowns, and zero interceptions.

The teams met again on November 1 in Green Bay, and the Vikings won again, 38–26. Rodgers went 26-for-41 for 287 yards with three touchdown passes and no interceptions. Favre went 17-for-28 for 244 yards with four touchdown passes and no picks.

Green Bay reached the playoffs, where they lost a crazy game to the Arizona Cardinals, 51–45 in overtime. Rodgers threw for 423 yards and four touchdowns. No one ever wondered again if he could play in the NFL.

Jonathan Daniel/Getty Images

Clay Matthews III

When your grandfather, father, and uncle all played in the NFL, it's hard not to say that you were born into the game. Clay Matthews III is not only carrying on the family tradition, but the family's first and last names.

A former University of Southern California All-American, Matthews III was drafted by the Packers in the first round in 2009. In his first four seasons in the lineup as a linebacker, he was chosen for the Pro Bowl each year.

Matthews wears his blond hair long, and when he pulls it back he more resembles a European rock star than a ferocious football player, even though he is 6-foot-3 and weighs 255 pounds.

Matthews' grandfather, the first Clay, played four years in the NFL. His dad, Clay Jr., played 19 seasons and was selected

All-Pro four times. Uncle Bruce Matthews was one of the all-time greats. He played 19 seasons, was chosen for 14 Pro Bowls, and was elected to the Pro Football Hall of Fame.

Casey Matthews, Clay III's younger brother, is on the roster of the Philadelphia Eagles, and they have three cousins playing college football.

"It's fun to continue on this legacy of players that have excelled in the NFL," Clay III said.

Matthews' distinctive hair has helped make him popular with certain fans, and he jokes that he has better hair than fellow Green Bay linebacker A. J. Hawk, who also has long blond hair. As a joke, blonde television reporter Erin Andrews once dressed as Matthews for Halloween.

Titletown for the 13th time!

G oing 10–6 in the regular season was not a record that promised tremendous excitement in the postseason, so going all the way was a grand surprise.

Aaron Rodgers was entrenched at quarterback, though his numbers were down a little to 3,922 yards and 28 touchdown passes. The running game's decline was alarming, though. Brandon Jackson was the leading rusher with 703 yards.

Ryan Grant injured his ankle in the opener, underwent surgery, and was gone for the season. As part of the early bad luck, the Packers in October lost in overtime on field goals to Washington and Miami.

Ignoring those discouraging developments, the Packers won four straight and closed strongly enough to make the playoffs. First up were the Philadelphia Eagles, and the Packers prevailed in the Wild Card game 21–16. Green Bay got an early lead and protected it.

Next came the Atlanta Falcons, also on the road. The Packers exploded for 28 points in the second quarter on the way to a 48–21 triumph. That set up the NFC Championship Game against the Bears in Chicago, the third straight playoff road trip for the Pack. Green Bay won 21–14 to advance to the Super Bowl.

Super Bowl XLV in Arlington, Texas, before 103,000 fans, was a classic game with considerable suspense. The Packers prevailed 31–25, as the Steelers fell short of a potential winning touchdown in the last two minutes. Rodgers was chosen MVP, and it was Green Bay's thirteenth NFL championship.

In Green Bay's season-opening win against Philadelphia, Clay Matthews tallied three sacks, a total he matched the following week against Buffalo, en route to a team-high 13.5 sacks on the year. His dominance of opposing quarterbacks earned him a selection as a first-team All-Pro. *Hunter Martin/Philadelphia Eagles/Getty Images*

2010

▶ **10–6   2nd place** ◀

Game-by-Game

9/12	**W**, 27–20, at Philadelphia Eagles
9/19	**W**, 34–7, vs. Buffalo Bills
9/27	**L**, 17–20, at Chicago Bears
10/3	**W**, 28–26, vs. Detroit Lions
10/10	**L**, 13–16 (OT), at Washington Redskins
10/17	**L**, 20–23 (OT), vs. Miami Dolphins
10/24	**W**, 28–24, vs. Minnesota Vikings
10/31	**W**, 9–0, at New York Jets
11/7	**W**, 45–7, vs. Dallas Cowboys
11/21	**W**, 31–3, at Minnesota Vikings
11/28	**L**, 17–20, at Atlanta Falcons
12/5	**W**, 34–16, vs. San Francisco 49ers
12/12	**L**, 3–7, at Detroit Lions
12/19	**L**, 27–31, at New England Patriots
12/26	**W**, 45–17, vs. New York Giants
1/2/11	**W**, 10–3, vs. Chicago Bears

Playoffs

1/9/11	**W**, 21–16, at Philadelphia Eagles
1/15/11	**W**, 48–21, at Atlanta Falcons
1/23/11	**W**, 21–14, at Chicago Bears
2/6/11	**W**, 31–25, vs. Pittsburgh Steelers

Team Scoring

388 points scored (10th)

240 points allowed (2nd)

Super Bowl XLV

Quarterback Aaron Rodgers, who only a few seasons earlier was wondering if he would ever get off the bench in Green Bay, led the Packers to the Super Bowl title on February 6, 2011, besting the Pittsburgh Steelers 31–25.

Rodgers was named Most Valuable Player at Cowboys Stadium in Texas by completing 24 of 39 passes for 304 yards and tossing three touchdowns with no interceptions. Attendance was 103,219 in the new stadium, just short of the all-time Super Bowl record of 103,985 at the Rose Bowl. Viewership topped 111 million people, more than watched the final episodes of *M*A*S*H* or *Cheers* or the "Who Shot J. R.?" *Dallas*.

It was Green Bay's thirteenth NFL title and fourth Super Bowl championship. The Packers led 14–0 after the first quarter and never trailed, but Pittsburgh always threatened.

A particularly demoralizing Packers touchdown for the Steelers was the second one. Immediately after Green Bay took its lead, Pittsburgh had the ball. Only the margin shot to 14–0 after quarterback Ben Roethlisberger was intercepted by Nick Collins.

Collins picked off the pass and ran it back 37 yards, and kicker Mason Crosby added another extra point. "I played high school running back, so I know what to do when the ball is in my hands," Collins said. "I made a couple of moves to get into the end zone. I was able to read Big Ben, and I got a nice jump on the ball."

"It's a dream come true," Rodgers said of salting away the crown. "It's what I dreamt about as a little kid watching Joe Montana and Steve Young."

Jordy Nelson (87) and Aaron Rodgers (12) celebrate their 29-yard touchdown play in the first quarter of Super Bowl XLV. *Kevin C. Cox/Getty Images*

MVP Books Collection

Rodgers completed two touchdown passes to Greg Jennings, one on a 21-yard throw and one on an eight-yard play. Emotional and happy, the religious Jennings kept repeating "To God be the glory" whenever he was asked about a play that worked against the Steelers.

The Packers were the only ones to hit paydirt in the first quarter, and the scoring play was a 29-yard pass from Rodgers to receiver Jordy Nelson. Rodgers had seen the way the defense was aligned and changed his original call. "It was actually a screen play," Nelson said, "but he checked to a go route. That's what we hit."

Nelson was Green Bay's catch leader with nine for 140 yards. Most of the offense for both teams came through the air, but Roethlisberger was intercepted twice. The Packers won pretty much without a ground game, netting only 50 yards rushing.

Knowing that Green Bay residents refer to their community as "Titletown," and that the winner's trophy is named after the most iconic figure in team history, made the victory sweeter for Packers players.

"We're going back to Titletown, baby," Collins said. "This is big. The Vince Lombardi Trophy is coming back home."

2011

▶ 15–1   1st place ◀

Game-by-Game

9/8	W, 42–34, vs. New Orleans Saints
9/18	W, 30–23, at Carolina Panthers
9/25	W, 27–17, at Chicago Bears
10/2	W, 49–23, vs. Denver Broncos
10/9	W, 25–14, at Atlanta Falcons
10/16	W, 24–3, vs. St. Louis Rams
10/23	W, 33–27, at Minnesota Vikings
11/6	W, 45–38, at San Diego Chargers
11/14	W, 45–7, vs. Minnesota Vikings
11/20	W, 35–26, vs. Tampa Bay Buccaneers
11/24	W, 27–15, at Detroit Lions
12/4	W, 38–35, at New York Giants
12/11	W, 46–16, vs. Oakland Raiders
12/18	L, 14–19, at Kansas City Chiefs
12/25	W, 35–21, vs. Chicago Bears
1/1/12	W, 45–41, vs. Detroit Lions

Playoffs

| 1/15/12 | L, 20–37, vs. New York Giants |

Team Scoring

560 points scored (1st)

359 points allowed (19th)

All-Pro Aaron Rodgers seemingly did it all in 2011, and against Denver in early October, he not only set a new career mark with 408 yards passing and threw for four touchdowns, he also ran in two TDs in the 49–23 thrashing of the Broncos. *Joe Amon/The Denver Post/Getty Images*

A season after winning the Super Bowl, the Packers looked even better. They compiled the finest regular-season record in their history, going 15–1. They scored a remarkable 560 points, averaging 35 points per game as the No. 1 offense in the NFL. Eleven times the Packers tallied at least 30 points in a game.

While the road to the Super Bowl the previous year had been a long one, with three games at other stadiums, the Packers earned a first-round playoff bye this season and earned home-field advantage throughout the NFC playoffs.

Although Green Bay fans did not quite disrespect Brett Favre enough to say "Brett who?," the new darling was definitely Aaron Rodgers, his successor. Rodgers had a fabulous season, throwing for 4,643 yards and 45 touchdowns while tossing just six interceptions.

Seven different receivers caught at least 25 passes, with Jordy Nelson at the top of the list with 68 catches. Nelson was a fourth-year man out of Kansas State, but he hadn't been a primary receiver before. He grabbed one more ball than Greg Jennings.

Rookie Randall Cobb from Eastern Kentucky added a new dimension to the return game. He averaged 11.3 yards per punt return, with one touchdown, and 27.7 yards per kickoff return, including a 108-yard touchdown, which equaled the NFL record for longest kickoff return.

For all of that, the Packers went out and lost in the first round of the playoffs, 37–20, to the New York Giants at Lambeau Field.

PACKERS HEADLINE

Dominating regular season ends with disappointing postseason loss.

Packers Season Tickets

Once a year, the Green Bay Packers front office sends out a postcard to update fans on where they rank on the season-ticket waiting list. That notorious Packers list runs around 96,000 people deep (though it changes so quickly that it might have jumped over 100,000 by now), and one estimate indicated it would take 956 years to get from the bottom to the top and have your name called.

Another estimate of it taking only 30 years is probably way optimistic. When some ticket buyers realized that because of their age they would never ascend to the top in their lifetimes, they began putting the names of newborn babies on the list in the hopes they would acquire what their parents couldn't.

Turnover on the ticket list is most usually attributable to death with no heirs. There are years when it is less than 100. A boomlet of opportunity occurred the first time personal seat licenses were required and 7,000 fans failed to renew.

The projected seating capacity for Lambeau Field for the 2013 season, once the latest round of renovations is completed, is 79,594. The previous capacity was 73,094. Despite minor stadium tweaks, the maximum attendance figure since 2003 has remained within several hundred seats of that mark.

Lambeau opened as the new City Stadium in 1957 with a capacity of 32,500. Including the 2013 change, it has been expanded nine times by at least 1,500 seats—and usually more—with each alteration.

Cheeseheads

You can't go to a Green Bay Packers game—or go anywhere in Wisconsin during football season—without seeing somebody wearing a piece of foam cheese on their head.

The campy, off-beat, cheese-shaped chunks of foam that were molded into hats were birthed by a man named Ralph Bruno at a Milwaukee Brewers–Chicago White Sox game in 1987. They were actually made from the stuffing of his mother's couch.

As they evolved as a fashion accessory, few could have predicted how widespread the cheesehead hat phenomenon would become as a symbol for passionate Packers fans.

The origin of the word *cheesehead* is traced to the 1969 book *Papillon*, in which it was used as an insult to describe someone from Wisconsin due to the huge production of cheese in the state.

Bruno, the hat's inventor, turned their manufacture into a business. Green Bay fans wear the colorful hats with pride and embrace the designation of cheesehead despite taunts from opposing sports fans.

Season tickets at Lambeau, as well as cheeseheads, are a multigenerational obsession for Packers fans. *Jonathan Daniel/Getty Images*

Donald Driver

One of the grandest of Green Bay careers came to an end at the conclusion of the 2012 season when Donald Driver announced his retirement. A virtual unknown out of Alcorn State when he was drafted in the last round in 1999, Driver closed the door on a four-time Pro Bowl career with 743 catches.

Right from the start, Driver did not take for granted that he would even make the team. He had some fortunate timing in that Robert Brooks retired.

"It's a big, sad thing right now that Robert retired, because I looked up to Robert," Driver said. "My biggest thing would still be making the team. I'm not guaranteed that I'll have a spot."

Yet Driver not only survived the cuts, he thrived. Players chosen 213th in the draft are long shots to make an NFL team, never mind become stars, but the 6-foot, 195-pound whiz beat the odds. Sixty-one of Driver's career catches went for touchdowns, and he surpassed 10,000 yards in receiving. One natural Driver skill was his leaping ability—in college he high jumped 7 feet, 6 1/2 inches—and that enhanced his overall catching ability. It was originally Driver's dream to represent the United States in the Olympics, and he participated in the 1996 trials.

While his high jumping was a superb achievement, Driver was lucky he lived to tell about it. When he was eight or nine, he used to wear a cape and emulate Superman—by jumping from the second story of apartment buildings as if he could fly. In high school in Houston, Driver was a kind of superman, winning 19 varsity letters in a variety of sports.

Before he had even tried it—and following in the footsteps of Brooks—Driver looked forward to scoring a touchdown that would lead to a Lambeau Leap.

"I'm going to jump straight up in the stands," he said.

Driver got to practice that kind of jumping more often than high jumping over the years. In 2002 and 2004, he tallied nine touchdowns each season. In 2006, Driver caught 92 passes, his career high. He caught more than 80 in a year three more times and 70 in a year another three times.

Driver also had seven seasons with at least 1,000 yards gained through the air.

By 2006, Driver had become the leader of the receiving corps. He was such an integral part of the team that the Packers, unsolicited, tore up an existing contract with time left on it to give him more money. General manager Ted Thompson told Driver, 'Hey, you deserved it."

"I know I had two years left and they didn't have to do anything at all," Driver said. "You have to feel good that a man like that feels that way about you."

Over time, all of Green Bay came to feel that way about Driver because of his work ethic, personality, and off-field charitable work. Driver won the Ed Block Courage Award, with teammates citing his inspirational nature, and the Packers' Walter Payton Man of the Year Award.

Ronald C. Modra/Sports Imagery/Getty Images

Aaron Rodgers leads Green Bay to the playoffs for the fourth straight year with another all-star season.

N ot as consistent as in 2011, and coping with serious injuries, the Packers got stronger as the season wore on, finishing 11–5 and winning the NFC North. They got healthy and were poised to make noise in the playoffs.

Aaron Rodgers was showing he was Brett Favre's equal at quarterback, once again running up more than 4,000 yards on pass plays and producing an almost unbelievable 40-touchdown to six-interception ratio.

Scoring was no problem, but the defense also shored up as the Packers won four out of their last five games. Heading into the postseason, they were viewed as one of the most dangerous clubs in the NFC with as good a chance as anyone else to make it back to the Super Bowl.

Although they lost to Minnesota on the last day of the regular season—allowing the Vikings to reach the playoffs—and had to face them again immediately, the postseason game was much different. Minnesota starting quarterback Christian Ponder was a last-minute scratch because of injury, and backup Joe Webb filled in after barely playing all season. Green Bay led 24–3 going into the fourth quarter and won 24–10.

The powerful San Francisco 49ers were on deck, and in a game that unfolded in a surprising manner, the 49ers piled up points and quarterback Colin Kaepernick, a starter for only half a season, continuously broke free, setting an NFL quarterback rushing record with 181 yards. The 49ers won 45–31 and went on to the Super Bowl.

Game-by-Game

9/9	L, 22–30, vs. San Francisco 49ers
9/13	W, 23–10, vs. Chicago Bears
9/24	L, 12–14, at Seattle Seahawks
9/30	W, 28–27, vs. New Orleans Saints
10/7	L, 27–30, at Indianapolis Colts
10/14	W, 42–24, at Houston Texans
10/21	W, 30–20, at St. Louis Rams
10/28	W, 24–15, vs. Jacksonville Jaguars
11/4	W, 31–17, vs. Arizona Cardinals
11/18	W, 24–20, at Detroit Lions
11/25	L, 10–38, at New York Giants
12/2	W, 23–14, vs. Minnesota Vikings
12/9	W, 27–20, vs. Detroit Lions
12/16	W, 21–13, at Chicago Bears
12/23	W, 55–7, vs. Tennessee Titans
12/30	L, 34–37, at Minnesota Vikings

Playoffs

1/5/13	W, 24–10, vs. Minnesota Vikings
1/12/13	L, 31–45, at San Francisco 49ers

Team Scoring

433 points scored (5th)

336 points allowed (11th)

James Jones leaps over a Vikings defender to haul in one of his league-leading 14 touchdowns in 2012. This TD grab helped lead the Pack to a 23–14 home win over Minnesota in early December. *Joe Robbins/Getty Images*

Team Leaders

(**Boldface** indicates league leader)

Scoring Leaders (Points)

2000: Ryan Longwell, 131
2001: Ryan Longwell, 104
2002: Ryan Longwell, 128
2003: Ahman Green & Ryan Longwell, 120
2004: Ryan Longwell, 120
2005: Ryan Longwell, 90
2006: Dave Rayner, 109
2007: Mason Crosby, **141**
2008: Mason Crosby, 127
2009: Mason Crosby, 129
2010: Mason Crosby, 112
2011: Mason Crosby, 140
2012: Mason Crosby, 113

Rushing Leaders (Carries / Yards / TDs)

2000: Ahman Green, 263 / 1,175 / 10
2001: Ahman Green, 304 / 1,387 / 9
2002: Ahman Green, 286 / 1,240 / 7
2003: Ahman Green, 355 / 1,883 / 15
2004: Ahman Green, 259 / 1,163 / 7
2005: Samkon Gado, 143 / 582 / 6
2006: Ahman Green, 266 / 1,059 / 5
2007: Ryan Grant, 188 / 956 / 8
2008: Ryan Grant, 312 / 1,203 / 4
2009: Ryan Grant, 282 / 1,253 / 11
2010: Brandon Jackson, 190 / 703 / 3
2011: James Starks, 133 / 578 / 1
2012: Alex Green, 135 / 464 / 0

Passing Leaders (Completions / Attempts / Yards)

2000: Brett Favre, 338 / 580 / 3,812
2001: Brett Favre, 314 / 510 / 3,921
2002: Brett Favre, 341 / 551 / 3,658
2003: Brett Favre, 308 / 471 / 3,361
2004: Brett Favre, 346 / 540 / 4,088
2005: Brett Favre, **372** / **607** / 3,881
2006: Brett Favre, 343 / **613** / 3,885
2007: Brett Favre, 356 / 535 / 4,155
2008: Aaron Rodgers, 341 / 536 / 4,038
2009: Aaron Rodgers, 350 / 541 / 4,434
2010: Aaron Rodgers, 312 / 475 / 3,922
2011: Aaron Rodgers, 343 / 502 / 4,643
2012: Aaron Rodgers, 371 / 552 / 4,295

Receiving Leaders (Receptions / Yards / TDs)

2000: Ahman Green, 73 / 559 / 3
2001: Ahman Green, 62 / 594 / 2
2002: Donald Driver, 70 / 1,064 / 9
2003: Donald Driver, 52 / 621 / 2
2004: Javon Walker, 89 / 1,382 / 12
2005: Donald Driver, 86 / 1,221 / 5
2006: Donald Driver, 92 / 1,295 / 8
2007: Donald Driver, 82 / 1,048 / 2
2008: Greg Jennings, 80 / 1,292 / 9
2009: Donald Driver, 70 / 1,061 / 6
2010: Greg Jennings, 76 / 1,265 / 12
2011: Jordy Nelson, 68 / 1,263 / 15
2012: Randall Cobb, 80 / 954 / 8

Interceptions (Number / Yards / TDs)

2000: Darren Sharper, 9 / 109 / 0
2001: Darren Sharper, 6 / 78 / 0
2002: Darren Sharper, 7 / 233 / 1
2003: Darren Sharper, 5 / 78 / 0
2004: Darren Sharper, 4 / 97 / 2
2005: Al Harris, 3 / 30 / 1
2006: Charles Woodson, 8 / 61 / 1
2007: Atari Bigby, 5 / 50 / 0
2008: Nick Collins, 7 / 295 / 3
　　　Charles Woodson, 7 / 169 / 2
2009: Charles Woodson, 9 / 179 / 3
2010: Tramon Williams, 6 / 87 / 0
2011: Charles Woodson, 7 / 63 / 1
2012: Casey Hayward, 6 / 81 / 0

First-Team All-Pros

2000: Darren Sharper, S
2004: William Henderson, RB
2009: Charles Woodson, CB
2010: Clay Matthews, LB
2011: Aaron Rodgers, QB
2011: Charles Woodson, CB

Pro Bowl Selections

2000: Darren Sharper, S
2001: Brett Favre, QB
2001: Bubba Franks, TE
2001: Ahman Green, RB
2002: Donald Driver, WR
2002: Brett Favre, QB
2002: Bubba Franks, TE
2002: Ahman Green, RB
2002: Marco Rivera, G
2002: Darren Sharper, S
2003: Brett Favre, QB
2003: Mike Flanagan, C
2003: Bubba Franks, TE
2003: Kabeer Gbaja-Biamila, DE
2003: Ahman Green, RB
2003: Marco Rivera, G
2004: Ahman Green, RB
2004: William Henderson, RB
2004: Marco Rivera, G
2004: Javon Walker, WR

2006: Donald Driver, WR
2006: Aaron Kampman, DE
2007: Chad Clifton, T
2007: Donald Driver, WR
2007: Brett Favre, QB
2007: Al Harris, CB
2007: Aaron Kampman, DE
2008: Nick Collins, S
2008: Al Harris, CB
2008: Charles Woodson, CB
2009: Nick Collins, S
2009: Clay Matthews, LB
2009: Aaron Rodgers, QB
2009: Charles Woodson, CB
2010: Chad Clifton, T
2010: Nick Collins, S
2010: Clay Matthews, LB
2010: Greg Jennings, WR
2010: Tramon Williams, CB
2010: Charles Woodson, CB
2011: John Kuhn, RB
2011: Clay Matthews, LB
2011: Greg Jennings, WR
2011: B. J. Raji, DT
2011: Aaron Rodgers, QB
2011: Scott Wells, C
2011: Charles Woodson, CB
2012: Clay Matthews, LB
2012: Aaron Rodgers, QB
2012: Jeff Saturday, C

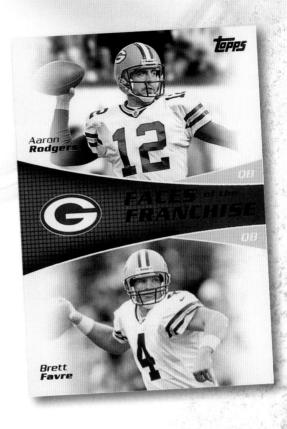

1st-Round Draft Picks

2000: Bubba Franks (14), TE, Miami
2001: Jamal Reynolds (10), DE, Florida State
2002: Javon Walker (20), WR, Florida State
2003: Nick Barnett (29), LB, Oregon State
2004: Ahmad Carroll (25), CB, Arkansas
2005: Aaron Rodgers (24), QB, California
2006: A. J. Hawk (5), LB, Ohio State
2007: Justin Harrell (16), DT, Tennessee
2008: No pick
2009: B. J. Raji (9), DT, Boston College; Clay Matthews III (26), LB, Southern California
2010: Bryan Bulaga (23), OT, Iowa
2011: Derek Sherrod (32), OT, Mississippi State
2012: Nick Perry (28), DE, Southern California

THE GREEN BAY PACKERS
ALL-TIME PLAYER ROSTER

Minimum 5 games played. Through the 2012 season.

Player name	Position	Seasons	Games	Player name	Position	Seasons	Games
Cliff Aberson	B	1946	10	Kevin Barry	T	2002–2005	59
George Abramson	G/T	1925	10	Norm Barry	B	1921	8
Ron Acks	LB	1974–1976	40	Don Barton	B	1953	5
Chet Adams	T	1943	10	Carl Barzilauskas	DT	1978–1979	21
Herb Adderley	CB	1961–1969	125	Myrt Basing	B	1923–1927	41
Bob Adkins	B	1940–1941, 1945	20	Lloyd Baxter	C	1948	11
William Afflis	G	1951–1954	48	Sanjay Beach	WR	1992	16
Louie Aguiar	P	1999	15	Ken Beck	DT	1959–1960	24
Chris Akins	S	2000–2001	13	Wayland Becker	E	1936–1938	30
Zac Alcorn	TE	2006	6	Don Beebe	WR	1996–1997	26
Ben Aldridge	B	1953	8	Bruce Beekley	LB	1980	15
Lionel Aldridge	DE	1963–1971	123	Albert Bell	WR	1988	5
Kurt Allerman	LB	1980–1981	29	Chris Bell	G/T	2000	6
Marty Amsler	DE	1970	9	Ed Bell	G/T	1947–1949	35
Norm Amundsen	G	1957	12	Edgar Bennett	RB	1992–1996	80
Bill Anderson	TE	1965–1966	24	Tony Bennett	LB	1990–1993	56
Donny Anderson	RB	1966–1971	84	Cedric Benson	RB	2012	5
John Anderson	LB	1978–1989	146	Paul Berezney	T	1942–1944	31
Marques Anderson	S	2002–2003	30	Ed Berry	DB	1986	16
Vickey Ray Anderson	FB	1980	7	Tom Bettis	LB	1955–1961	84
Joe Andruzzi	G	1998–1999	23	David Beverly	P	1975–1980	86
Charlie Ane	C	1981	15	Josh Bidwell	P	2000–2003	64
Lester Archambeau	DE	1990–1992	36	Atari Bigby	S	2005–2010	46
Billy Ard	G/T	1989–1991	35	Lewis Billups	CB	1992	5
Mike Arthur	C	1995–1996	16	Tom Birney	K	1979–1980	13
Rodney Artmore	S	1999	5	Desmond Bishop	LB	2007–2011	69
Marion Ashmore	T	1928–1929	21	Will Blackmon	CB	2006–2009	32
Bert Askson	TE	1975–1977	42	Ed Blaine	G	1962	14
Steve Atkins	RB	1979–1981	19	Michael Blair	RB	1998	11
Hise Austin	DB	1973	9	Carl Bland	WR	1989–1990	30
Buddy Aydelette	G	1980	9	Shaun Bodiford	WR	2006–2007	9
				Bill Boedeker	B	1950	9
Byron Bailey	HB	1953	10	Vaughn Booker	DE/DT	1998–1999	30
Karsten Bailey	WR	2002–2003	8	Billy Bookout	DB	1955–1956	19
Bill Bain	T	1975	14	J. R. Boone	B	1953	8
Roy Baker	B	1928–1929	13	Nate Borden	DE	1955–1959	57
Frank Balasz	B	1939–1941	13	Jim Bowdoin	G	1928–1931	45
Al Baldwin	E	1950	12	Matt Bowen	S	2001–2002	21
Herb Banet	B	1937	7	David Bowens	DE	2000	14
Bob Barber	DE	1976–1979	60	Ken Bowman	C	1964–1973	123
Allen Barbre	G	2007–2009	25	Jerry Boyarsky	NT	1986–1989	29
Don Barclay	G/T	2012	16	Greg Boyd	DE	1983	12
Bryan Barker	P	2004	16	Jarrett Boykin	WR	2012	10
Gary Barnes	E	1962	13	Don Bracken	P	1985–1990	80
Nick Barnett	LB	2003–2010	107	Charlie Brackins	QB	1955	7
Solon Barnett	T	1945–1946	5	Corey Bradford	WR	1998–2001	42
Nate Barragar	C	1931–1932, 1934–1935	41	Dave Bradley	G	1969–1971	15
Al Barry	G	1954, 1957	24	Jeff Brady	LB	1992	8

Player name	Position	Seasons	Games	Player name	Position	Seasons	Games
Byron Braggs	DE	1981–1983	41	Tony Carter	FB	2002	12
Kent Branstetter	T	1973	9	Ron Cassidy	WR	1979–1981, 1983–1984	60
Zeke Bratkowski	QB	1963–1968, 1971	43	Chuck Cecil	S	1988–1992	66
Ray Bray	G	1952	12	Don Chandler	K	1965–1967	42
Gene Breen	LB	1964	6	Antonio Chatman	WR/KR	2003–2005	48
Diyral Briggs	LB	2010	5	Louis Cheek	T	1991	12
Charley Brock	C/LB	1939–1947	92	Bill Cherry	C	1986–1987	28
Lou Brock	B	1940–1945	58	Brandon Chillar	LB	2008–2010	34
Matt Brock	DE/DT	1989–1994	76	Mark Chmura	TE	1993–1999	89
John Brockington	RB	1971–1977	85	Paul Christman	QB	1950	11
Bucky Brooks	CB	1996–1997	5	Gus Cifelli	T	1953	12
Robert Brooks	WR	1992–1998	96	Bob Cifers	B	1949	9
Aaron Brown	DE	1973–1974	10	Jack Clancy	WR	1970	14
Allen Brown	TE	1966–1967	19	Allan Clark	RB	1982	5
Bob Brown	DT	1966–1973	104	Jessie Clark	FB	1983–1987	60
Buddy Brown	G	1953–1956	47	Vinnie Clark	CB	1991–1992	32
Carlos Brown	QB	1975–1976	26	Shannon Clavelle	DE	1995–1997	15
Dave Brown	CB	1987–1989	44	Mark Clayton	WR	1993	16
Gary Brown	T	1994–1996	25	Cal Clemens	B	1936	9
Gilbert Brown	DT	1993–1999, 2001–2003	125	Ray Clemons	G	1947	9
Ken Brown	C	1980	7	Chad Clifton	T	2000–2011	165
Robert Brown	LB/DE	1982–1992	164	Jack Cloud	FB	1950–1951	13
Tom Brown	DB	1964–1968	70	Randall Cobb	WR	2011–2012	30
Ross Browner	DE/NT	1987	11	Reggie Cobb	RB	1994	16
Hank Bruder	B	1931–1939	98	Ed Cody	B	1947–1948	20
Mike Bucchianeri	G	1941, 1944–1945	14	Junior Coffey	RB	1965	13
Willie Buchanon	CB	1972–1978	80	Paul Coffman	TE	1978–1985	119
Howard "Cub" Buck	T	1921–1925	49	Colin Cole	DT	2004–2008	57
Terrell Buckley	CB	1992–1994	46	Keo Coleman	LB	1993	12
Larry Buhler	B	1939–1941	21	Daryn Colledge	G/T	2006–2010	80
Bryan Bulaga	T/G	2010–2012	37	Steve Collier	T	1987	10
Hank Bullough	G	1955, 1958	20	Albin Collins	HB	1951	7
Art Bultman	C	1932–1934	37	Brett Collins	LB	1992–1993	15
Ronnie Burgess	DB	1985	7	Nick Collins	S	2005–2011	95
Morgan Burnett	S	2010–2012	36	Patrick Collins	RB	1988	5
Paul Burris	G	1949–1951	29	Derek Combs	CB	2003	8
Blair Bush	C	1989–1991	48	Irv Comp	B	1943–1949	69
Jarrett Bush	CB	2006–2012	110	Rudy Comstock	G	1931–1933	40
Bill Butler	B	1959	11	Jack Concannon	QB	1974	14
Frank Butler	C/T	1934–1936, 1938	26	Fred Cone	FB/K	1951–1957	82
LeRoy Butler	CB/S	1990–2001	181	Kelly Cook	RB	1987	11
Mike Butler	DE	1977–1982, 1985	95	Ted Cook	E/DB	1948–1950	35
				Bill Cooke	DE	1975	5
Brian Cabral	LB	1980	7	Kerry Cooks	S	1998	9
Mossy Cade	DB	1985–1986	30	Mark Cooney	LB	1974	13
Lee Roy Caffey	LB	1964–1969	83	Junius Coston	T/G	2005–2007	16
Tiny Cahoon	T	1926–1929	31	Frank Coughlin	T	1921	5
Rich Campbell	QB	1981–1984	7	Larry Coutre	HB	1950, 1953	19
James Campen	C	1989–1993	61	Ron Cox	LB	1996	16
Tony Canadeo	B	1941–1944, 1946–1952	116	Tom Crabtree	TE	2010–2012	46
Mark Cannon	C	1984–1989	68	Larry Craig	E/B	1939–1949	121
Jim Capuzzi	B	1955–1956	9	Keith Crawford	CB/WR	1995, 1999	13
Joe Carey	G	1921	6	Leon Crenshaw	DT	1968	10
Al Carmichael	HB	1953–1958	68	Bernie Crimmins	G/B	1945	6
Lew Carpenter	B	1959–1963	66	Tiny Croft	T	1942–1947	51
Fred Carr	LB	1968–1977	140	Tommy Cronin	HB	1922	5
Alphonso Carreker	DE	1984–1988	72	Mason Crosby	K	2007–2012	96
Ahmad Carroll	CB	2004–2006	34	Dave Croston	T	1988	16
Leo Carroll	DE	1968	6	Ray Crouse	RB	1984	16
Paul Ott Carruth	RB	1986–1988	43	Tommy Crutcher	LB	1964–1967, 1971–1972	80
Carl Carter	CB	1992	7	Ward Cuff	B	1947	10
Jim Carter	LB	1970–1975, 1977–1978	106	Jim Culbreath	FB	1977–1979	29
Joe Carter	E	1942	11	Tyrone Culver	S	2006	14

Player name	Position	Seasons	Games	Player name	Position	Seasons	Games
George Cumby	LB	1980–1985	80	Dave Drechsler	G	1983–1984	32
Mike Curcio	LB	1983	13	Wally Dreyer	B	1950	12
Dan Currie	LB	1958–1964	90	Donald Driver	WR	1999–2012	205
Bill Curry	C	1965–1966	28	Chuck Drulis	G	1950	11
Scott Curry	T	1999	5	Bill DuMoe	E	1921	6
Andy Cvercko	G	1960	12	Paul Duhart	B	1944	8
Hec Cyre	T	1926	10	Jamie Dukes	C	1994	6
				Red Dunn	B	1927–1931	58
Tom Dahms	T	1955	12				
Carroll Dale	WR	1965–1972	111	Ralph Earhart	B	1948–1949	24
Joe Danelo	K	1975	12	Jug Earp	C	1922–1932	120
Ave Daniell	T	1937	5	Roger Eason	G	1949	12
Mike Daniels	DE	2012	14	Enrique Ecker	T	1950–1951	19
Ernie Danjean	LB	1957	12	Antuan Edwards	CB/S	1999–2003	53
Chris Darkins	RB	1997	14	Earl Edwards	DT	1979	9
Bernard Darling	C	1927–1931	36	Gary Ellerson	FB	1985–1986	31
Najeh Davenport	RB/FB	2002–2005	39	Carlton Elliott	E	1951–1954	48
Don Davey	DE/DT	1991–1994	50	Gerry Ellis	FB	1980–1986	103
Ben Davidson	DE	1961	14	Ken Ellis	CB	1970–1975	83
Anthony Davis	LB	1999	14	Tiny Engebretsen	G	1934–1941	64
Dave Davis	WR	1971–1972	24	Wuert Engelmann	B	1930–1933	44
Harper Davis	B	1951	12	Rex Enright	FB	1926–1927	19
Kenneth Davis	RB	1986–1988	35	Phil Epps	WR	1982–1988	85
Pahl Davis	G	1922	7	Joe Ethridge	T	1949	12
Ralph Davis	G	1947–1948	22	Dick Evans	E	1940, 1943	17
Rob Davis	LS	1997–2007	167	Doug Evans	CB	1993–1997	79
Tyrone Davis	TE	1997–2002	69	Lon Evans	G	1933–1937	57
Willie Davis	DE	1960–1969	138				
Gib Dawson	HB	1953	7	Tony Falkenstein	FB	1943	10
Jim DeLisle	DT	1971	9	Mike Fanucci	DE	1974	13
Walter Dean	FB	1991	9	Hal Faverty	C/LB	1952	11
Don Deeks	T	1948	8	Brett Favre	QB	1992–2007	255
Bob Dees	T	1952	9	Greg Feasel	T	1986	15
Jim Del Gaizo	QB	1973	8	Howie Ferguson	FB	1953–1958	65
Al Del Greco	K	1984–1987	46	Robert Ferguson	WR	2001–2006	60
Jeff Dellenbach	C/G	1996–1998	33	Bill Ferrario	G	2002	16
Patrick Dendy	CB	2005–2006	16	Lou Ferry	T	1949	12
Preston Dennard	WR	1985	16	Jermichael Finley	TE	2008–2012	64
Burnell Dent	LB	1986–1992	95	Tony Fisher	RB	2002–2005	60
Dick Deschaine	P	1955–1957	36	Paul Fitzgibbons	B	1930–1932	24
Ty Detmer	QB	1993, 1995	7	Dick Flaherty	E	1926	12
Ray DiPierro	G	1950–1951	18	Mike Flanagan	C/T	1998–2005	98
Lynn Dickey	QB	1976–1977, 1979–1985	105	Jim Flanigan Sr.	LB	1967–1970	40
Clint Didier	TE	1988–1989	31	Jim Flanigan	DT	2001	16
Evan Dietrich-Smith	G/C	2009, 2011–2012	45	Marv Fleming	TE	1963–1969	95
Na'il Diggs	LB	2000–2005	84	Bob Flowers	C/LB	1942–1949	63
Bobby Dillon	DB	1952–1959	94	Bobby Jack Floyd	FB	1952	12
Anthony Dilweg	QB	1989–1990	10	Matt Flynn	QB	2008–2011	34
Lavern Dilweg	E	1927–1934	98	Tom Flynn	S	1984–1986	38
Antonio Dingle	DT	1999	6	Lee Folkins	DE	1961	14
Leo Disend	T	1940	5	Herman Fontenot	RB	1989–1990	30
John Dittrich	G	1959	12	Len Ford	DE	1958	11
Waldo Don Carlos	C	1931	12	Bill Forester	LB	1953–1963	138
Mike Donohoe	TE	1973–1974	27	Aldo Forte	G	1947	10
Matthew Dorsett	CB	1995	10	Bob Forte	B	1946–1953	80
John Dorsey	LB	1984–1988	76	Chris Francies	WR	2006–2007	8
Earl Dotson	T	1993–2002	120	Joe Francis	B	1958–1959	24
Santana Dotson	DT	1996–2001	88	Robert Francois	LB	2010–2012	35
Bobby Douglass	QB	1978	12	Bubba Franks	TE	2000–2007	114
Mike Douglass	LB	1978–1985	119	Todd Franz	S	2002, 2005	7
Corey Dowden	CB	1996	9	Paul Frase	DE	1997	9
Steve Dowden	T	1952	12	Antonio Freeman	WR	1995–2001, 2003	116
Boyd Dowler	WR	1959–1969	150	Bobby Freeman	DB	1959	12

Player name	Position	Seasons	Games	Player name	Position	Seasons	Games
Sherwood Fries	G/LB	1943	5	Darryl Haley	T	1988	13
Ted Fritsch	B	1942–1950	99	Charlie Hall	CB	1971–1976	83
Derrick Frost	P	2008	12	Korey Hall	FB	2007–2010	48
Ed Frutig	E	1941, 1945	9	Lamont Hall	TE	1999	14
Curtis Fuller	S	2003–2004	10	Mark Hall	DE	1989–1990	10
Joe Fuller	CB	1991	16	Ron Hallstrom	G	1982–1992	162
Brent Fullwood	RB	1987–1990	45	Ruffin Hamilton	LB	1994	5
Chuck Fusina	QB	1986	7	Dave Hampton	RB	1969–1971	33
				Dave Hanner	DT	1952–1964	160
Samkon Gado	RB	2005–2006	9	Don Hansen	LB	1976–1977	20
Harry Galbreath	G	1993–1995	48	Leon Harden	S	1970	8
Milt Gantenbein	E	1931–1940	103	Roger Harding	C	1949	6
Eddie Garcia	K	1983–1984	19	Kevin Hardy	DT	1970	14
Gus Gardella	FB	1922	7	Justin Harrell	DT	2007–2008, 2010	14
Milton Gardner	G	1922–1926	55	Willard Harrell	RB	1975–1977	40
Bobby Garrett	QB	1954	9	Al Harris	CB	2003–2009	102
Len Garrett	TE	1971–1973	30	Bernardo Harris	LB	1995–2001	111
Ron Gassert	DT	1962	10	Corey Harris	WR/CB/KR	1992–1994	37
Lester Gatewood	C	1946–1947	23	Jack Harris	B	1925–1926	21
Buck Gavin	B	1921, 1923	9	Jackie Harris	TE	1990–1993	60
Kabeer Gbaja-Biamila	DE	2000–2008	124	Leotis Harris	G	1978–1983	74
Charlie Getty	T	1983	15	Raymont Harris	RB	1998	8
Jim Gillette	B	1947	10	Tim Harris	LB	1986–1990	76
Gale Gillingham	G	1966–1974, 1976	128	Doug Hart	DB	1964–1971	112
Matt Giordano	S	2009	5	Maurice Harvey	S	1981–1983	29
Earl Girard	B	1948–1951	46	Matt Hasselbeck	QB	1999–2000	32
Chris Gizzi	LB	2000–2001	23	Dave Hathcock	DB	1966	14
Leland Glass	WR	1972–1973	26	Tim Hauck	S	1991–1994	58
Terry Glenn	WR	2002	15	Dennis Havig	G	1977	7
Ed Glick	B	1921–1922	6	A. J. Hawk	LB	2006–2012	110
Derrel Gofourth	G/C	1977–1982	85	Mike Hawkins	CB	2005	11
Buckets Goldenberg	G/B	1933–1945	120	Michael Hawthorne	CB/S	2003–2004	30
Brett Goode	LS	2008-12	80	Aaron Hayden	RB	1997	14
Herbert Goodman	RB	2000–2001	12	Dave Hayes	E	1921–1922	13
Les Goodman	RB	1973–1974	19	Gary Hayes	DB	1984–1986	42
Clyde Goodnight	E	1945–1949	38	Norbert Hayes	E	1923	6
Darrien Gordon	CB/KR	2002	13	Bill Hayhoe	T	1969–1973	61
Lou Gordon	T	1936–1937	22	Spencer Havner	TE/LB	2008–2010	21
Ken Gorgal	DB	1956	5	George Hays	DE	1953	9
Jim Grabowski	RB	1966–1970	63	Casey Hayward	CB	2012	16
David Grant	DE	1993	7	Tom Hearden	B	1927–1928	5
Ryan Grant	RB	2007–2012	67	Stan Heath	QB	1949	12
Johnnie Gray	S	1975–1983	124	Larry Hefner	LB	1972–1975	34
Ahman Green	RB	2000–2006, 2009	104	Jerry Helluin	DT	1954–1957	48
Alex Green	RB	2011-2012	16	William Henderson	FB	1995–2006	188
Howard Green	NT	2010-2011	25	Dutch Hendrian	B	1924	11
Tiger Greene	S	1986–1990	72	Ted Hendricks	LB	1974	14
Norm Greeney	G	1933	7	Urban Henry	DT	1963	14
Tom Greenfield	C/LB	1939–1941	22	Craig Hentrich	P	1994–1997	64
David Greenwood	S	1986	9	Arnie Herber	B	1930–1940	109
Forrest Gregg	T	1956, 1958–1970	187	Noah Herron	RB	2005–2006	21
Hank Gremminger	DB	1956–1965	123	Larry Hickman	FB	1960	12
Hal Griffen	C	1928	5	Don Highsmith	RB	1973	7
Billy Grimes	HB	1950–1952	36	Jim Hill	DB	1972–1974	41
Dan Grimm	G	1963–1965	42	John Hilton	TE	1970	14
Earl Gros	FB	1962–1963	28	Dick Himes	T	1968–1977	135
Roger Grove	B	1931–1935	51	Clarke Hinkle	FB	1932–1941	113
Jim Gueno	LB	1976–1980	75	Abdul Hodge	LB	2006	8
				Carlyle Holiday	WR	2006–2007	5
Dale Hackbart	DB	1960–1961	14	Darius Holland	DT/DE	1995–1997	42
Joey Hackett	TE	1987–1988	20	Johnny Holland	LB	1987–1993	103
Michael Haddix	FB	1989–1990	32	Vonnie Holliday	DE	1998–2002	66
John Hadl	QB	1974–1975	22	Lamont Hollinquest	LB	1996–1998	46

Player name	Position	Seasons	Games	Player name	Position	Seasons	Games
Darick Holmes	RB	1998	11	Joe Johnson	HB	1954–1958	53
Jerry Holmes	CB	1990–1991	29	Keshon Johnson	CB	1994, 1997	7
Estus Hood	DB	1978–1984	104	Kenneth Johnson	DB	1987	12
Charles Hope	G	1994	6	LeShon Johnson	RB	1994–1995	14
Don Horn	QB	1967–1970	20	Marvin Johnson	DB	1952–1953	12
Paul Hornung	B	1957–1962, 1964–1966	104	Quinn Johnson	FB	2009–2010	20
Jason Horton	CB	2004–2005	23	Reggie Johnson	TE	1994, 1997	13
Davon House	CB	2011–2012	11	Tom Johnson	DT	1952	8
Desmond Howard	WR/KR	1996, 1999	24	Chester Johnston	B	1931, 1934–1938	26
Tubby Howard	B	1921–1922	12	Johnny Jolly	DT	2006–2009	48
John Howell	B	1938	6	Mike Jolly	S	1980, 1982–1983	35
Billy Howton	E	1952–1958	80	Bobby Jones	G	1934	12
Cal Hubbard	T	1929–1933, 1935	75	Brad Jones	LB	2007–2012	51
Harlan Huckleby	RB	1980–1985	84	Bruce Jones	G	1927–1928	22
Bob Hudson	RB	1972	12	Daryll Jones	DB	1984–1985	24
Tim Huffman	G/T	1981–1985	47	James Jones	WR	2007–2012	90
Tom Hull	LB	1975	12	Ron Jones	TE	1969	6
Donnie Humphrey	DE	1984–1986	48	Sean Jones	DE	1994–1996	47
Tory Humphrey	TE	2005–2006, 2008	24	Terry Jones	NT	1978–1984	85
Cletidus Hunt	DT/DE	1999–2004	85	Tom Jones	G	1938	8
Ervin Hunt	DB	1970	6	Charles Jordan	WR	1994–1995, 1999	20
Mike Hunt	LB	1978–1980	22	Henry Jordan	DT	1959–1969	139
Art Hunter	C	1954	12	Carl Jorgensen	T	1934	10
Jason Hunter	DE	2006–2008	42	Seth Joyner	LB	1997	11
Scott Hunter	QB	1971–1973	35	Bhawoh Jue	CB/S	2001–2004	51
Paul Hutchins	T	1993–1994	17	John Jurkovic	NT	1991–1995	69
Don Hutson	E/DB	1935–1945	116				
Bob Hyland	C	1967–1969, 1976	56	Bob Kahler	B	1942–1944	19
				Royal Kahler	T	1942	7
Ken Iman	C	1960–1963	54	Aaron Kampman	DE	2002–2012	112
Robert Ingalls	C/LB	1942	10	Jeremy Kapinos	P	2008–2009	20
Darryl Ingram	TE	1992–1993	18	Leo Katalinas	T	1938	8
Mark Ingram	WR	1995	16	Kani Kauahi	C	1988	16
Cecil Isbell	B	1938–1942	54	Jim Keane	E	1952	11
Eddie Lee Ivery	RB	1979–1986	72	Emmett Keefe	T	1921	23
				Jim Kekeris	T	1948	5
Chris Jacke	K	1989–1996	126	Paul Kell	T	1939–1940	20
Brandon Jackson	WR	2007–2010	52	Bill Kelley	E	1949	12
Grady Jackson	DT	2003–2005	34	Joe Kelly	LB	1995	13
Keith Jackson	TE	1995–1996	25	Perry Kemp	WR	1988–1991	6
Melvin Jackson	G	1976–1980	64	Bill Kern	T	1929–1930	18
Allen Jacobs	HB	1965	14	Ken Keuper	B	1945–1947	31
Jack Jacobs	B	1947–1949	36	Blair Kiel	QB	1988, 1990–1991	8
Harry Jacunski	E	1939–1944	55	Walt Kiesling	G	1935–1936	18
Van Jakes	CB	1989	16	Bobby Kimball	WR	1979–1980	8
Claudis James	WR	1967–1968	15	J. D. Kimmel	DT	1958	12
Ed Jankowski	B	1937–1941	50	Billy Kinard	B	1957–1958	24
John Jefferson	WR	1981–1984	50	Randy Kinder	CB	1997	12
Norman Jefferson	DB	1987–1988	14	Don King	DT	1956	6
Noel Jenke	LB	1973–1974	10	Jack Kirby	B	1949	6
Billy Jenkins	S	2001	6	Syd Kitson	G	1980–1981, 1983–1984	49
Cullen Jenkins	DT/DE	2004–2010	93	Adrian Klemm	G/T	2005	16
Greg Jennings	WR	2006–2012	96	Gary Knafelc	E	1954–1962	90
M. D. Jennings	S	2011–2012	31	Lindsay Knapp	G	1996	9
Jim Jensen	RB	1981–1982	23	Gene Knutson	DE	1954, 1956	18
Travis Jervey	RB	1995–1998	56	Steve Knutson	T	1976–1977	25
Bob Jeter	DB	1963–1970	107	Matt Koart	DE	1986	6
Bill Johnson	DE	1941	6	Greg Koch	T	1977–1985	133
Charles Johnson	DT	1979–1980, 1983	45	Mark Koncar	T	1976–1977, 1979–1981	53
Ezra Johnson	DE	1977–1987	148	George Koonce	LB	1992–1999	112
Glenn Johnson	T	1949	8	Dave Kopay	RB	1972	14
Howard Johnson	G/LB	1940–1941	22	Ron Kostelnik	T	1961–1968	110
Joe Johnson	DE	2002–2003	11	Eddie Kotal	B	1925–1929	46

Player name	Position	Seasons	Games	Player name	Position	Seasons	Games
Jerry Kramer	G	1958–1968	130	Nolan Luhn	E	1945–1949	56
Ron Kramer	TE	1957, 1959–1964	89	Steve Luke	DB	1975–1980	90
Ken Kranz	B	1949	7	Dewey Lyle	E	1922–1923	11
Larry Krause	RB	1970–1971, 1973–1974	51	Del Lyman	T	1941	5
Ryan Krause	TE	2007	9	Billy Lyon	DT/DE	1998–2002	59
Bob Kroll	S	1972–1973	5				
Bob Kuberski	DT	1995–1998	21	Bill Maas	NT	1993	14
Rudy Kuechenberg	LB	1970	6	Tom MacLeod	LB	1973	10
John Kuhn	FB	2007–2012	92	Red Mack	WR	1966	8
Joe Kurth	T	1933–1934	20	Don Majkowski	QB	1987–1992	68
Bill Kuusisto	G	1941–1946	54	Grover Malone	B	1921	6
				Tony Mandarich	T	1989–1991	45
Matt LaBounty	DE	1995	14	Chris Mandeville	DB	1987–1988	6
Curly Lambeau	B	1921–1929	77	Leon Manley	G	1950–1951	24
Pete Lammons	TE	1972	12	Bob Mann	E	1950–1954	38
Walt Landers	FB	1978–1979	13	Roy Manning	LB	2005	15
Sean Landeta	P	1998	16	Terrell Manning	LB	2012	5
MacArthur Lane	RB	1972–1974	41	Marquand Manuel	S	2006	16
T. J. Lang	G/T	2009–2012	59	Chester Marcol	K	1972–1980	102
Danny Lansanah	LB	2008	5	Larry Marks	B	1928	11
Bill Larson	TE	1980	9	Bud Marshall	DT	1965	14
Fred Larson	C	1925	13	Torrance Marshall	LB/FB	2001–2004	51
Kurt Larson	LB	1991	13	Charles Martin	DE	1984–1987	48
Jim Laslavic	LB	1982	8	David Martin	TE	2001–2006	70
Kit Lathrop	DT	1979–1980	17	Derrick Martin	S	2009–2010	19
Jamari Lattimore	LB	2011–2012	23	Ruvell Martin	WR	2006–2008	41
Larry Lauer	C	1956–1957	18	John Martinkovic	DE	1951–1956	72
Jim Laughlin	LB	1983	15	Russell Maryland	DT	2000	16
Joe Laws	B	1934–1945	120	Dave Mason	DB	1974	12
Walt LeJeune	G	1925–1926	19	Joel Mason	E	1942–1945	41
Vonta Leach	FB	2004–2006	23	Larry Mason	RB	1988	15
Bill Lee	T	1937–1942, 1946	53	Carlton Massey	DE	1957–1958	14
Charles Lee	WR	2000–2001	22	Norm Masters	T	1957–1964	104
Donald Lee	TE	2005–2010	92	Tim Masthay	P	2010–2012	48
James Lee	DT	2004	9	Charlie Mathys	B	1922–1926	47
Mark Lee	CB	1980–1990	157	Pat Matson	G	1975	14
Pat Lee	CB	2008, 2010–2011	32	Al Matthews	DB	1970–1975	84
ReShard Lee	RB	2005	7	Aubrey Matthews	WR	1988–1989	20
Charlie Leigh	RB	1974	10	Clay Matthews III	LB	2009–2012	58
Paris Lenon	LB	2002–2005	64	Frank Mayer	G	1927	10
Bobby Leopold	LB	1986	12	Derrick Mayes	WR	1996–1998	29
Darrell Lester	C	1937–1938	16	Jack McAuliffe	HB	1926	8
Russ Letlow	G	1936–1942, 1946	71	Tod McBride	CB/S	1999–2002	61
Dorsey Levens	RB	1994–2001	102	Bob McCaffrey	C	1975	11
Verne Lewellen	B	1924–1932	102	Larry McCarren	C	1973–1984	162
Cliff Lewis	LB	1981–1984	57	Dave McCloughan	CB	1992	5
Gary Lewis	TE	1981–1984	44	Mike McCoy	DB	1976–1983	110
Mark Lewis	TE	1985–1987	18	Mike McCoy	DT	1970–1976	94
Mike Lewis	NT	1980	10	Hurdis McCrary	B	1929–1933	52
Ron Lewis	WR	1992–1994	21	John McDowell	G	1964	12
Tim Lewis	CB	1983–1986	51	Scott McGarrahan	S	1998–2000	44
Cully Lidberg	FB	1926, 1929–1930	26	Clarence McGeary	DT	1950	12
Paul Lipscomb	T	1945–1949	57	Max McGee	E	1954, 1957–1967	148
Dale Livingston	K	1970	14	Rich McGeorge	TE	1970–1978	116
James Lofton	WR	1978–1986	136	Lenny McGill	CB	1994–1995	21
Dick Logan	G	1952–1953	19	Gene McGuire	C	1996	8
Bob Long	WR	1964–1967	35	Lamar McHan	QB	1959–1960	24
Ryan Longwell	K	1997–2005	144	Don McIlhenny	HB	1957–1959	36
Ace Loomis	B	1951–1953	33	Guy McIntyre	G	1994	10
Jack Losch	HB	1956	12	Paul McJulien	P	1991–1992	25
Nick Luchey	FB	2003–2004	27	Roy McKay	B	1944–1947	35
Bill Lucky	DT	1955	12	Keith McKenzie	DE/LB	1996–1999, 2002	62
Bill Lueck	G	1968–1974	90	Mike McKenzie	CB	1999–2004	70

Player name	Position	Seasons	Games	Player name	Position	Seasons	Games
Raleigh McKenzie	G	1999–2000	19	Dimitri Nance	RB	2010	12
Lee McLaughlin	G	1941	8	Tom Nash	E	1928–1932	53
Mike McLeod	DB	1984–1985	20	Hannibal Navies	LB	2003–2004	31
Jim McMahon	QB	1995–1996	6	Ed Neal	DT/T	1945–1951	68
Herb McMath	DT	1977	8	Frankie Neal	WR	1987	12
Steve McMichael	DT	1994	16	Mike Neal	DE	2010–2012	20
Ernie McMillan	T	1975	12	Bill Neill	NT	1984	16
Jerron McMillian	S	2012	16	Bob Nelson	NT	1988–1990	46
Dexter McNabb	FB	1992–1993	32	Jim Nelson	LB	1998–1999	16
John "Blood" McNally	B	1929–1933, 1935–1936	75	Jordy Nelson	WR	2008–2012	73
Forrest McPherson	T	1943–1945	14	Tom Neville	G/T	1986–1988, 1992	38
Mike Meade	FB	1982–1983	18	Marshall Newhouse	G/T	2011–2012	32
Rondell Mealey	RB	2001–2002	14	Craig Newsome	CB	1995–1998	46
Steve Meilinger	E	1958, 1960	24	Hamilton Nichols	G	1951	9
Ruben Mendoza	G	1986	6	Hardy Nickerson	LB	2002	16
Chuck Mercein	RB	1967–1969	22	Walter Niemann	C	1922–1924	22
Mike Mercer	K	1968–1969	16	Ray Nitschke	LB	1958–1972	190
Casey Merrill	DE	1979–1983	59	Doyle Nix	DB	1955	12
Frank Mestnik	FB	1963	11	Fred Nixon	WR	1980–1981	23
Lou Michaels	K	1971	10	Brian Noble	LB	1985–1993	117
Walt Michaels	G	1951	12	Danny Noonan	NT	1992	6
Mike Michalske	G	1929–1935, 1937	95	Al Norgard	E	1934	10
John Michels	T	1996–1997	24	Jerry Norton	DB	1963–1964	28
Terry Mickens	WR	1994–1997	47	Marty Norton	B	1925	10
Terdell Middleton	RB	1977–1981	71	Bob Nussbaumer	B	1946, 1951	14
Lou Midler	DE	1940	7	Rick Nuzum	C	1978	16
Don Milan	QB	1975	7	Chukie Nwokorie	DE	2003	14
John Miller	T	1960	5	Lee Nystrom	T	1974	13
Ookie Miller	C	1938	11				
Paul Miller	B	1936–1938	32	Harry O'Boyle	B	1928, 1932	21
Stan Mills	B	1922–1923	17	Bob O'Connor	T	1935	7
Paul Minick	G	1928–1929	18	Pat O'Donahue	DE	1955	12
Brandon Miree	FB	2006	10	Richard O'Donnell	E	1924–1930	74
Basil Mitchell	RB	1999–2000	17	Ed O'Neil	LB	1980	12
Roland Mitchell	CB/S	1991–1994	48	Dwayne O'Steen	CB	1983–1984	11
Bo Molenda	B	1928–1932	45	Carleton Oats	DT	1973	8
Tony Moll	T/G	2006–2008	39	Cyril Obiozor	LB	2009	5
Bob Monnett	B	1933–1938	62	Steve Odom	WR/KR	1974–1979	75
Michael Montgomery	DE	2005–2010	58	Urban Odson	T	1946–1949	44
Allen Moore	E	1939	5	Alfred Oglesby	NT	1992	7
Blake Moore	C/G	1984–1985	27	Steve Okoniewski	DT	1974–1975	28
Rich Moore	DT	1969–1970	20	Larry Olsonoski	G	1948–1949	16
Tom Moore	HB	1960–1965	78	Dan Orlich	E	1949–1951	36
Rich Moran	G	1985–1993	108	Dave Osborn	RB	1976	6
Vernand Morency	RB	2006–2007	26				
Tim Moresco	DB	1977	14	Tony Palmer	G	2006–2007	8
Anthony Morgan	WR	1993–1996	37	Sam Palumbo	LB/C	1957	9
Jim Bob Morris	DB	1987	11	Ernie Pannell	T	1941–1942, 1945	22
Lee Morris	WR	1987	5	Babe Parilli	QB	1952–1953, 1957–1958	48
Jim Morrissey	LB	1993	114	De'Mond Parker	RB	1999–2000	19
Mike Morton	LB	2000	16	Keith Paskett	WR	1987	12
Dom Moselle	B	1951–1952	20	George Paskvan	B	1941	7
Dezman Moses	LB	2012	16	Shawn Patterson	DE	1988–1991, 1993	48
Russ Mosley	B	1945–1946	8	Ricky Patton	RB	1979	6
Perry Moss	QB	1948	6	Tony Paulekas	C	1936	10
Roderick Mullen	CB/S	1995–1997	38	Bryce Paup	LB	1990–1994	64
Carl Mulleneaux	E	1938–1941, 1945–1946	46	Ken Payne	WR	1974–1977	44
Lee Mulleneaux	C	1938	5	Francis Peay	T	1968–1972	62
Mark Murphy	S	1980–1985, 1987–1991	147	Doug Pederson	QB	1996–1998, 2001–2004	66
Jab Murray	T	1921–1924	22	Ray Pelfrey	E	1951–1952	13
				Charlie Peprah	S	2006–2008, 2010–2011	67
Romanus Nadolney	G	1922	8	Don Perkins	FB	1944–1945	17
Craig Nall	QB	2003–2004, 2007	7	Tom Perko	LB	1976	14

Player name	Position	Seasons	Games	Player name	Position	Seasons	Games
Claude Perry	T	1927–1935	89	Rudy Rosatti	T	1924, 1926–1927	27
Nick Perry	LB	2012	6	Al Rose	E	1932–1936	48
Dick Pesonen	DB	1960	12	Ken Roskie	B	1948	6
Kenny Peterson	DE/DT	2003–2005	34	Dan Ross	TE	1986	15
Les Peterson	E	1932, 1934	20	Jeremy Ross	WR	2012	5
John Petitbon	DB	1957	12	Allen Rossum	CB/KR	2000–2001	22
Kenny Pettway	DE	2008	8	Tobin Rote	QB	1950–1956	84
David Petway	S	1981	6	Aaron Rouse	S	2007–2009	27
Ryan Pickett	DT	2006–2012	103	John Rowser	DB	1967–1969	42
Elijah Pitts	RB	1961–1969, 1971	126	Larry Rubens	C	1982–1983	25
Ron Pitts	CB	1988–1990	44	Paul Rudzinski	LB	1978–1980	33
Brady Poppinga	LB	2005–2010	81	Grey Ruegamer	C/G	2003–2005	43
Guy Prather	LB	1981–1985	73	Ken Ruettgers	T	1985–1996	156
Merv Pregulman	G	1946	11	Howie Ruetz	DT	1951–1953	20
Roell Preston	WR/KR	1997–1998	17	Gordon Rule	DB	1968–1969	15
Mike Prior	S	1993–1998	80	Clive Rush	E	1953	11
Steve Pritko	E	1949–1950	20	Steve Ruzich	G	1952–1954	36
Joe Prokop	P	1985	9	Jon Ryan	P	2006–2007	32
Fred Provo	B	1948	9				
Jim Psaltis	DB	1954	11	Brandon Saine	RB	2011–2012	14
Pid Purdy	B	1926–1927	17	Jim Salsbury	G	1957–1958	24
Dave Pureifory	DL	1972–1977	78	Chuck Sample	B	1942, 1945	10
Frank Purnell	FB	1957	9	Howard Sampson	DB	1978–1979	31
				B. J. Sander	P	2005	14
Andrew Quarless	TE	2010–2011	23	Dan Sandifer	B	1952–1953	13
Jess Quatse	T	1933	9	John Sandusky	T	1956	12
Jeff Query	WR	1989–1991	48	Al Sarafiny	C	1933	7
Bill Quinlan	DE	1959–1962	52	Jeff Saturday	C	2012	14
				George Sauer	B	1935–1937	20
Ken Radick	E	1930–1931	5	Russ Saunders	FB	1931	9
B. J. Raji	NT	2009–2012	60	Hurles Scales	DB	1975	7
Al Randolph	DB	1971	14	Zud Schammel	G	1937	8
Terry Randolph	DB	1977	14	Bernie Scherer	E	1936–1938	26
Keith Ranspot	E	1942	5	Walt Schlinkman	FB	1946–1949	46
Baby Ray	T	1938–1948	116	Art Schmaehl	FB	1921	6
Dave Rayner	K	2006	16	George Schmidt	C	1952	7
Pete Regnier	B	1922	5	John Schmitt	C	1974	14
Bill Reichardt	FB	1952	12	Herm Schneidman	B	1935–1939	40
Floyd Reid	HB	1950–1956	78	Bill Schroeder	WR	1994, 1997–2001	74
Bill Renner	P	1986–1987	6	Bill Schroll	G	1951	12
Jamal Reynolds	DE	2001–2003	18	Carl Schuette	C/DB	1950–1951	24
Jay Rhodemyre	C/LB	1948–1949, 1951–1952	45	Harry Schuh	T	1974	14
Allen Rice	RB	1991	6	Jeff Schuh	LB	1986	12
Gary Richard	DB	1988	10	Charles Schultz	T	1939–1941	21
Sean Richardson	S	2012	5	Ade Schwammel	T	1934–1936, 1943–1944	46
Ray Riddick	E	1940–1942, 1944	26	Patrick Scott	WR	1987–1988	24
Jim Ringo	C	1953–1963	131	Randy Scott	LB	1981–1986	78
Andre Rison	WR	1996	5	Bucky Scribner	P	1983–1984	32
Marco Rivera	G	1997–2004	125	Champ Seibold	T	1934–1938, 1940	48
John Roach	QB	1961–1963	23	Clarence Self	B	1952, 1954–1955	26
Tootie Robbins	T	1992–1993	27	Wash Serini	G	1952	11
Dave Robinson	LB	1963–1972	127	Jim Shanley	HB	1958	12
Eugene Robinson	S	1996–1997	32	Sterling Sharpe	WR	1988–1994	112
Koren Robinson	WR	2006–2007	13	Darren Sharper	CB/S	1997–2004	121
Michael Robinson	CB	1996	6	Derek Sherrod	T	2011	5
Alden Roche	DE	1971–1976	83	Sam Shields	CB	2010–2012	39
Aaron Rodgers	QB	2005–2012	85	Vai Sikahema	RB/KR	1991	11
Del Rodgers	RB/KR	1982, 1984	23	Dave Simmons	LB	1979	16
Nick Rogers	LB	2004	10	John Simmons	DB	1986	6
Herm Rohrig	B	1941, 1946–1947	25	Wayne Simmons	LB	1993–1997	64
Dave Roller	DT	1975–1978	48	Ron Simpkins	LB	1988	7
Mark Roman	S	2004–2005	32	Nate Simpson	RB	1977–1979	43
Al Romine	HB	1955, 1958	16	Joe Sims	T/G	1992–1995	47

Player name	Position	Seasons	Games	Player name	Position	Seasons	Games
Josh Sitton	G	2008–2012	73	John Symank	DB	1957–1962	76
Daryle Skaugstad	NT	1983	9	Len Szafaryn	T	1950, 1953–1956	55
Joe Skibinski	G	1955–1956	24				
Gerald Skinner	T	1978	15	Jerry Tagge	QB	1972–1974	18
Bob Skoglund	DE	1947	9	Damon Tassos	G	1947–1949	26
Bob Skoronski	T	1956, 1959–1968	146	Mark Tauscher	T/G	2000–2010	134
Elmer Sleight	T	1930–1931	26	Aaron Taylor	G	1995–1997	46
Barry Smith	WR	1973–1975	41	Ben Taylor	LB	2006	10
Barty Smith	RB	1974–1980	67	Cliff Taylor	RB	1976	7
Ben Smith	E	1933	9	Jim Taylor	FB	1958–1966	118
Bruce Smith	B	1945–1948	23	Kitrick Taylor	WR	1992	10
D. J. Smith	LB	2011–2012	22	Ryan Taylor	TE	2011–2012	31
Dave Smith	RB	1970	7	George Teague	S	1993–1995	47
Ed Smith	HB	1948–1949	15	Jim Temp	DE	1957–1960	43
Ernie Smith	T	1935–1937, 1939	40	Bob Tenner	E	1935	11
Jermaine Smith	DT	1997, 1999	19	Pat Terrell	S	1998	16
Larry Smith	DT/DE	2003–2004	13	Deral Teteak	LB/G	1952–1956	49
Ollie Smith	WR	1976–1977	25	Keith Thibodeaux	CB	2001	7
Perry Smith	DB	1973–1976	47	John Thierry	DE	2000–2001	28
Red Smith	G	1927, 1929	10	Ben Thomas	DE	1986	9
Rod Smith	CB	1998	8	Ike Thomas	DB	1972–1973	25
Malcolm Snider	T/G	1972–1974	42	Joey Thomas	CB	2004–2005	20
Matt Snider	FB	1999–2000	24	Robert Thomas	LB	2005	10
Vic So'oto	LB	2011–2012	8	Bobby Thomason	QB	1951	11
Glen Sorenson	G	1943–1945	27	Jeff Thomason	TE	1995–1999	75
John Spagnola	TE	1989	6	Arland Thompson	G	1981	9
Ron Spears	DE	1983	13	Aundra Thompson	WR	1977–1981	63
Joe Spencer	T	1950–1951	14	Darrell Thompson	RB	1990–1994	60
Ollie Spencer	T	1957–1958	24	Jeremy Thompson	DE/LB	2008–2009	15
John Spilis	WR	1969–1971	40	John Thompson	TE	1979–1982	34
Jack Spinks	G	1955–1956	7	Andrae Thurman	WR	2004–2005	12
Jason Spitz	G	2006–2010	65	Fred Thurston	G	1959–1967	112
Dennis Sproul	QB	1978	6	George Timberlake	LB/G	1955	6
Ray Stachowicz	P	1981–1982	25	Adam Timmerman	G	1995–1998	61
Jon Staggers	WR	1972–1974	39	Gerald Tinker	WR	1975	6
Dick Stahlman	T	1931–1932	27	Pete Tinsley	G/LB	1938–1939, 1941–1945	50
Walter Stanley	WR	1985–1988	48	Nelson Toburen	LB	1961–1962	24
Don Stansauk	T	1950–1951	15	Chuck Tollefson	G	1944–1946	18
Ken Starch	RB	1976	6	Mike Tomczak	QB	1991	12
James Starks	RB	2010–2012	22	Tom Toner	LB	1973, 1975–1977	53
Bart Starr	QB	1956–1971	196	Clayton Tonnemaker	LB/C	1950, 1953–1954	36
Ben Starret	B	1942–1945	27	Eric Torkelson	RB	1974–1979, 1981	93
Ben Steele	TE	2004–2005	17	Keith Traylor	LB	1993	5
Rebel Steiner	DB	1950–1951	24	R-Kal Truluck	DE	2004	13
Jan Stenerud	K	1980–1983	45	Esera Tuaolo	NT/DE	1991–1992	20
Scott Stephen	LB	1987–1991	72	Walter Tullis	WR	1978–1979	32
John Stephens	RB	1993	5	Emlen Tunnell	S	1959–1961	37
Dave Stephenson	G/C	1951–1955	49	Richard Turner	NT	1981–1983	30
Ken Stills	S	1985–1989	65	Wylie Turner	DB	1979–1980	28
Barry Stokes	G/T	2000–2001	24				
Tim Stokes	T	1978–1982	63	Keith Uecker	G/T	1984–1985, 87–88, 90–91	64
John Stonebraker	E	1942	8	Brandon Underwood	CB	2009–2010	23
Fred Strickland	LB	1994–1995	30	Marviel Underwood	S	2005	16
Lyle Sturgeon	T	1937	7	Andy Uram	B	1938–1943	62
John Sullivan	DB	1986	6	Alex Urban	E	1941, 1944–1945	11
Bob Summerhays	B	1949–1951	35	Eddie Usher	B	1922, 1924	6
Bud Svendsen	C	1937, 1939	21				
George Svendsen	C/LB	1935–1937, 1940–1941	52	Bruce Van Dyke	G	1974–1976	29
Brett Swain	WR	2009–2010	22	Hal Van Every	B	1940–1941	20
Karl Swanke	T/C	1980–1986	84	Greg Van Roten	G	2012	7
Erwin Swiney	CB	2002–2003	9	Clyde Van Sickle	C	1932–1933	9
Veryl Switzer	B	1954–1955	24	Pete Van Valkenburg	RB	1974	5
Harry Sydney	FB	1992	16	Phil Vandersea	LB/DE	1966, 1968–1969	38

Player name	Position	Seasons	Games	Player name	Position	Seasons	Games
Vernon Vanoy	DT	1972	13	Brian Williams	LB	1995–2000	45
Fred Vant Hull	G	1942	8	Clarence Williams	DE	1970–1977	111
Randy Vataha	WR	1977	6	Corey Williams	DT	2004–2007	56
Alan Veingrad	T	1986–1987, 1989–1990	59	D. J. Williams	LB	2011–2012	26
Ross Verba	T/G	1997–2000	59	Howie Williams	DB	1962–1963	10
Carl Vereen	T	1957	12	K. D. Williams	LB	2000–2001	28
George Vergara	E	1925	12	Mark Williams	LB	1994	16
Fred Vinson	CB	1999	16	Perry Williams	RB	1969–1973	69
Evan Vogds	G	1948–1949	27	Tramon Williams	CB	2007–2012	95
Lloyd Voss	DT	1964–1965	28	Travis Williams	RB/KR	1967–1970	48
Tillie Voss	E	1924	11	Tyrone Williams	CB	1996–2002	111
				Matt Willig	T	1998	16
Jude Waddy	LB	1998–1999	27	James Willis	LB	1993–1994	25
Bryan Wagner	P	1992–1993	23	Jeff Wilner	TE	1994–1995	13
Steve Wagner	DB	1976–1979	57	Ben Wilson	FB	1967	14
Mike Wahle	T/G	1998–2004	97	C. J. Wilson	DE	2010–2012	42
Erik Walden	LB	2010–2012	40	Charles Wilson	WR	1990–1991	30
Cleo Walker	C/LB	1970	11	Gene Wilson	E/DB	1947–1948	21
Frank Walker	CB	2007	12	Marcus Wilson	RB	1992–1995	48
Javon Walker	WR	2002–2005	48	Milt Wilson	G	1921	6
Malcom Walker	C	1970	11	Mule Wilson	B	1930–1931	13
Randy Walker	P	1974	14	Abner Wimberly	E	1950–1952	35
Rod Walker	DT	2001–2003	31	Rich Wingo	LB	1979, 1981–1984	69
Sammy Walker	CB	1993	8	Francis Winkler	DE	1968–1969	21
Val Joe Walker	DB	1953–1956	46	Randy Winkler	G	1971	7
Wesley Walls	TE	2003	14	Paul Winslow	HB	1960	12
Tyson Walter	T/G	2006	5	Blaise Winter	DE/NT	1988–1990	45
Steve Warren	DT	2000, 2002	25	Frank Winters	C/G	1992–2002	156
Elbert Watts	DB	1986	9	Wimpy Winther	C	1971	11
Nate Wayne	LB	2000–2002	44	Jerron Wishom	CB	2005	5
Clarence Weathers	WR	1990–1991	28	Cal Withrow	C	1971–1973	42
Jim Weatherwax	DT	1966–1967, 1969	34	Earl Witte	B	1934	5
Gary Weaver	LB	1975–1979	63	Alex Wizbicki	B	1950	11
Mike Weddington	LB	1986–1990	52	Willie Wood	S	1960–1971	166
Ray Wehba	E	1944	10	Whitey Woodin	G	1922–1931	86
Dick Weisgerber	B	1938–1940, 1942	24	Jerry Woods	S	1990	16
Clayton Weishuhn	LB	1987	9	Keith Woodside	RB	1988–1991	64
Mike Wellman	C	1979–1980	20	Charles Woodson	CB	2006–2012	100
Don Wells	E	1946–1949	38	Vince Workman	RB	1989–1992	56
Scott Wells	C/G	2004–2011	111	Jerel Worthy	DE	2012	14
Terry Wells	RB	1975	13	Keith Wortman	G	1972–1975	46
Ed West	TE	1984–1994	167	Randy Wright	QB	1984–1988	46
Bryant Westbrook	CB	2002	6	Steve Wright	T	1964–1967	56
Ryan Wetnight	TE	2000	10	DeShawn Wynn	RB	2007–2009	16
Cowboy Wheeler	E	1921–1923	22	Jarius Wynn	DE	2009–2011	36
Bill Whitaker	DB	1981–1982	25				
Adrian White	S	1992	15	Gust Zarnas	G	1939–1940	14
Gene White	DB	1954	9	Roger Zatkoff	LB	1953–1956	48
Reggie White	DE	1993–1998	95	Joe Zeller	G	1932	14
Tracy White	LB	2006–2008	32	Max Zendejas	K	1987–1988	18
David Whitehurst	QB	1977–1983	54	Lance Zeno	C	1993	5
James Whitley	S	2003–2004	9	Frank Zombo	LB	2010–2012	25
Jesse Whittenton	DB	1958–1964	88	Jim Zorn	QB	1985	13
William Whitticker	G	2005	15	Dave Zuidmulder	B	1929–1931	7
Ron Widby	P	1972–1973	26	Merle Zuver	C	1930	10
Doug Widell	G	1993	16				
Dick Wildung	T	1946–1951, 1953	74				
Matt Wilhelm	LB	2010	7				
Elmer Wilkens	E	1925	6				
Bruce Wilkerson	T	1996–1997	30				
Gabe Wilkins	DE/DT	1994–1997	60				
Marcus Wilkins	LB	2002–2003	12				
A. D. Williams	E	1959	12				

INDEX